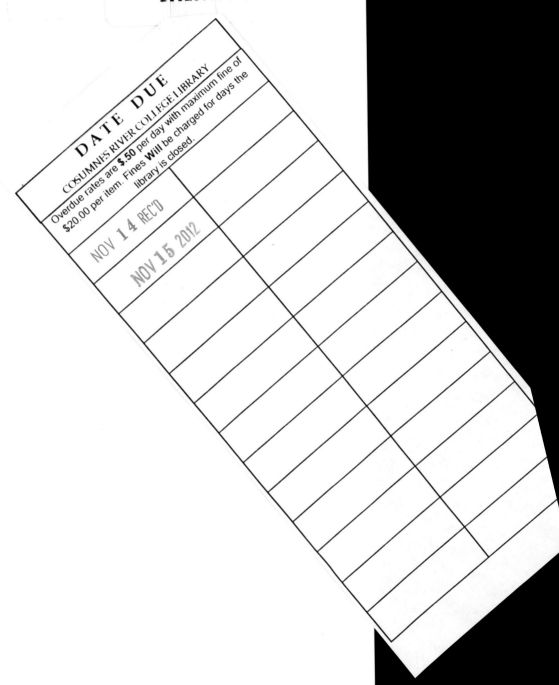

DATE DUE

COSUMNES RIVER COLLEGE LIBRARY

Overdue rates are **$.50** per day with maximum fine of $20.00 per item. Fines **will** be charged for days the library is closed.

NOV 14 REC'D

NOV 15 2012

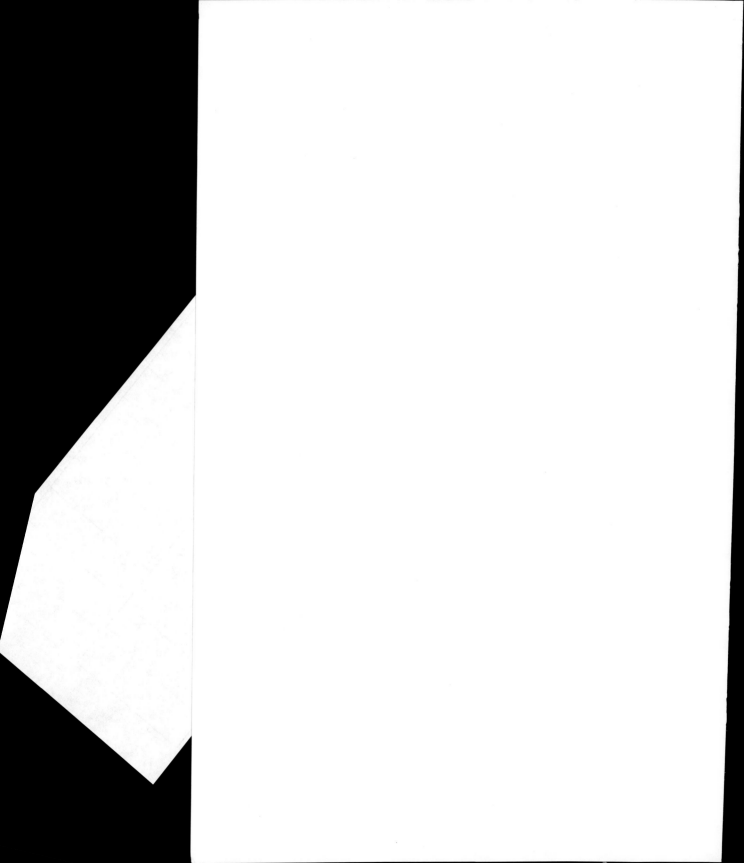

Obedience to Authority

Current Perspectives
on the
Milgram Paradigm

Obedience to Authority

Current Perspectives
on the
Milgram Paradigm

Edited by

Thomas Blass

University of Maryland, Baltimore County

LEA LAWRENCE ERLBAUM ASSOCIATES, PUBLISHERS
2000   Mahwah, New Jersey   London

Lawrence Erlbaum Associates, Inc., Publishers
10 Industrial Avenue
Mahwah, NJ 07430

Cover design by Kathryn Houghtaling Lacey

Library of Congress Cataloging-in-Publication Data

Obedience to authority : current perspectives on the
Milgram paradigm / edited by Thomas Blass.
      p. cm.
      Includes bibliographical references and index.
      ISBN 0-8058-2737-4 (cloth: alk. paper)
      ISBN 0-8058-3934-8 (paper : alk. paper)
      1. Authority. 2. Obedience. 3. Milgram, Stanley.
      Obedience to authority. I. Blass, Thomas.
HM1251.O24   1999
    303.3'6—dc21
                                                    99-30504
                                                    CIP

Books published by Lawrence Erlbaum Associates are printed
on acid-free paper, and their bindings are chosen for strength
and durability.

Printed in the United States of America
10   9   8   7   6   5   4   3   2   1

She opens her mouth with wisdom,
and the lesson of kindness is on her tongue.
—Proverbs 31:26

In memory of my mother,
Maria Blass
She had the clarity of vision to see through
a malevolent authority's false reality
and the courage to defy its orders,
saving our lives during the Holocaust.

Contents

Preface   ix

1 My Personal View of Stanley Milgram   1
   Alexandra Milgram

2 How Stanley Milgram Taught About Obedience   9
   and Social Influence
   Harold Takooshian

3 Professor Stanley Milgram—Supervisor, Mentor, Friend   25
   Judith Waters

4 The Milgram Paradigm After 35 Years: Some Things   35
   We Now Know About Obedience to Authority
   Thomas Blass

5 Impression Management and Identity Construction   61
   in the Milgram Social System
   Barry E. Collins and Laura Ma

6 Captain Paul Grueninger: The Chief of Police Who   91
   Saved Jewish Refugees by Refusing To Do His Duty
   François Rochat and Andre Modigliani

7 Self-Destructive Obedience in the Airplane Cockpit   111
   and the Concept of Obedience Optimization
   Eugen Tarnow

8 The Role of the Obedience Experiments in Holocaust   125
Studies: The Case for Renewed Visibility
Ann L. Saltzman

9 A Science Museum Exhibit on Milgram's Obedience   145
Research: History, Description, and Visitors' Reactions
Caryl Marsh

10 The Dynamics of Obeying and Opposing Authority: 161
A Mathematical Model
François Rochat, Olivier Maggioni, Andre Modigliani

11 Reflections on the Stanford Prison Experiment: 193
Genesis, Transformations, Consequences
Philip G. Zimbardo, Christina Maslach, Craig Haney

Author Index   239

Subject Index   245

Preface

One of the most important and widely known research programs of our times is Stanley Milgram's work on obedience to authority. Although conducted in the early 1960s, its revelatory power—showing the ease with which ordinary people can be induced by a legitimate authority to act with extraordinary cruelty against an innocent victim—shows no signs of weakening. In fact, what is remarkable about the obedience experiments is just how large and wide their domain of relevance is. Thus one can find discussions of the experiments in publications in disciplines as wide ranging as business ethics, philosophy, nursing, and law—in addition to publications in psychology, of course.

The aim of this book is to demonstrate the vibrancy of the obedience paradigm by presenting to readers a variety of its most important and stimulating contemporary uses and applications. Paralleling Milgram's own eclecticism in the content and style of his research and writing, the contributions comprise a potpourri of styles of research and presentation, ranging from personal narratives, through conceptual analyses, to randomized experiments.

The first three chapters set the stage for the rest, which are grounded in various ways in the obedience research. Although approaching their subject matter from different perspectives, these first chapters paint verbal portraits of the person behind the obedience experiments. This manner of beginning the book is based on the premise that coming to know Stanley Milgram, the human being, can contribute to a fuller understanding of Stanley Milgram, the scientist, and his most famous work and its sequelae.

As Stanley Milgram's wife (and, therefore, unparalleled authority on his life), Alexandra Milgram brings a unique perspective to the book's first chapter. In it, she traces—among other things—Stanley's development from childhood to adulthood and shows how his personal interests and experiences can be seen as antecedents to some of his research. I am grateful to her for agreeing to share her valuable recollections and insights through her contribution to this book. Harold Takooshian was a doctoral student in social psychology at City University of New York (CUNY) when Milgram was chairman of that program. He took virtually every course and seminar taught by Milgram, who also chaired his doctoral dissertation. Drawing on his experiences, as well as those of some other former students, Takooshian presents in chapter 2 a nuanced description of the content and style of Stanley's classroom activities when teaching about obedience, as well as other subjects in social psychology. Chapter 3 is by Judith Waters, another former student. Milgram had been her mentor and research supervisor, and they remained friends after she received her doctorate. In her chapter, she weaves a tapestry of vignettes and lessons learned, and, reading it, one ends up with a better appreciation of the complex human being that Milgram was.

In chapter 4, I review our current state of knowledge regarding certain questions and issues connected with the Milgram obedience paradigm, (e.g., sex differences in obedience and whether or not obedience rates have changed over time). It is meant to complement and round out my other literature reviews on the obedience paradigm that have appeared in the *Journal of Personality and Social Psychology, Advances in Experimental Social Psychology,* and the journal *Holocaust and Genocide Studies.* Chapter 5, by Barry Collins and Laura Ma, presents a new obedience paradigm that extends Milgram's work to the realm of person-perception. Collins and colleagues filmed reenactments of one of Milgram's baseline conditions, which they varied in outcome (obedience vs. disobedience) and style of disobedience (polite vs. defiant). The chapter presents the latest developments in their research program: experimental results that show how these variations affect perceivers' personality impressions of the three interactants in the obedience experiment—teacher, experimenter, and learner.

An important reason for the durability—decades after they were conducted—of the obedience studies is their usefulness in illuminating real-world events and phenomena involving authority–subordinate relationships. The subsequent two chapters represent strikingly different instances of the application of the obedience paradigm in this manner. In chapter 6, François Rochat and Andre Modigliani present a case study of a heroic individual, Swiss police captain Paul Grueninger, who went against his government's orders and allowed about 3,000 Jewish refugees fleeing the persecution of the Third Reich to enter Switzerland. As a result, he lost his job and pension and died in poverty. The authors shed some new light on his behavior by drawing parallels between his defiance of unjust authority and the participants who disobeyed Milgram's experimenter. Chapter 7, by Eugen Tarnow, presents an analysis of a troubling phenomenon—airplane crashes that are attributable to crew members' reluctance to challenge the captain's authority. He shows that aspects of the experimenter–participant relationship that contributed to excessive obedience in the Milgram experiment can also sometimes characterize the relationship between the captain and first officer in the airplane cockpit.

It is not uncommon to hear persons who have learned about the obedience research describe it as a valuable learning experience, alerting them to the surprising power of authority or even giving them the inner strength to resist a superior's immoral orders. In fact, Milgram used testimonials of this sort, provided by some participants, as part of his rebuttal to Baumrind's ethical critique of the obedience experiments (both of which appeared in the *American Psychologist* in 1964). Chapters 8 and 9 deal with two large-scale educational uses of the obedience experiments. In chapter 8, Ann Saltzman, a former student of Milgram and now codirector of the Center for Holocaust Study at Drew University, writes about the incorporation of the obedience studies into Holocaust education curricula. The appearance of the obedience experiments in Holocaust Studies curricula should be quite appropriate, because an attempt to understand the inhumane obedience of the perpetrators of the Holocaust was one of the factors that led Milgram to conduct his experiments. And today, Milgram's approach, derived from his experimental findings, is regarded as one of the legitimate viewpoints in debates about how best to explain the behavior of the perpetrators of the Holocaust, as can be seen in the following quote from a book review of Daniel Goldhagen's book, *Hitler's Willing Executioners*: "[Goldhagen] now claims he deserves a place alongside Hannah Arendt, Stanley Milgram, Raul Hilberg, and Yehuda Bauer, the great fathomers of the Holocaust" (Marc Fisher, *Washington Post*, p. C1, April 25, 1996). In her chapter, Saltzman presents the results of her quantitative content analysis of Holocaust curricula and finds, surprisingly, that the obedience studies appear in only a small percentage of them.

She then makes a strong case for their increased representation in such educational materials.

A different sort of educational use of the obedience experiments is described by Caryl Marsh in chapter 9. A social psychologist and an exhibitions curator, she was the director of a traveling museum exhibition launched by the American Psychological Association in 1992 to mark the organization's 100th anniversary. Among its 40 hands-on exhibits is one that provides a clever participatory learning experience about the obedience experiments and includes Milgram's original shock machine. Among other things, she describes visitors' strong reactions to the exhibit and the very high rate of visitors' obedience to some rather arbitrary instructions. In a way, these results can be seen as an informal conceptual replication of the original obedience experiments.

Chapter 10 represents perhaps one of the most unique contemporary uses of the obedience experiments, in that here the word *uses* is meant quite literally: It is based on the close analysis of the actual audiotaped recordings of the experimental sessions of one of the conditions in Milgram's series of obedience experiments. The work it describes is the innovative outcome of a productive collaboration among two social psychologists, François Rochat and Andre Modigliani, and an applied mathematician, Olivier Maggioni, who has done research in the field of dynamical systems. Using the data from the audio recordings of the Bridgeport condition, the authors created a mathematical model, described in their chapter, which shows how participants behave over the course of the experiment. The result has been twofold: The model provides both a better understanding of the paths taken by Milgram's experimental participants and the ability to simulate their behavior as the experiment unfolds.

The last chapter is about the Stanford Prison Experiment. Rich in detail, analysis, and insights, it is the most comprehensive presentation of that work to date—a collaborative effort of Philip Zimbardo, Christina Maslach, and Craig Haney. Each author has written a portion of the chapter, to which he or she brings his or her own experiences with, and perspectives on, the prison experiment. The result is truly a totality that is greater than the sum of its parts. The reader might wonder how a chapter on the Stanford Prison Experiment fits into a book about the contemporary relevance of Milgram's obedience experiments. The answer is that, although they constituted two separate research programs, there are important connections between them. Foremost is the fact that the two studies have historically been considered by social psychologists and others to be the prime examples of the ability of situational factors to override personal dispositions as determinants of behavior. Also, the fact is that Milgram's research contributed importantly to the spirit of the times that spawned the Stanford Prison Experiment. As Craig Haney writes in this chapter, "his work provided a preexisting context for ours, helping to expand our sense of what it was possible to accomplish in an experimental setting and even to embolden us in the critical uses to which we were willing and able to put our laboratory-based empirical knowledge." Indeed, this is a fitting closing chapter to a book about the continuing impact of—in the words of Harvard social psychologist Roger Brown—"the most famous series of experiments in social psychology."

Thomas Blass
Baltimore, Maryland

1

My Personal View of Stanley Milgram*

Alexandra Milgram
Riverdale, New York

It is a pleasure to contribute to this book by presenting my personal view of Stanley.

Let me begin with a brief synopsis of Stanley's life. He was born on August 15, 1933. He grew up primarily in the Bronx, which at the time was considered a pleasant place to live for middle-class immigrant families. His Hungarian father and Romanian mother were hardworking people who emphasized to their three children the importance of education, of having a profession, and of maintaining relations with the family. Stanley's sister Margie was 1½ years older than he, and his brother Joel was 5 years younger. For whatever reason, Stanley seemed closer to his brother; the two had fun playing various kinds of games and pranks.

At an early age Stanley began to show signs of his great mental abilities. I remember Stanley's mother saying that when Stanley was in kindergarten he would stand next to her at night while she helped his sister with the next day's assignment. In those days, Lincoln's and Washington's birthdays were observed as separate holidays, not just as a single holiday labeled President's Day. Thus, when Stanley was in kindergarten, he learned about President Abraham Lincoln at night from his mother. The next day when Stanley's teacher asked his class what they

*This chapter is based on an invited talk given at the annual convention of the American Psychological Association on August 21, 1993, in Toronto, Canada, Copyright 1999 Alexandra Milgram

1

knew about Abraham Lincoln, Stanley raised his hand and recited what he had learned the previous night. The teacher was so impressed that she had little Stanley taken around to all the classes in the school to give his speech about the great president.

Stanley went on to James Monroe High School, where he became an editor of the *Science Observer* (a school paper). He also enjoyed working on stagecraft for school productions. And, as might be expected, he was a member of Arista, an honor society.

By the time Stanley graduated from high school, his family was already living in Queens. He attended Queens College, where he majored in political science. He became vice president of both the International Relations Club and the Debating Club. He graduated Phi Beta Kappa. I remember Stanley speaking of Queens College with positive memories. While there, he became interested in music and art.

During his last year at Queens College, Stanley applied for and was accepted into a graduate program at the School of International Affairs at Columbia University that would prepare him for the foreign service. However, a dean of Queens College had heard Stanley give a speech just prior to commencement. He asked him if he had considered going on to the Department of Social Relations at Harvard University. Not having heard of the department before, Stanley obtained a catalogue. After noting the interesting courses in social psychology, sociology, and social anthropology, Stanley decided to change his plans and applied to the program for a PhD. He was not accepted because he had not taken a single psychology course. He did not accept the rejection. After a discussion with the faculty of the Department of Social Relations, it was agreed that if Stanley took prerequisite psychology courses during the summer he would be permitted to enter Harvard in September as a special nonmatriculating student. If he did well, he would be permitted to matriculate. That summer, Stanley worked very diligently, taking a number of courses in three different colleges—Hunter, Brooklyn, and New York University. Then, after doing well in his courses at Harvard in the fall semester, he was permitted to continue for his PhD in social psychology.

His years at Harvard provided a wonderful, enjoyable, and very expansive experience for Stanley. His mentors in social psychology were Jerome Bruner, Roger Brown, Solomon E. Asch, and Gordon Allport. He became interested in cross-cultural research and did his thesis on conformity in Oslo and Paris. Also during his years at Harvard, he became interested in writing librettos for musicals.

After graduating from Harvard University, Stanley became an assistant professor at Yale University in the Psychology Department, where he conducted his most famous research, on obedience to authority. While he was at Yale, Stanley and I met at a party in Manhattan. After a long-distance courtship commuting between New York and New Haven, we were married on December 10, 1961.

Stanley returned to the Department of Social Relations at Harvard in 1963, where he continued teaching and doing research. We both enjoyed living in Cambridge, developing various friendships. Both of our children, Michele and Marc, were born during those years. Stanley was very excited to become a father and enjoyed playing with and caring for his children.

In 1967 Stanley became a full professor at the Graduate Center of the City University of New York, where he continued his career teaching, doing research, writing, and also making films on social psychology. We were happy to return to the New York area where we both had family and friends and could pursue our numerous interests in art, movies, and theater, as well as simply exploring the various areas of the city and its environs. In 1980 Stanley was appointed Distinguished Professor at the Graduate Center.

Stanley passed away December 20, 1984, at the age of 51, after suffering for 4 years with cardiac problems.

Now I elaborate on how some of the interests that Stanley had from boyhood through adulthood can be thought of, perhaps, as influences on, or even bases for some of his research.

Stanley's interests in news and politics can be traced to his youth. He often spoke of how his parents listened to the news on the radio. (There was no television then.) As a youngster growing up in the 1930s, Stanley was very much aware of his family's concerns about Nazi Germany and World War II. Stanley's father had some family still living in Europe at the time. As an undergraduate at Queens College, Stanley majored in political science. Some readers might even be aware of an article he wrote in which he described himself as a "news addict." Besides reading *The New York Times* every day and weekly news magazines, he liked to watch the news on television. He felt he was keeping informed of the latest events, as well as sometimes seeing history in the making.

With this knowledge of Stanley's interest in news and history, plus his strong Jewish identity, we can understand his deep concern about the Holocaust, which led to his best known research—obedience to authority. He wondered, as did many people, about Germany, a country in which so many Jews were integrated into society as professionals and businessmen. Who were all the men who pushed the levers to let the gas into the chambers of Auschwitz and Dachau? It was not just one crazy man.

Initially, when Stanley was designing the obedience experiment, he, like the 40 psychiatrists he interviewed at Yale University, believed that most Americans would not continue pressing the levers down but would break off the experiment early. In fact, he originally thought that, after conducting the experiment in the United States, he would then replicate it in Germany to see if there was a cultural difference in how people responded. During the pilot study in which he used Yale students, he thought that their proceeding to press the levers until they reached the end of the shock generator could be explained as the behavior of just "Yalies." However, during the regular running of the experiment, he was surprised to observe the numerous participants—men and some women, 20 to 50 years of age—going until the end without breaking off, even though some participants expressed concern and a desire to stop. Thus Stanley found it necessary to design different conditions in order to find out under what circumstances people would break off before reaching the last lever of the shock generator marked 450 volts. He never went to Germany to replicate the experiment there.

Stanley's desire to do cross-cultural research perhaps grew out of his interest in different cultures. At age 19, in order to improve his French, he spent the summer studying the language at the Sorbonne University in Paris. This first trip to Europe was very exciting to him, culminating in his traveling on a motorized bike from Paris to Spain and then on to Italy.

The cross-cultural study of conformity that Stanley did in Oslo and Paris for his PhD thesis was a very meaningful experience to him. Besides setting up experiments in foreign countries, with all the problems and intricacies that this entailed, he also developed a first-hand knowledge of two different cultures just by living in them for many months. Stanley wanted to continue doing cross-cultural research and originally conceived of the obedience experiment as one to be done cross-culturally.

After he had his first taste of travel at 19, Stanley continued to enjoy it throughout his life. We traveled around South America for our honeymoon and spent many vacations with the family traveling to different parts of Europe, the Caribbean, the United States, Israel, and Morocco.

Often we would rent a house or apartment for our vacation and stay in one area and explore it in depth. We enjoyed walking through the different sections of Paris, discovering charming little streets and numerous beautiful parks.

Stanley's love of cities—especially Paris and New York—led to his studies of psychological maps of these two cities. For readers who are not familiar with these studies, Stanley requested that the participants draw a map of their city indicating where the rich live, where it is frightening to go, as well as the path of their favorite walk, and so forth.

Stanley's interest in politics was an influence on his Lost Letter studies, done in New Haven to determine the sentiment of the residents toward communism in the 1960s and in Asia to find out how the overseas Chinese felt about mainland China.

As a youngster, Stanley was given a chemistry set by an older cousin. I recall Stanley describing how exciting it was for him to mix the various chemicals and to observe the results. At times friends joined him in performing these experiments. They were careful not to perform dangerous experiments at home but would take the chemicals to a safe place in the nearby Bronx Park to see if they would explode. This interest in science persisted into high school. Throughout his adult life, Stanley continued reading about the latest scientific breakthroughs and also about the scientists involved.

In his social psychological experiments, Stanley was interested in the methodology—designing experiments to precisely measure what he was looking for. He was very careful in keeping records. In the obedience experiment, not only did he observe how far each participant went, but he also had a machine hooked up to the shock generator to measure how long each person held down each lever. He also firmly believed that if an experiment produced results different from what was predicted, it would indicate a significant finding. This was certainly the case with the results of the obedience experiment.

Stanley was also a family man. He loved us dearly. Evenings, weekends, and vacations were times for us to be together. He insisted on my being by his side while he was watching TV. Not only did he like to watch the news and analysis of it, but also comedy, drama, some sports, and the latest shows. Weekends were devoted to family outings to museums, parks, and movies or to visiting our mothers or sisters who lived in the area. I recall Stanley keeping Michele up at night to talk to her alone without the distraction of others. And I remember him teaching

Marc to ride a bike. He enjoyed playing chess and Monopoly with the family. And he enjoyed going out with me to the movies or gourmet restaurants.

Now you may wonder what influence his family might have had on his research. As an example, once when my mother was visiting us she asked Stanley why young people no longer get up in a bus or subway to give their seat to a white-haired lady. Stanley then asked her if she ever asked for a seat. She looked at him in surprise that he could ask such a question. The next week, when Stanley met with his class in experimental social psychology, he designed with them the Subway study. In this experiment, pairs of students would enter subway cars in New York. One would ask a seated passenger, "Excuse me, may I have your seat?" The other student would record what happened. It was a surprise to most people that in the New York subways the majority of people gave up their seats if requested. Stanley found that when he personally participated in this experiment, the most difficult task was for him to ask for a seat. He felt compelled to pretend he was sick.

Stanley liked to think of himself as a Renaissance man. Besides his very full professional life as an experimental social psychologist, he also spent time thinking about different inventions that he carefully recorded. For instance, he thought it very wasteful and expensive that carbon ribbons for his Selectric IBM typewriter could only be used once. He thought of a small machine for rewinding the ribbons so that they could be reused. For people who forget to take their letters with them to mail, he designed a simple plastic envelope to be attached to the inside of the door of the home into which letters to be mailed could be placed. These are just two of numerous inventions that Stanley created.

He also designed various games. One was a board game dealing with the art world, with its auctions, collections, and so on. Another game was based on tenure of professors.

Stanley also wrote children's stories. One was about how a little boy learned to put a coffeepot together after it came apart. Another was about an American Jewish boy coming to terms with his identity.

During his years as a graduate student at Harvard, Stanley wrote a libretto for a musical based on the O. Henry story "The Gift of the Magi." After finishing the project with a young musician who was also at Harvard, they went to see a producer in New York with a sample of their endeavors. After they had been waiting for a while, the producer rushed in very excited, announcing that he had just heard a marvelous musical by

Leonard Bernstein—"West Side Story." The competition was too great for Stanley and his musical friend Victor Ziskin. In later years, Stanley wrote the libretto for another musical based on the well-known story "The Man Without a Country."

Despite various efforts, Stanley was not successful in getting his children's stories published or his musicals produced. And his ideas for inventions remain in the record book he kept.

In art, Stanley favored the works of such diverse artists as Rembrandt, Klee, and Picasso. He enjoyed collecting contemporary Japanese wood-block prints, as well as the works of contemporary Argentinian painters. And in music his tastes ran from Bach's *Brandenburg Concertos* to Lerner and Loewe musicals. I remember Stanley saying at times that he wished he had been born a composer.

Stanley had a great zest for learning about most things. He could be serious and reflective. At other times he was playful, and he enjoyed children of all ages.

The world will continue to know about Stanley's work as a social psychologist through writings and films by him and others. Those of us who had the good fortune to know him were aware of the energy, numerous interests, and abilities that he possessed.

2

How Stanley Milgram Taught About Obedience and Social Influence

Harold Takooshian
Fordham University

"What was he like?" This is the question almost invariably heard by a few dozen U.S. social psychologists, when someone discovers they studied with Stanley Milgram. Such curiosity is understandable, considering that Milgram was such a widely-known researcher who taught so few students, and that only a small number of psychologists knew Milgram as anything but the larger-than-life scientist who created the obedience experiments. "What was he like?" is indeed an excellent question, because those of us who studied with Milgram saw much more than a researcher. As a doctoral student in the Social-Personality Psychology program at the graduate school of the City University of New York (CUNY), I completed some half-dozen of Milgram's courses, and he chaired my dissertation committee. This chapter cumulates my recollections, supplemented by those of some of his other students, to describe Milgram's work in the classroom—his teaching in general, and his teaching about obedience and social influence in particular.

STANLEY MILGRAM, PROFESSOR

There is no question of Stanley Milgram's pre-eminence as a behavioral researcher (Blass, 1992, 1996), the architect of "the most well-known

9

research in social psychology, perhaps all of psychology" (Brock & Brannon, 1994, p. 259). An introductory psychology textbook would be incomplete without mention of Milgram's obedience experiments (Perlman, 1980). A social psychology course without them would be unthinkable (Perlman, 1979). Some prominent social psychologists have been unreserved in recognizing a unique quality in Milgram's obedience research, that applies to no other study within the field. For example, Muzafer Sherif (1975) said, "Milgram's obedience experiment is the single greatest contribution to human knowledge ever made by the field of social psychology, perhaps psychology in general." And at Milgram's eulogy in December, 1984, his close colleague Irwin Katz noted "When viewed in relation to the main body of psychology ..., Stanley Milgram's work on obedience stands by itself—an indestructible monolith on an uninhabited plain." Besides the obedience studies, which he conducted in his twenties, he went on to do other pioneering research on city life, the media, cognitive maps, and a score of diverse topics (Blass, 1992), that made him one of the few social scientists to directly impact our popular culture—including Broadway theater and feature films (Takooshian, 1998), and a television play based on the obedience experiments (Milgram, 1976).

Yet the fact is that Milgram was also a teacher throughout his career—first at Yale (1960–1963), then at Harvard (1963–1967), and finally at the City University of New York (1967–1984). In fact, his teaching at CUNY began at age 33, as a full professor and head of the social psychology doctoral program, and ended by chairing a student's defense of her dissertation at 2 pm on December 20, 1984, a few hours before he succumbed to heart failure. His 24 continuous years of teaching were punctuated only by a few sabbaticals and, starting in 1980, some brief medical leaves interspersed among his 4 heart attacks. His teaching materials fill some 106 boxes in the Yale University archives. Soon after his untimely death, the American Psychological Foundation (APF) considered Milgram's nomination by his students for its annual award for Distinguished Teaching in Psychology, but APF policy ultimately excluded a posthumous Award. (See Appendix.)

Despite Milgram's dedication to teaching, the alumni who studied with him number in the dozens rather than the hundreds, for at least a few reasons. Like his father, he left this world at an early age (51), "achieving so much in the short time allotted him" (Florence and Solomon Asch, 1993).*[1] His intense years at Yale and Harvard were too few to allow him to serve on more than a handful of dissertation committees, despite his popularity as "a bright young professor who connected with students" (Silver, 1993). His years at CUNY were almost exclusively with doctoral students in small classes of as few as 3 students, averaging only 15 or so in his two classes per semester. Milgram himself (1980b) acknowledged that, unlike other key social psychologists, he headed no theoretical "school" of social psychology that would attract students into a systematic research program, comparable to the theories of cognitive dissonance or attribution. Not least of all, he had a reputation as a demanding advisor and teacher, who expected from his students the same intensity for research that he himself felt, thus attracting only a certain type of student for his classes and dissertation research. Consequently, the extensive literature on Milgram's research (e.g., Miller, Collins, & Brief, 1995), eclipses what little there is on his teaching (Blass, 1996; Silver, 1993; Takooshian, 1993).

It is notable that the modest number of graduate students who studied closely with Milgram contain many who made their mark in psychology, and include several who stayed within academic social psychology. Among these are: Charles D. Korte (North Carolina State University), Barry Wellman (University of Toronto), Alan C. Elms (University of California–Davis), Leon Mann (University of Melbourne, Australia), Elliot Turiel (University of California–Berkeley), Eli Baker (Cornell Medical College), Annette Benedict (Ramapo College), Leonard Bickman (Vanderbilt University), Sidney Callahan (Mercy College), David C. Carraher (University of Pernambuco, Brazil), Benzion Chanowitz (Brooklyn College, CUNY), Lirio S. Covey (Columbia School of Public Health), Rita S. Dytel (Mount St. Vincent College), Samuel L. Gaertner (University of Delaware), David C. Greene (Ramapo College), Susan Harter (University of Denver), Shelley H. Juran (Pratt Institute), Ansley W. Lamar (New Jersey City University), Carl W. Malinowski (Pace University), Robert F. Massey (Seton Hall University), Margot B. Nadien (Fordham University), Robert A. Panzarella (John Jay College, CUNY), John Sabini (University of Pennsylvania), Ann L. Saltzman (Drew University), Kathleen Schiaffino (Fordham

---

[1]The asterisks for this and subsequent quotes indicate remembrance letters sent by Milgram's students and colleagues in August, 1993, celebrating his life and work at the annual meeting of the American Psychological Association in Toronto. This was a series of four events to mark both the thirtieth anniversary of the first publication of his obedience research, and what would have been his sixtieth birthday on August 15, 1993.

University), Jeffrey S. Shaw (NYU), Laura S. Sidorowicz (Nassau Community College), Maury Silver (St. Francis College), Harold Takooshian (Fordham University), Christina J. Taylor (Sacred Heart University), and Judith A. Waters (Fairleigh Dickinson University–Madison).

Certainly those close to Milgram saw more than a researcher. In fact, his flair for research was one of a unique combination of several equally rare talents.

Researcher.   He had no peer as an inventive researcher, in both the insightful topics he extracted from everyday life, and the creative methods he developed to study these—unbound by any specific theory or method (McGuire, 1997). His alumnus Samuel Gaertner* described him as "a social scientific artist whose research illustrates and clarifies human reality using methods we have never encountered before."

Thinker.   Like DaVinci, his powerful mind probed and integrated an immense ken, ranging from brain physiology and video technology to abstract art and virtual reality.

Speaker.   He was a riveting and popular lecturer, who could communicate nuances in so few words that a transcribed tape-recording of his speech often reads like finished prose.

Writer.   He was a suasive author, a wordmaster equally comfortable in many genres—technical reports, essays, screenplays, short stories, poetry, even librettos—who showed a certain visible joy for writing that some composers like Haydn and Mozart show in their music. While most of us must squeeze our thoughts into the right words, he was a wordsmith with that rare gift in which his use of words actually seemed to hone his thoughts.

Teacher.   In class, his sometimes scintillating, semistructured Socratic approach could involve students so thoroughly that they often continued discussion long after the hour ended.

Personal style.   Not least of all, he himself embodied the very opposite of obedience; he was an archenemy of convention, always full of surprises. Like Maslow's (1987) "self-actualizing" person, he could sometimes be as icy to longtime friends as he could be warm to total strangers.

MILGRAM IN THE CLASSROOM

In teaching it is the method and not the content that is the message—
the drawing out, not the pumping in.
                                                    —Ashley Montagu

There was nothing extraordinary about the printed syllabi in Milgram's courses, which assigned the traditional readings in the field.[2] What made his courses unforgettable was his style inside the classroom[3], which was intense in many ways.

First, he was clearly the unquestioned authority in his classroom. The very opposite of boring, his approach was highly personal, involving, and interactive. He would tell a student to remove his sunglasses, so his eyes were as visible as others' during class discussion. He typically tolerated no food, drink, or smoking in his class, and students were instructed to finish their refreshments outside, once class was about to start. He often challenged students by name, in a way that did not happen in other courses. About crowd behavior, for example, he would ask, "What if you were in a crowded theater and a muscular fellow like Mr. Takooshian here began to shove you?" Or once, when discussing attitude research, he asked: "Would a message sway you less if it came from an ardent feminist like Miss Smith here?"

During student discussions, he was quite candid in his comments, praising new insights while openly deriding shallow comments. With his agile mind and razor tongue, he could be caustic, even devastating, with a surgical precision that cut to the quick. Oddly, this did not stifle discussion, as students realized there was no personal animus in the criticism, and instead vied for his praise of their insights. In no class was student participation more lively, crackling with new insights. Milgram did not discourage this; he encouraged students to spar with him and each other. Even those students who felt he was authoritarian in class would acknowledge that he actively solicited constructive criticism. For

---

[2]The courses Milgram taught were all within social psychology, and research-oriented. Some were required: Advanced social, Social relations, Research methods, Experimental social, International social, and Independent research. Others were specialized electives created by him: Urban research, Authority and the individual, Photography and film, and Mass media. At CUNY, a few were team-taught with others: Irwin Katz, Stuart Albert, Jack Sansolo, and Steven Cohen.

[3]With CUNY's 10 doctoral programs in Psychology, Milgram's social psychology program had more than its share of noted teachers, including at various times: Morton Bard, Edgar F. Borgatta, Florence L. Denmark, Barbara Snell Dohrenwend, Howard Ehlichman, Irwin Katz, Leonard Kogan, Ellen Langer, and Samuel Messick.

example, after giving a detailed presentation of Diana Baumrind's (1964) caustic critique of the ethics of his obedience experiments, he challenged the class as an assignment: "How would you redesign the obedience experiment, to reduce or eliminate deception without compromising its value?" The more compelling the students' efforts, the better he liked them. Indeed, one of Milgram's students undertook such a redesign for his dissertation, testing whether or not role-playing would produce findings comparable to the original experiments (Geller, 1975).

Milgram was a maestro at communicating "incomplete understanding," a Socratic technique often used to draw out discussion in industrial focus groups (Bellenger, 1976). There was some question he simply could not resolve by himself—if only we students could help him—such as, "Why did some subjects in the obedience experiments (as depicted in Milgram's documentary film, *Obedience*) giggle as they administered shocks to the protesting learner?" He was able to ask in such a way that students outdid each other and themselves to probe the issues he presented, leaving the 2-hour seminars with far more insight than before. Readings came alive in Milgram's classes. Somehow he was able to motivate students to feel the same intensity that he obviously felt about the "whys" of human behavior. In critiquing the validity of one oft-cited study on "severity of initiations" (Aronson & Mills, 1959), Milgram challenged his students about whether an experimenter could truly induce stress in college students simply by forcing them to swear, by probing: "What is the filthiest phrase in the English language?" Students' initial competition eventually segued into an odd take-home assignment that proved to be quite a learning experience about not taking at face value all published research. He was particularly critical of what he called "cardboard studies," that is, studies low in mundane realism. Whereas some teachers manage to make a lively topic dull, Milgram's opposite gift made even queues and mental maps topics of fascination.

Milgram had a distinctive nonverbal mannerism which played a large role in his face-to-face interactions—a display worthy of an impressionist. At reflective moments during a discussion, he would go through a three-fold sequence, which can be glimpsed when he appears in his films (e.g., *Obedience, The City and the Self*). He would raise and quiver his right hand with forefinger slightly extended; knit his eyebrows in an unusual way, sloped upward in the middle and downward at the sides (like an inverted V); stammer in halting, soft tones. This display was quite distinctive, and somehow effectively signaled to his group during lively give-and-takes to restore him as its center of atten-tion, ready to hear his forthcoming insight. One interviewer described Milgram's hand motions as follows: "Milgram speaks with precise hand gestures, as if he were stitching a cloud or conducting an adagio" (Tavris, 1974, p. 75).

No professor could match Milgram's warmth at times. As one stu-dent told Tavris (1974): "He can be utterly charming on unexpected occasions" (p.75). His alumna Elyse V. Goldstein* reminisces, "Stanley was ... so playful that no graduate career could have had so much hu-mor and wit. I remember most barreling in laughter with Stanley." On one especially jocose day, he replaced his speech with song for the en-tire day, and refused to listen to anyone unless they too sang their words to him. Indeed, his classes could become riotously funny, and he was of-ten intensely playful with those around him. Milgram (1980a) recalled his own Harvard mentor Gordon Allport's gentle gift for cheering up frazzled students, and he emulated this nice habit of rousing students who seemed blue. His alumnus Maury Silver* noted that he actually followed Milgram from Harvard to CUNY in the 1970s because of "that sense of excitement, playfulness, and intellectual adventure that he al-most always radiated."

Still, Milgram could be equally harsh. Colleagues and students weighed his words carefully. As one of his students put it, "Where he hurts, no grass grows" (Tavris, 1974, p. 75). One telling example of this occurred one afternoon when Milgram pointed out to me a gaping hole just to one side of the handsome black couch in his office, and asked my opinion of it. Milgram explained that a disgruntled former student had been sitting there earlier that morning, furtively grinding this hole in the couch with a pen while the two chatted eye to eye. Milgram mused about the perverse pleasure this former student must have felt, to amia-bly maintain eye contact with Milgram while perpetrating a vandalism that would surely be discovered minutes later.

Milgram seemed to take for granted his ambivalent image, ranging somewhere between a charming St. Nick and Ivan the Terrible. For ex-ample, one day in his office he was to meet seven-year-old Jackie Mo-naco, "the lost child" in his students' urban field experiment (Takooshian, Haber, & Lucido, 1977). Before Jackie could shake his hand, her mother first asked the creator of the obedience experiments, "Do you like children?" Milgram quickly detected her concern and re-plied, "Oh yes, I love children, especially with salt and pepper."

Why was Milgram's classroom teaching style unique in so many ways? Upon analysis, this was not so much an effort on his part, or a calculated technique, but rather it seemed to flow naturally from his temperament—in fact a constellation of traits already evident to those who knew him in his youth. His younger brother, Joel Milgram (1993), remembered his prankish sense of humor within the family; Philip Zimbardo described his James Monroe High School classmate Stanley as a cerebral youngster with a clear bent for empirical science (Zimbardo, 1993) and an unusually subtle sense of humor (Zimbardo, 1999); his wife Alexandra (1993) recalled his passion for understanding the whys of social behavior. Milgram himself recalled that his scientific interests began during his childhood years (Tavris, 1974).

RESEARCH, TEACHING, AND PERSONAL EXPERIENCE

I hear and I forget. I see and I remember. I do and I understand.
—Chinese proverb

Whereas most psychology professors have research programs quite separate from their teaching (Murray, 1997), Milgram made no attempt to separate his teaching from his research (Takooshian, 1990) or, for that matter, his personal life. There was a continual interplay among these three, in at least three ways.

First, his teaching fed his research, routinely spawning new ideas. Since his Yale years, so many of Milgram's most intriguing publications were based on ideas born in his classes—the small world problem, the lost letter technique, the familiar stranger, the lost child, the drawing power of crowds, social intrusion, cognitive maps, urban overload, queues, the image-freezing machine, cyranoids, and the urban simulator. Most of these appear in Milgram's (1977, 1992) anthology of his writings. It is notable that Milgram rarely co-authored research with his teaching colleagues, yet frequently co-authored research publications with his students. His Harvard alumnus Charles Korte* recalls, "Stanley Milgram was without a doubt the most significant influence on my career as a social psychologist. ... I was treated as a collaborator, a role I didn't expect to have so early in my graduate school career." Just as Milgram was a fount for innovative ideas, he also absorbed others' ideas quickly. In his "Authority and the individual" class, I asked if obedience would drop if the learner and teacher had shaken hands just before the research started, given the symbolism of a handshake? Within 1 week, students in Milgram's other course, "Urban psychology", were extending their outstretched hands to pedestrians on the streets of New York, to test how many Manhattanites would shake hands with a smiling stranger (Milgram, 1992).

Second, prior research fed his teaching. He routinely probed his past research in class, as if anew, focusing particularly on unresolved issues or alternate explanations. A clear example of this was his first offering of a new course, "Authority and the individual", mentioned earlier, in Spring, 1974, coincident with the release of his long-awaited volume, *Obedience to authority: An experimental view* (Milgram, 1974). The first 4 weeks of the course probed the first 12 experiments in the book step by step, as students delved into each permutation, even to excess. For example, the question arose: "Can the authority's personal appearance affect the obedience rate?" As one student wondered at length whether or not obedience would rise if the experimenter wore a priest's collar, another finally asked if it would decline if he was wearing a gorilla suit. In the remaining 12 weeks of the course, under Milgram's supervision, the class worked to draft a lexicon to define and distinguish some 100 terms related to social influence, although this was never finalized for publication.

Third, he was constantly open to personal experiences that exposed new questions to be researched. In one class, he asked students what they thought activated the lighted buttons in the CUNY elevators—touch, heat, electricity? When no one could answer, this became the object of the class' experimental study—using ice cubes, matches, batteries, and all sorts of systematic methods. So too with the Dinkie Bird, a 5-inch plastic toy which Times Square tourist shops once used to draw customers which bobs up and down for unclear reasons. He once said, "I do believe that a Pandora's box lies just beneath the surface of everyday life" (Milgram, 1992, pp. xxii–xxiii). He credits his mother-in-law's casual observation—how hard it is to find a seat in the subway—with his series of experiments in which subway riders were asked to give up their seats (Milgram & Sabini, 1978).

Although Milgram could be forceful in class, he could also be unusually tolerant of disagreements. One strong example stands out in my experience, because it involved the ethics of research, a sensitive issue in Milgram's career. In 1972, Milgram co-taught Experimental Social Psychology with an assistant professor. They assigned us all to go into the subways in teams of two to ask subway riders for their seats, and have the data collected by the time Milgram returned from a trip in 3 weeks. Many students found this request hard, even excruciating to the point of nausea, but Milgram's co-teacher dutifully prodded us to complete the task by his return. However, one student spotted what he felt was an ethical problem in the study—deceiving participants without later debriefing them—and asked for guidance from Milgram's co-teacher, but he was firmly told he was not authorized to deviate from Milgram's parting instructions. Unsatisfied, this student quickly devised a small "debrief card" suitable to give participants after the trial was completed, and he asked his classmates who had not yet completed their trials if they would consider using his adaptation. No classmate objected to this, but none joined him either, leaving this student feeling alone and very uneasy prior to Milgram's return. Upon his return, Milgram did not object to this departure from his instructions; instead, to this student's great relief, Milgram showed tolerance in praising the debrief card as a creative touch, and went on to credit two of this student's other innovations in his later writings on the subway experiment (Milgram & Sabini, 1978).

TEACHING ABOUT OBEDIENCE

Beware the steel cobwebs of convention.
—Thoreau

How did Milgram teach his students about obedience? He did so on at least two levels.

On a surface level, his syllabi contained his review of classic studies and traditional concepts. Consider a typical semi-structured class, such as one on the meaning of "obedience," and how it might relate to other concepts such as cooperation, trust, conformity, compliance. Students had been assigned several apt readings by Kelman, Hollander, Asch, French and Raven. But early in the class discussion, Milgram began to pose a half-dozen scenarios for analysis, starting with this one: A physician tells a distraught mother to reduce her baby's high fever by holding it underwater. The father comes home and hears the wife explain the baby's death as, "I trusted the doctor." Similarly, did Milgram's participants obey or simply trust the experimenter, even in his excesses? Can there be obedience without trust? Or are the experimenter and obedient participant cooperating? Can cooperation apply to actors of unequal as well as equal status? What if Milgram's experimenter started giggling? Or sounding vindictive, like "Shock him when he screams." Or confused about how to proceed? Would these certainly lower obedience rates? In the course of a 2-hour class, Milgram typically integrated the readings and concepts into the Socratic give-and-take, and the lively discussion often continued after the end of class. From this, Milgram would occasionally assign a brief take-home essay, to allow students to integrate the discussion in a position paper for him. Students in his class felt very capable of handling the actual ideas, rather than simply the literature about these ideas. It should be noted that Milgram was unusually conscientious in providing students with detailed written feedback on their exams and reports, often typewritten.

On a deeper level, though, Milgram taught experientially. Any discussion of how Milgram taught about obedience would be incomplete if it overlooked what might be called his "wonders"—unusual activities that made his students and colleagues openly and continuously wonder about his motives: "Why did he do that?"; "What will he do next?" A few classroom examples suffice.

At our first meeting of Advanced Social Psychology, Milgram noted he did not receive the classroom he expected, and for fully half of the 2-hour class he had us rearrange the tables and chairs into different shapes to see which "felt" best—octagon, rectangle, square. For all 14 of us, this was our first day at CUNY Graduate School, and with the illustrious Professor Milgram. So this bizarre display had us all very privately wondering what on earth was happening—as he had us repeatedly moving furniture, asking how we liked it now, welcoming new suggestions, then issuing new commands. It certainly increased interaction among us strangers, as we lifted and talked quite a bit. It allowed Milgram to demonstrate his control of the class, since none of us voiced our private thoughts. It displayed Milgram's remarkable ability to draw his students out, as we came to vie enthusiastically for his approval, volunteering new suggestions as each furniture arrangement fell miserably short. In the end we settled on a simple square. There was never any formal "debriefing" of this never-repeated exercise, nor ever another word about furniture. Even a quarter of a century later, this remains an unforgettable first class at CUNY.

Another wondrous exercise Milgram introduced into at least two Advanced Social Psychology classes was peer-grading. In an end-of-semester discussion of person perception, Milgram noted that this class was itself a group, subject to the principles of social psychology. He instructed each of us to help him by writing the names of all 13 class members, and assigning each the grade we think he or she deserved for this course. We all seemed stunned, but no one openly objected, and within 1 minute we were all writing. Milgram then collected the grade sheets, and asked aloud, "Why are there 13 of you and only 12 sheets?" One student diffidently replied, "I don't think students should be grading each other," to which Milgram simply shrugged "OK," then proceeded to read aloud students' names, and the grades they received from their classmates. Although a few students wrote A for everyone, others graded from A through C, so some students received lower grades than others, and many wondered long afterwards about the propriety of the exercise they had quietly completed. (Interestingly, the student who did not participate averaged the lowest grade from his peers, and also felt some pride at not participating in what seemed to him an obedience exercise.)

As mentioned previously, in Experimental Social Psychology, Milgram assigned us to ask people on the subway for their seats, which turned out to be an arduous task. As Milgram later noted about himself when he approached a subway-rider for his seat, "The words seemed lodged in my trachea and would simply not emerge. I stood there frozen" (Milgram, 1992, p. xxiv). After his students spent a month of struggling to complete the data collection, Milgram probed students' tensions in class in an unexpected way: Was your request illegal, or immoral? Why your pangs of conscience? Did your participants appear uneasy? Why did you do something you didn't want to do? How did you get through it? One student's report of the subway experiment captured the classroom dialog this way:

> "Each and every experimenter reported experiencing great and disproportionate amounts of tension. This tension even resembled the extremes produced in Milgram's (1965) experiment on obedience, where Ss were asked to electrically shock a fellow S complaining of a weak heart. For example, at least two of the female Ss reported uncontrollable laughter during the trials, similar to that found in the obedience study. One E agreed with his professor about becoming "dissociated" from his actions, and another noted that he naturally got more and more involved in the techniques of making his request, just as the obedient S had become more involved in the mechanics of flipping the shock levers. When asked the well-put question, "Well why did you go on despite the discomfort you felt?" one E responded "Well I had to do it for the course," so she surmounted her discomfort and completed the experiment." (Takooshian, 1972, pp. 10–11)

From Milgram's probing, it became clear to us students how much we resembled the subjects in his obedience experiment in almost every statement.

Both in and out of class, Milgram's unexpected activities often left his students and colleagues wondering about his motives, while also recognizing the insights these activities produced, particularly about obedience and other processes of social influence. Milgram's past achievements clearly endowed him with an ample supply of what has been termed "idiosyncrasy credit" (Hollander, 1958)—the ability to do unconventional activities that were simply unheard of in other courses, but which revealed their own unique insights.

CONCLUSION

One of the more unusual notebooks on Professor Milgram's shelf was a collection of letters he received over the years from some of the 1,000 participants in the obedience experiment on how his experiment touched their lives, often in unexpected and profound ways. Although some of these letters were negative, the greater number shared positive sentiments with him. Similarly, not all of Professor Milgram's students remember him the same way; yet we must all agree his classroom was a unique place, where abstract ideas took life, and where we learnt about social influence, obedience, and ourselves on more than one level. Like his research participants, there are many former students like me who say as I do, "Thank you, Professor Milgram."

REFERENCES

Aronson, E., & Mills, J. (1959). The effect of severity of initiation on liking for a group. *Journal of Abnormal and social psychology*, *59*, 177–181.

Baumrind, D. (1964). Some thoughts on ethics of research: After reading Milgram's "Behavioral study of obedience." *American Psychologist*, *19*, 421–423.

Bellenger, D.N. (1976). *Qualitative research in marketing*. Chicago: American Marketing Association.

Blass, T. (1991). Understanding behavior in the Milgram obedience experiment: The role of personality, situations, and their interactions. *Journal of Personality and Social Psychology*, *60*, 398–413.

Blass, T. (1992). The social psychology of Stanley Milgram. In M. P. Zanna (Ed.), *Advances in experimental social psychology* (Vol. 25, pp. 277–329). San Diego CA: Academic Press.

Blass, T. (1996). Stanley Milgram: A life of inventiveness and controversy. In G.A. Kimble, C.A. Boneau, & M. Wertheimer (Eds.). *Portraits of pioneers in psychology, Volume 2.* (pp. 315–331). Washington, DC, and Mahwah NJ: American Psychological Association and Lawrence Erlbaum Associates.

Brock, T. C., & Brannon, L. A. (1994). Milgram's last call. *Contemporary Psychology, 39,* 258–259.

Geller, D. M. (1975). *A role-playing simulation of obedience: Focus on involvement.* Doctoral dissertation, City University of New York. *Dissertation Abstracts International, 36,* 3671B: (University Microfilms No. 76–276)

Hollander, E. P. (1958). Conformity, status, and idiosyncrasy credit. *Psychological Review, 65,* 117–127.

Maslow, A. H. (1987). *Motivation and personality* (3rd ed.). New York: Harper & Row.

McGuire, W. J. (1997). Creative hypothesis generating in psychology: Some useful heuristics. In J. T. Spence, J. M. Darley, and D. J. Foss (Eds.), *Annual Review of Psychology, 48,* 1–30. Palo Alto, CA: Annual Reviews.

Milgram, A. (1993, August). A personal view. In H. Takooshian (Chair), *Stanley Milgram—His legacy for all of psychology,* Symposium conducted at the meeting of the American Psychological Association, Toronto.

Milgram, J. (1993, October). My brother Stanley. In H. Takooshian (Chair), *The legacy of Stanley Milgram's work,* Symposium conducted at Fordham University.

Milgram, S. (1963). *Obedience* (a film). Distributed by the New York University Film Library.

Milgram, S. (1965). Some conditions of obedience and disobedience to authority. *Human Relations, 18,* 57–75.

Milgram, S. (1973). *The city and the self* (a film). Distributed by Time-Life.

Milgram, S. (1974). *Obedience to authority: An experimental view.* New York: Harper & Row.

Milgram, S. (1976, August 21). Obedience to authority. *TV Guide,* pp. 24–25.

Milgram, S. (1977). *The individual in a social world: Essays and experiments.* Reading, MA: Addison-Wesley.

Milgram, S. (1980a, February 17). Response during the celebration of his appointment as CUNY Distinguished Professor of Psychology, Rendezvous Restaurant, New York City.

Milgram, S. (1980b, May 3). *Social psychology in the Eighties.* Keynote presentation to the eighth meeting of the New York Social Psychologists, Fordham University.

Milgram, S. (1992). *The individual in a social world: Essays and experiments.* (2nd Ed.). New York: McGraw-Hill. (Coedited posthumously by J. Sabini & M. Silver)

Milgram, S., & Sabini, J. (1978). On maintaining social norms: A field experiment in the subway. In A. Baum, J. E. Singer, and S. Valins (Eds.), *Advances in environmental psychology,* (Vol. 1, pp. 31–40). Hillsdale, NJ: Lawrence Erlbaum Associates.

Miller, A. G., Collins, B. E., & Brief, D. E. (1995). *Perspectives on obedience to authority: The legacy of the Milgram experiments.* [Special issue.] *Journal of Social Issues, 51* (3), 1–19.

Murray, B. (1997, August). Educators call for adding more research to classes. *APA Monitor,* p. 50.

Perlman, D. (1979). Rear end analysis: The uses of social psychology textbook citation data. *Teaching of psychology, 6,* 101–103.

Perlman, D. (1980). Who's who in psychology: Endler et al.'s SSCI scores versus a textbook definition. *American Psychologist, 35,* 104–106.

Sherif, M. (1975, August 31). *Social movements as effective vehicles of change: Social and personal.* Invited address to the annual meeting of the American Psychological Association, Chicago.

Silver, M. (1993, October). Stanley Milgram, teacher. In H. Takooshian (Chair), *The legacy of Stanley Milgram's work.* Symposium conducted at Fordham University.

Takooshian, H. (1972). *An experimental study of norms in the New York City subway.* Unpublished report, City University of New York.

Takooshian, H. (1990). Research, teaching, and the question of interaction. *New York State Psychologist, 41*(4), 44, 56.

Takooshian, H. (1993, August). *Stanley Milgram, professor.* In H. Takooshian (Chair), *Stanley Milgram—His legacy for all of psychology,* Symposium conducted at the annual meeting of the American Psychological Association, Toronto.

Takooshian, H. (1998). Stanley Milgram. In K. T. Jackson, K. E. Markoe, & A. Markoe (Eds.), *The Scribner encyclopedia of american lives* (Vol. 1, pp. 563–564). New York: Scribner's.

Takooshian, H., Haber, S., & Lucido, D. J. (1977, February). Who wouldn't help a lost child? You maybe. *Psychology Today,* pp. 67–68, 88.

Tavris, C. (1974, June). A man of 1,000 ideas: A sketch of Stanley Milgram. *Psychology Today,* pp. 74–75.

Zimbardo, P. G. (1993, August 21). *Discussant.* In H. Takooshian (Chair), *Stanley Milgram, His legacy for all of psychology,* Symposium conducted at the annual meeting of the American Psychological Association, Toronto.

Zimbardo, P. G. (1999, May). *Personal reflections on the joys of being a psychologist.* Invited presentation at the annual meeting of the Western Psychological Association, Irvine, CA.

APPENDIX: STUDENTS' NOMINATION OF STANLEY MILGRAM FOR THE 1985 APF AWARD FOR DISTINGUISHED TEACHING IN PSYCHOLOGY

Of the seven criteria for distinguished teaching in psychology, Stanley Milgram's contributions seem to fit at least four of them.

1. Teaching Materials.   He was one of the pioneers in the production of pedagogical films, to extend the teaching of psychology out of the classroom, while also enriching classroom teaching. (a) *Obedience* (NYU Film Library) has been seen by millions of Americans since its appearance in 1965, and is the most circulated film in the NYU Film Library. It is a uniquely powerful teaching tool, and it is hard to find a psychology student in college who has not seen it by the time of graduation. (b) There is also the *City and the self* (Time–Life, 1973) and (c) the four-film Harper & Row series in social psychology in the 1970s: *Invitation to Social Psychology, Conformity and independence, Human aggression, and Nonverbal communication.* Milgram conceived and produced these films in a simple, forceful way, and they have received several awards.

2. Classroom Teacher.   Among his doctoral students, he earned a reputation as a scintillating teacher, whose seminars often had an electric quality to them. He was brilliant in leading seminar discussions, asking the most probing questions, in expressing the most subtle ideas precisely, in seeing directly to the heart of an issue. In these, he seemed to have no peer, even in a department which had more than its share of excellent teachers.

3. Innovative Courses.   Milgram's restless imagination was continuously the source of new courses—Authority; Urban Psychology; Psychology and Photography; Media Psychology ... He seemed to develop a new course almost annually which was prescient of a growth of a new area of psychology; an indication of this is that research done in those courses was commonly published by him and the students in the course—contagion in crowds; the small world; the lost letter; the lost child; requesting a seat on the subway; urban overload; mental maps of New York and Paris; city steam; queue behavior.

4. Influence on Future Psychologists.   Milgram's courses at CUNY were required of incoming doctoral students the first year (Social Psychology, and Experimental Social Psychology), and there is little question they stimulated students toward enthusiastic careers in research and teaching. At his age of 51, he did not have a "full" career as a college teacher. It is somewhat arbitrary to identify some of the many alumni of his who are now psychology teachers/researchers, yet some of these are: Leonard Bickman, Alan Elms, Sam Gaertner, Daniel Geller, Charles Korte, Maury Silver. His colleagues of his time at Harvard are surely aware of a larger list, and Milgram's imprint has visibly shaped the careers of those he mentored.

3

Professor
Stanley Milgram—
Supervisor, Mentor, Friend

Judith Waters
Fairleigh Dickinson University, Madison

Since the obedience studies were first published in 1963, faculty and students, as well as reporters and members of the public at large, have been trying to interpret the results and to fathom the mind of an incredible individual, Dr. Stanley Milgram. Whereas most of the chapters in this book address theoretical and research issues, the first three attempt to supply some of the puzzle pieces that are needed to form a clear and cohesive picture of the unique and complex human being behind the obedience experiments. There has been a tendency to depict Dr. Milgram as that cliché, "larger than life," but although his work was creative and original, he lived in the normal world of academia and family. My goal is to present a balanced view from the perspective of a graduate assistant, doctoral student, and, later, friend.

If anyone were to ask me for a simplified observation of Dr. Milgram that I formulated during the years when I was his graduate assistant and a doctoral student in the Social/Personality Psychology Program at The Graduate School of the City University of New York (CUNY), I would say, "It must have been very difficult just being Stanley Milgram." In actuality, I don't think that he ever anticipated the level of notoriety that the obedience studies would generate, nor was he prepared for the nature of the criticisms, which sometimes included very personal and vituperative attacks. Even without the challenges to the ethics of the studies and their credibility (i.e., whether participants actually believed that the shocks and the learner's suffering were real), his fame alone created problems. Being so young in an academic community of venerable and accomplished researchers and becoming well known at such an early stage in his career interfered with his ability to judge the quality of his projects subsequent to the obedience studies. Quite simply, he was always trying to live up to himself. He could be alternately defensive and self-critical. But my story is getting ahead of itself.

STANLEY MILGRAM, SUPERVISOR

In the fall of 1968, Stanley Milgram was professor of Social/Personality Psychology at CUNY's Graduate Center. The first time that I actually saw him was at an interview that had been arranged by Dr. Harold M. Proshansky, first executive officer of the Psychology Program, later provost, and finally president of the Graduate School. The purpose of the meeting was for Dr. Milgram (in all the years that I worked for him and even after I graduated, I never called him "Stanley") to decide if he wanted to supervise my fellowship and have me as a graduate assistant. He agreed to let me follow in the footsteps of Leonard Bickman (who is presently a well-respected professor at Vanderbilt University), and thus began a relationship that lasted until Dr. Milgram died and perhaps, in a strange way, exists even now. Whenever I begin a new project, I wonder what he would think of it and how he would have designed the study. Knowing his standards and his creative approach to research sharpens my own thinking and drives me to justify my methods, even to myself, very carefully. The only difference between then and now is that now I seem to win more arguments.

There is still as much curiosity about Stanley Milgram as there was when he was alive. My own students now, my peers at the time, and colleagues have often asked what it was like to be Stanley Milgram's graduate assistant. I frequently wonder if they actually hope to hear that he used electric shock on me! The truth of the matter is that he behaved like many other faculty members. He didn't send me for coffee (he didn't drink coffee) or on any other trivial errands. When he was displeased with anyone, including me, he made no effort to disguise his feelings. Moreover, he was perfectly democratic. It didn't matter if the person was a student, a colleague, or even an invited guest speaker—he could be equally sharp in his comments.

Stanley Milgram was not noted for his patience. When I was still a graduate assistant, I attended a conference with Dr. Herbert Kelman of Harvard University, coauthor of *Crimes of Obedience* (Kelman & Hamilton, 1989), who asked me if Stanley was "still the same." Without further clarification, we both dissolved into laughter. Dr. Kelman quickly told me a story about how Dr. Milgram as a graduate student at Harvard had deposited a draft copy of his dissertation on Dr. Kelman's desk for review. He returned within hours to get Dr. Kelman's opinion. He actually expected immediate feedback.

Dr. Milgram's letters of recommendation for graduates seeking employment often left something to be desired. I will not present too many accounts here, but one of us was depicted as "strange looking but brilliant" (a paraphrase). My own letter said something in the nature of "despite the fact that she returned to school very late in life [I was 28 years old], her achievements are impressive." Because Stanley Milgram was an internationally famous authority figure, his words carried a great deal of weight. I have always wondered what image prospective employers formed of us from those letters.

The question that I must ask myself now that I have 25 years of faculty experience is, "Was Dr. Milgram more authoritarian than anyone else would have been in that position?" The answer is probably "no." In the end, he returned more in terms of his time and guidance than he demanded in terms of instant obedience. My individual problem was that I was already the parent of three children and found the traditional role of doctoral student a poor fit. I held onto the myth that I, too, was an authority figure. Therefore, it should come as no surprise to any of my fellow doctoral students nor to the faculty in the department that my professional relationship with Dr. Milgram did not always proceed smoothly. However, now that I look back on the experience from the perspective of a full professor and program director, I am surprised that he tolerated my challenges and even took the time to discuss his own germinating ideas with me. Given the pressures of running a program, I don't always have the opportunity to devote much time to nurturing my own graduate assistants.

When an apprentice works for a master long enough, they both need a respite. At the end of the first full year that I worked for Dr. Milgram, we were both happy to be going on vacation, but we avoided identifying, even generally, where we were going. In the back of my mind, I probably thought he would find something for me to do wherever I went. And, of course, he certainly didn't need to account to me for his time. On the first day of our vacation, my husband and I were climbing the hill to the Parthenon in Athens. It doesn't take much intuition to figure out who was sitting on the steps of that ancient monument. We greeted each other with restrained enthusiasm. The next day, I suggested to my husband that we pick a less popular tourist place to visit—in fact, probably the least popular site in Athens. Needless to say, Dr. and Mrs. Milgram were at the Military Museum, too. We all had dinner that evening, exchanged itineraries, and went merrily on our way, planning to meet on the last day and compare experiences. If I never heard the phrase "small world" again, I would not be devastated.

In the acknowledgment section of this chapter, I state that I owe Dr. Milgram's favorite charity $19. Let me now explain why. At one point in class, I had used a personal anecdote to illustrate a theoretical point, a habit I still haven't been able to cure. Because Dr. Milgram did not approve of the use of personal examples, he began to charge me $1 each time I transgressed. There are 19 stories in this chapter. I will cheerfully pay my debt for telling "Dr. Milgram stories," because I believe that understanding the individual will assist readers in understanding his work.

MENTOR

From the very beginning of my tour of duty as Stanley Milgram's assistant, he expressed the hope that my research would follow his own interests in the study of obedience to authority. The more he pressed, the more I resisted. In retrospect, I acted like an academic adolescent who argues against authority in order to establish her independence. I wish it were possible to communicate with him now and tell him that both my research and counseling practice interests have returned to important concepts associated with authority, albeit on a more pragmatic level. When I worked for him, my own perspective on the issues of authority differed from Dr. Milgram's basic orientation. He was concerned, and rightfully so, with unreasoning conformity, compliance, and obedience to authority figures, especially punitive and irrational leaders. I worry now, and did so 30 years go, about disrespect, defiance, and disobedience to rational authority figures (Roberts & Waters, 1998). Being involved in drug addiction counseling and the criminal justice system, I see the consequences of the denigration of teachers, law enforcement officers, and, most especially, parents, many of whom are more than worthy of being obeyed when such behavior is necessary (Waters, Morgen, Schmitt, Kuttner, & Schwartz, 1996; Waters, Roberts, & Morgen, 1997). The problems associated with socializing children both to respect and to question authority and the issues of the quality of the leadership in our society are beyond the scope of this article, but I can truly say that I still miss the opportunity to discuss these issues with him the way that I did when I was a graduate student. Now, of course, I am supposed to be the expert with a few, if not all of the right answers.

My focus in the study of authority is derived, at least partially, from my experience working as a researcher and counselor in a drug therapeutic community (TC) in Newark, New Jersey. TCs are residential treatment programs that generally, but not exclusively, deal with indigent and disadvantaged clients. The philosophy of a TC incorporates the concept of respect for rational authority figures. The model is that of a treatment program in which the residents are members of a functional family (DeLeon, 1994). Progress through the drug treatment program is marked by steps. Clients must earn their way by completing specific tasks at each level. The TC is run by staff (many of whom are "recovering" and are also graduates of the TC) and by residents who have achieved respect and positions of responsibility by virtue of their exemplary behavior. "Dissing" a staff member will result in a "pull up" (lower level criticism) for lesser transgressions and "haircuts" for more serious offenses. Haircuts once involved actually shaving peoples' heads, but they are now symbolic. One theoretical basis of the TC is that many of the residents have never been properly socialized in the first place and are in need of "habilitation," not rehabilitation. Dr. Milgram questioned my involvement both with drug abuse and with the criminal justice system. For him, pure academic research was the most valuable endeavor to which one could aspire. He met several of my colleagues from a local police force in New Jersey, and although he was certainly interested in what they did, I was never sure that he was totally comfortable with people from the "real world."

Not many people know that Stanley Milgram wrote children's books. Because I had done the line drawings for *Obedience to Authority* (Milgram, 1974a), he asked me to illustrate a book titled *Charlie's Coffeepot*. I felt that he should have a professional illustrator work with him and declined. He actually had more confidence in me than I had. That was, however, not the only project I declined. When he was making such educational films as *Invitation to Social Psychology* (Milgram, 1975), he asked if I wanted to assist him—without pay—just for the experience. I chose to teach summer session at Brooklyn College instead. As advice to students who may read this chapter, my strong suggestion is that, unless the money is critical, learn whatever you can and add to your portfolio of marketable skills and experience regardless of the pay.

When I was still a student, Dr. Milgram critiqued my papers by saying that my work was like listening to Haydn's Surprise Symphony; no one knew, until at least the third or fourth page, what the project was all about! I have transmitted this advice to my students: Let the reader know in the first paragraph where you are going. I recently passed the classroom of one of my former students who is now an adjunct faculty member. She was giving instructions for the term paper in her class and began by referring to the story that I had told her class about the Surprise Symphony. I just hope they've heard of the Surprise Symphony.

The city of New York had always fascinated me, perhaps even as much as the experience of living in cities interested Dr. Milgram. We had both grown up in New York City. In class, I tried to show the advantages of urban living, whereas the rest of my peers emphasized the superior quality of life in suburban areas. There I was again, always going in the opposite direction. However, I think Dr. Milgram was secretly pleased. A fellow student, Kathleen Hughes, and I did a study of discrimination in housing against gay men, which appeared in Dr. Milgram's (1970) article in *Science* magazine. We attempted to show that gay men would find it more comfortable to live in cities than in suburban or rural areas. We sent out letters written for us by a gay activist group that stated that we were two gay men trying to purchase a house either in cities, suburbs, or farm areas across the country. The letters were addressed to 200 real estate agents in those three locations. The results were in the predicted direction; that is, that living in the cities provides opportunities otherwise unavailable to people with what Goffman (1963) called a "spoiled identity." Our study was gratifying to Dr. Milgram, because the rest of the students found that people in the areas outside of cities were more helpful than urbanites.

Whenever there wasn't a particularly pressing project that needed to be completed, Dr. Milgram and I would play a sort of word game that he invented. For example, he would give me a simple title or phrase and I would turn it into a complex version in "psychologese." Thus Goffman's (1963) title, *Stigma*, became "the relative acceptance of a potentially discreditable person," and the words "I guess" were transformed into the statement: "Based on the previous assumptions as enumerated above, it is possible to hypothesize that the following outcomes will obtain under certain limited conditions"! At one point, I was sure that Dr. Milgram was in the process of designing a study of scientific language and the fine art of obscuring one's meaning from the uninitiated (i.e., anyone without an advanced degree). He was frequently concerned about how inaccessible the results of scientific studies were to the general public.

Because I had demonstrated an interest in studying cities, I designed a project that involved mapping out New York City in terms of Lynch's (1960) work on nodes (most frequented areas of a city) and pathways. I photographed sites all over the borough and then showed them to students from City College to see how many sites they could identify. One afternoon, after that study had been completed, I was sitting in the reception area outside of Dr. Milgram's office waiting for another student to go to lunch. Dr. Milgram came out and started asking me questions about how I had designed the New York study and if I was familiar with Paris. After a few minutes, he switched to speaking French. How grateful I was that I hadn't taken Spanish. At the end of our conversation, he asked if I wanted to go to Paris and repeat the New York study. This time I was much smarter and agreed immediately, even though I didn't know how the expenses would be covered. I ended up spending 6 weeks in Paris, taking 5,000 photographs, courtesy of the grants office at the Graduate Center. It was an experience that I will never forget. It fueled our conversations for years to come, because Dr. Milgram loved Paris even more than I did. He included the drawings that I had made of major monuments and the maps in an exhibition of his work in a gallery in Paris.

Along with other graduate students, I worked on the book on obedience, sometimes reviewing the debriefing forms and letters sent by participants and sometimes working on the illustrations, a few of which have become covers for foreign editions (Milgram, 1974b, 1982). When the book was published, my husband and I had a small dinner party in our home for Dr. and Mrs. Milgram. The book sat in a prominent place on the cocktail table. One of my sons, Mitchell, was about 12 years old at the time. Dr. Milgram asked him if he had read the book, to which Mitchell replied in the affirmative. Dr. Milgram then asked him his opinion, as though a 12-year-old were the most important reader he could have. They discussed all aspects of the book for about a half hour when Mitchell summarized his own evaluation. He essentially said that in the beginning of the book when Dr. Milgram was first describing the experiment it was excellent but that, in Mitchell's estimation, the interpretation at the end went far beyond the actual data! Dr. Milgram took his comments good-naturedly and added that his own editor had said much the same thing. He treated my children with respect from the first time that he met them, when they were all young.

By the time the obedience book was published, Dr. Milgram's and my relationship had mellowed. Before that, however, we still had some turbulent times. On one occasion, my way of responding to what I considered unreasonable behavior was to cover a sheet of paper with the symbols that comic book artists use to depict curses and then shove the paper under his door. On another occasion, when I entered Dr. Milgram's office, the chairs appeared to be in strange positions, not only out of their usual places opposite his desk but also out of alignment with each other, so that anyone sitting in them would have to stare at a wall and not face another person. I promptly moved the chairs around, at which point he demanded to know why I had moved his chairs without his permission. I laughed and said that he really didn't mean that and then asked what he was "up to". Of course, the strange placement of the chairs was to be used as a demonstration of his hypothesis that no one (no graduate student, at least) would even consider moving the chairs, and certainly not without his permission. There I was, the troublemaker again. Perhaps he kept me as a graduate assistant because he could count on me to be contrary.

FRIEND

When I was up for tenure and promotion to associate professor at Fairleigh Dickinson University, one of the criteria was—and remains—having a "national reputation," something that I had not yet acquired. To help me develop such a reputation, Dr. Milgram suggested that I chair a conference to be sponsored by the New York Area Social Psychologists featuring a famous keynote speaker. He volunteered to be that speaker, without a fee, when by that point in his career he was being paid in the thousands for lecturing. With the help of Harold Takooshian, who arranged for Fordham University to be the conference site, I did become the chair. There were an impressive number of people in the audience, thanks also to Florence Denmark and Victor Sanua. At the end of Dr. Milgram's address, he scanned that audience, which included many of his former students, and said that, although many of us might be having problems at our various institutions, we should not be discouraged. He also said that we should continue to contribute to our field despite the opinions of others. We all thought he was talking to each one of us alone, but we also knew that he was bringing up old and painful memories.

For years after I graduated, I would visit the Graduate Center to see Dr. Milgram whenever I was in Manhattan. The last time is a day that I will never forget—December 20, 1984. I was to meet my sister for lunch at the Hotel Algonquin (two blocks from the Graduate Center) for my birthday, but traffic from New Jersey was heavy, probably due to the upcoming Christmas holidays. Consequently, I arrived later than I anticipated. When I got to Dr. Milgram's office, he had already left for a dissertation defense, according to one of the secretaries. She suggested that if I ran I could catch up to him, and I thought "the days that I run after him are over. I'll see him next time." Of course, there was to be no "next time." That night when I got home, the phone rang, and my husband, who answered it, said that Joan Gerver was calling. Joan Gerver was a graduate student in the Social and Personality graduate program, but what was more salient was that she was Stanley Milgram's sister-in-law. I knew even before I took the phone that he had lost his battle with heart disease; he was only 51 years old. We had talked about his heart condition many times. He had told me how he hated his medication and that he felt his life and accomplishments were all behind him. No matter how hard I tried, I couldn't convince him otherwise. We are fortunate that he left us the legacy that he did. How I wish I had run after him one more time.

With an individual as creative as Stanley Milgram, it was difficult to select the most representative (not necessarily the most dramatic) events during my tenure as his graduate assistant and even beyond. There were so many stories. His mind can be compared to the salt machine depicted in "The Sorcerer's Apprentice" production of *Fantasia*. The tale of the sorcerer's apprentice is an old legend that dates back to the time when salt was a valuable commodity (remember "worth his salt"). The sorcerer has a book of incantations, including the one to activate the salt machine. The apprentice, as typical of apprentices, is both curious and mischievous. He finds the incantation that starts the machine. The problem is that he hasn't learned how to shut it off. Soon, every room in the castle is filled to overflowing with salt. In order to escape the wrath of the sorcerer and to avoid punishment, the apprentice drags the machine to a boat and rows it out into the ocean, where it sinks to the bottom, remaining there until the present day. And that, as the legend goes, is how the sea became salty. Stanley Milgram's mind was a salt machine of ideas.

ACKNOWLEDGMENTS

I wish to thank Tom Blass for his patience and encouragement in what proved to be a more difficult task than I had anticipated. I also owe Dr. Milgram's favorite charity $19 (which will be adjusted for inflation) for writing this article and telling stories.

REFERENCES

DeLeon, G. (1994). Therapeutic communities. In M. Galanter & H. Kleber (Eds.). *The American Psychiatric Press textbook of substance abuse treatment* (pp. 391–414). Washington, DC: American Psychiatric Press, Inc.

Goffman, E. (1963). *Stigma: Notes on the management of a spoiled identity*. New York: Simon & Schuster.

Kelman, H. C., & Hamilton, V. L. (1989). *Crimes of obedience: Toward a social psychology of authority and responsibility*. New Haven, CT: Yale University Press.

Lynch, K. (1960). *The image of the city*. Cambridge, MA: MIT Press.

Milgram, S. (1970, March 13). The experience of living in cities. *Science*, 1461–1468.

Milgram, S. (1974a). *Obedience to authority: An experimental view*. New York: Harper & Row.

Milgram, S. (1974b). *Grenzeloze gehoorzaamheid: Een experimenteel onderzoek* [Limitless obedience: An experimental inquiry]. Utrecht/Antwerpen: Bruna & Zoon.

Milgram, S. (Producer and writer). (1975). Invitation to social psychology [Film]. New York: Harper & Row.

Milgram, S. (1982). *Das Milgram-experiment: Zur Gehorsamsbereitschaft gegenuber Autoritat* [The Milgram experiment: On obedience-readiness toward authority]. Reinbek bei Hamburg, Germany: Rowohlt Vevlag GmbH.

Roberts, A. R., & Waters, J. (1998). The coming storm: Factors in juvenile violence and justice system responses. In A. R. Roberts (Ed.), *Juvenile justice: Policies programs, and services* (pp. 40–72). Chicago: Nelson Hall.

Waters, J., Morgen, K., Schmitt, B., Kuttner, P., & Schwartz, A. (1996). "Guiding Adolescents to Prevention": An HIV prevention program in a youth detention center. *Crisis Intervention and Time-Limited Treatment, 5*, 85–96.

Waters, J., Roberts, A. R., & Morgen, K. (1997). High risk pregnancies: Teenagers, poverty, and drug abuse. *Journal of Drug Issues, 27*, 541–562.

4

The Milgram Paradigm After 35 Years: Some Things We Now Know About Obedience to Authority*

Thomas Blass
University of Maryland, Baltimore County

What have I learned from my investigations? First, that the conflict be-tween conscience and authority is not wholly a philosophical or moral is-sue. Many of the subjects felt, at the philosophical level of values, that they ought not to go on, but they were unable to translate this conviction into action. ... It may be that we are puppets—puppets controlled by the strings of society. But at least we are puppets with perception, with aware-ness. And perhaps our awareness is the first step to our liberation. (Milgram, 1974b, p. 568)

SAFER: Are you suggesting that—that it could happen here?

MILGRAM: I would say, on the basis of having observed a thousand peo-ple in the experiment and having my own intuition shaped and informed by these experiments, that if a system of death camps were set up in the United States of the sort we had seen in Nazi Germany, one would be able

---

*Reprinted with permission from the *Journal of Applied Social Psychology*, 1999, Vol. 29, pp. 955–978.

to find sufficient personnel for those camps in any medium-sized American town. (CBS News, *Sixty Minutes*, March 31, 1979)

Milgram conducted the obedience studies early in his professional career and then went on to apply his innovative touch to a variety of other phenomena, such as the "small world" problem and the effects of televised antisocial behavior. Yet clearly the obedience work has overshadowed his other research—it remains his best known and most widely discussed work. Of the approximately 140 invited speeches and colloquia he gave during his lifetime, more than one third dealt, directly or indirectly, with obedience.[1] Milgram was still giving invited colloquia on the topic in 1984, the year he died—22 years after he completed them: one at LaSalle College on April 7 and the other at the University of Tennessee at Martin on April 26. In fact, it is somewhat ironic that his very last publications, both appearing posthumously in 1987, dealt with obedience. One appeared in the *Concise Encyclopedia of Psychology* (Milgram, 1987a) and the other in *The Oxford Companion to the Mind* (Milgram, 1987b).

Given the widespread familiarity of Milgram's obedience studies, it should not be surprising to find the obedience research discussed or referred to in publications as diverse as the *Archives of Internal Medicine* (Green, Mitchell, Stocking, Cassel, & Siegler, 1996) and the *Indian Journal of the History of Science* (Laurent, 1987), nor to see it brought into discussions of topics as wide- ranging as business ethics (Browne, Kubasek, & Giampetro-Meyer, 1995/1996; Ferrell & Gardiner, 1991; MacLellan & Dobson, 1997), military psychology (Guimond, Kwak, & Langevin, 1994; Spector, 1978), economics (Anderson & Block, 1995), Holocaust studies (e.g., Browning, 1992; Goldhagen, 1996; Katz, 1993), philosophy (Assiter, 1998; Morelli, 1983), and law (Koh, 1997). Perhaps it should not even be surprising to find it in the title of a song ("We Do What We're Told—Milgram's 37" by rock musician Peter Gabriel, on his 1986 album, *So*) or featured prominently in a French film, *I Comme Icare* (*I as in Icarus*), starring Yves Montand. The obedience experiments were the focus of the fall 1995 issue of the *Journal of Social Issues*, and they continue to fascinate the reading public (e.g., French, 1997; Masters, 1996).

The interest generated by the obedience research has crossed not only disciplinary boundaries but also language barriers. Early on,

---

[1]Quotes from letters and most information given without citation are from the Stanley Milgram Papers, Yale University Archives.

Milgram's (1965b) article, "Some Conditions of Obedience and Dis-obedience to Authority," was translated into German (Milgram, 1966) and Hebrew (Milgram, 1967). The book *Obedience to Authority: An Experimental View* (Milgram, 1974a) has been translated into 11 languages. During the past few years, a social psychologist at the Russian State University of the Humanities, Alexander Voronov, has been introducing Milgram's work to Russian audiences through his teaching and newspaper articles (e.g., Voronov, 1993) and through Milgram's documentary film *Obedience* (1965a), with a Russian voice-over added.

The obedience research is clearly among the best known and most widely discussed work in the social sciences. Undoubtedly, an important reason for this is that it has been a source of usable insights and lessons for both self and society. As his colleague Irwin Katz described the obedience studies at Milgram's funeral:

> After two decades of critical scrutiny and discussion, they remain one of the most singular, most penetrating, and most disturbing inquiries into human conduct that modern psychology has produced in this century. Those of us who presume to have knowledge of man are still perplexed by his findings, with their frightful implications for society.

The purpose of this chapter is to provide a detailed examination of a number of salient questions and issues surrounding the Milgram obedience experiments that are still in need of systematic attention. (For reviews and analyses related to other aspects of the obedience paradigm and of other facets of Milgram's life and work, the reader is referred to Blass, 1991, 1992b, 1993, 1996b; see also Miller, 1986.) Specifically, I draw on about 35 years of accumulated research and writings on the obedience paradigm to present a status report on four questions and issues. Although each of the questions and issues could be addressed independently of the others, what unites them is that, in their totality, their answers should help advance our knowledge of research using the Milgram paradigm and its implications.

First I address the question of how to construe the nature of authority in the obedience experiment. This is a fundamentally important question because the kinds of authority–subordinate relationships to which the findings from the obedience experiments are generalizable hinge on the answer to that question. In pursuit of that answer, I review the various views on this question. Then, in an attempt to provide at least an indirect resolution of the conflicting viewpoints, I present the results of a person-perception experiment I conducted using an edited version of Milgram's (1965a) documentary film, *Obedience*. Second, I review the evidence regarding the apparent inability of naive respondents to predict the high degree of obedience Milgram found in his standard conditions. The tendency for those unfamiliar with the obedience experiments to vastly underestimate the actual obedience rates reported by Milgram has contributed importantly to the revelatory power of the experiments. The prediction-versus-outcome dichotomy is also important because it is closely intertwined with a controversy regarding how to interpret the obedient participants' behavior—as representing destructive obedience, as Milgram saw it, or as involving a more benign view centered on participants' trust in the experimenter, as represented in Mixon's approach. Third, I present a review of all the methodological replications of Milgram's standard or baseline conditions that allowed comparisons of males and females in rates of obedience. As will be shown, the totality of the findings of my review are consistent with those of Milgram, although there are a couple of discrepant results that pose a challenge to understanding. Finally, this chapter provides an empirical answer to the question of whether or not obedience rates have changed since Milgram first conducted his experiments in 1961–1962. The answer not only has practical usefulness for those of us who have often fielded this question from students when teaching about the obedience experiments but also has theoretical importance: It provides data-based input regarding the validity of Gergen's "enlightenment effects" notion.

HOW SHOULD WE CONSTRUE THE NATURE OF AUTHORITY IN THE OBEDIENCE EXPERIMENT?

How to characterize the kind of authority embodied by Milgram's experimenter is a fundamentally important question, since the kind of authority-subordinate relationships the experiments have implications for, depend on the answer to that question. I first examine Milgram's view of the authority figure in his experiments, as well as differing perspectives. Then I present the findings from an experiment that provide a rapprochement between the conflicting viewpoints, at least indirectly.

Milgram saw his experimenter as representing a legitimate authority, one who is seen as having a right to issue commands and to whom one feels an obligation to obey. As Milgram (1974a) put it, "an authority system ... consists of a minimum of two persons sharing the expectation that one of them has the right to prescribe behavior for the other" (pp. 142–143). He also notes that a legitimate authority is one who is "perceived to be in a position of social control within a given situation" (p. 138) and that "the power of an authority stems not from personal characteristics but from his perceived position in a social structure" (p. 139). And what is it about a legitimate authority that, according to Milgram, enables him to elicit destructive obedience, the kind that bears a kinship to the behavior of a Nazi storm trooper? First is the ability of a legitimate authority to define reality for the person who accepts his or her authority. As Milgram put it: "There is a propensity for people to accept definitions of action provided by legitimate authority. That is, although the subject performs the action, he allows authority to define its meaning" (1974a, p. 145). Earlier, (Milgram, 1965b), he had made the point even more strongly:

> With numbing regularity good people were seen to knuckle under the demands of authority and perform actions that were callous and severe. Men who are in everyday life responsible and decent were seduced by the trappings of authority, by the control of their perceptions, and by the uncritical acceptance of the experimenter's definition of the situation, into performing harsh acts. (p. 74)

The other factor that enables a legitimate authority to evoke destructive obedience, according to Milgram, is the shift of participants into a different experiential state—the agentic state—that enables them to relinquish responsibility to the authority and therefore to follow his or her orders without regard to their morality. As Milgram (1974a) put it: "The most far-reaching consequence of the agentic shift is that a man feels responsible *to* the authority directing him but feels no responsibility *for* the content of the actions that the authority prescribes" (pp. 145–146).

A main differing perspective on the nature of authority in the obedience experiment is to see him as an expert authority. Morelli (1983), a critic of Milgram, succinctly captures the difference between a legitimate authority and an expert authority as the difference between saying someone is *in* authority, that is, in charge, or *an* authority, that is, someone with expertise on some topic.

One of several writers (Greenwood, 1982; Helm & Morelli, 1985; Morelli, 1983; Penner, Hawkins, Dertke, Spector, & Stone, 1973) who express the authority-as-expert point of view is Patten (1977), a philosopher, and in doing so he argues for a distinction between the obedience of participants in the Milgram experiments and obedience in carrying out mass killings. He argues that there is a difference between the type of authority represented by Milgram's experimenters and the kind wielded by a Hitler. The former possess what Patten calls "expert-command" authority; that is, they are able to command obedience by means of their presumed expertise regarding learning and shock machinery. The latter, more worrisome, kind of authority wields what he calls a "simple-command" authority; that is, the power to command and to exact obedience is based on legal or quasi-legal considerations, not on any special expertise regarding the task at hand. According to Patten, knowledge about how a person might react to expert-command authority cannot tell us about that individual's behavior in relation to a simple-command authority.

Milgram clearly distinguished between his conception of his experimenter as a legitimate authority and authority based on expertise. In an interview conducted by Evans (1976), he said, "When we talk about a medical authority, we're talking about someone with expertise. That's not quite the same as the kind of authority I was studying, which is someone perceived to have the right to control one's behavior" (p. 349).

What is interesting about this comment is that there is evidence provided by Milgram himself—although it is anecdotal—that for some of his own participants the authority's expertise may have been his salient attribute. In his book (Milgram, 1974a), he quotes an exchange between a participant, a Mr. Rensaleer, and the experimenter. The participant had just stopped at 255 volts, and the experimenter tried to prod him on by saying, "There is no permanent tissue damage." Mr. Rensaleer answers, "Yes, but I know what shocks do to you. I'm an electrical engineer, and I have had shocks ... and you get real shook up by them—especially if you know the next one is coming. I'm sorry" (1974a, p. 51). What this participant seems to be doing is pitting his own expertise against the experimenter's expertise as a way of undermining the latter's power.

It is also worth noting that Milgram was not entirely consistent in his view about the source of his experimenter's power as an authority. Or, more precisely, he seemed to have shifted his position somewhat later in his career. In 1983, in one of the last things he wrote about obedience before his death, here is what he said in reply to a critical article by Morelli (1983):

In regard to the term "authority," Morelli states I did not adequately distinguish between the expert knowledge of "an" authority and a person who is "in" authority (in the sense that he occupies an office or position). I fully agree with Morelli that this is an important distinction. ... Within my own study, how would the experimenter be classified in terms of these two types of authority? As frequently happens, real life is more complex than textbooks: both components co-exist in one person. The experimenter is both the person "in charge" and is presumed by subjects to possess expert knowledge. One could envision a series of experiments that attempt to empirically disentangle these two elements and I am all for such inquiry. (Milgram, 1983, pp. 191–192)

I recently conducted an experiment that tried to assess the perceived roles played by expertise and legitimacy in the obedience experiment (Blass, 1992a). I studied my participants' *judgments* about obedience rather than their *own* obedience, so it is not exactly the kind of experiment Milgram had in mind that would "empirically disentangle [the] two elements." Still, I hoped that it would serve as useful input into the issue. (I should note that there is a study, a doctoral dissertation by Frederick Miller, 1975, that is probably closer to the kind that Milgram had in mind. It pitted the experimenter's expertise and legitimacy against each other in a factorial design, and obedient vs. defiant behavior of the participant served as the dependent variable. However, its focus was on self-inflicted pain, which probably involves different underlying dynamics than does obedience to inflict pain on another person.)

The conceptual framework I worked with is French and Raven's (1959) classic formulation regarding the bases of social power. There is a natural affinity between French and Raven's schema and the obedience work, for a couple of reasons. First, many social psychology textbooks discuss them together. Second, Raven (1965; Raven & Rubin, 1983) in later publications actually cites the obedience experiment as an illustration of legitimate power, one of the types of power in French and Raven's system. (For a recent statement on the bases of social power, see Raven, 1992.) For my purposes, their conceptualization is also useful because expert power is another one of their categories. A further potential benefit of using French and Raven's schema is that they actually distinguish among *six* different types of power: besides legitimate and expert power, there are reward, coercive, referent, and informational power. So by using French and Raven's framework, we might also learn about the perceived role of other attributes besides expertise and legitimacy as determinants of the authority's power. The sources of power are listed, with their meanings, in the first and second columns of Table 4.1.

The college-student participants in the experiment were shown a 12-minute videotape, a shortened, edited version of Milgram's (1965a) documentary film *Obedience*, similar to ones I have used in other studies that focused on attributional processes in the Milgram experiment (Blass, 1990, 1995). The end of the segment the students saw shows a

TABLE 4.1

Mean Rankings of Bases of Social Power as Explanations for an Obedient Participant's Behavior in the Milgram Experiment

Power Categories	Meanings: Participants are influenced because ...	Explanation	Mean Ranks
Reward	they see the E as a potential source of rewards.	Because the experimenter is a figure of authority, his positive evaluations are especially rewarding. So the participant carries out the experimenter's wishes, thereby hoping to win his approval.	4.46^b
Coercive	they see the E as a potential source of punishments.	The experimenter urged the participant to continue, using such phrases as: "The experiment requires that you go on." For the participant, such phrases seemed to warn of negative consequences if he didn't continue.	2.71^a
Legitimate	they believe that the E has a legitimate right to prescribe behavior for them.	Because the experimenter represents the authority of science and the participant agreed to be a participant, he believes that the experimenter has a right to control his actions, and so the participant feels obliged to comply with the experimenter's wishes.	2.40^a
Referent	they identify with, or like, the E.	The participant has respect and admiration for the experimenter, identifies with him, and would like to be such a person.	5.86^c
Expert	they perceive the E as having some special knowledge or expertise.	As a scientific expert, the experimenter has the faith and trust of the participant, so, when the experimenter tells him that "although the shocks may be painful, they're not dangerous," the participant feels reassured and continues with the procedure.	2.31^a
Informational	the information the E provides is intrinsically compelling or convincing.	The introductory information, provided by the experimenter, about the goal of the experiment—namely, to learn more about the effect of punishment on memory—convinces the participant that the study has value and, therefore, that his cooperation is important.	3.23^a

Note. Means sharing a superscript do not differ significantly from each other.

participant, referred to in Milgram's (1974a) book by the pseudonym Fred Prozi, administering the sequence of shocks beginning with 90 volts. In the full version of the film, he is shown ending up completely obedient (i.e., giving the 450-volt shock). In the edited version shown to my participants, the tape was stopped right after Prozi administered the 180-volt shock.

Participants were then asked to indicate why they thought the man they just saw kept on following the experimenter's instructions and continued to shock the learner. To answer that question, they were provided with a set of six cards, each of which contained a different explanation that was meant to capture a specific social power category. These explanations are listed in the third column of Table 4.1. (I am indebted to Forsyth, 1987, and Raven and Rubin, 1983, for some of the ideas and wording that I used in developing the explanations.) The participants were asked to indicate which reason they thought was the most likely one, then the next most likely one, and so on.

Participants' choices were assigned rank scores of 1 through 6, with the most likely explanation receiving a rank score of 1. The data were analyzed by means of a one-way repeated-measures analysis of variance, with social power category as the independent variable and assigned rank as the dependent variable, yielding a highly significant $F(5, 170) = 42.77, p < .0001$. Dependent t-tests using the Bonferroni test correction were then conducted to test for differences between pairs of mean rank scores. The mean rank scores are presented in the last column of Table 4.1. As can be seen, the expert-power explanation was seen as most likely, followed very closely by legitimate power, whereas coercive power was seen as the third and informational power as the fourth most likely explanation. These differences, however, were not significant. Reward power came next, and referent power was seen as the least likely reason for the participants' compliance.

Several conclusions can be drawn from the findings, tempered by the obvious caution that they are based on data from external perceivers about 30 years after the fact and not from actual participants in the Milgram experiments. First, it is reassuring to know that the two attributes of the experimental authority seen as most salient by naive perceivers are the same ones that have been pointed to over the years by more scholarly perspectives—that is, legitimacy and expertise. Second, rather than deciding between legitimacy and expertise, the results suggest that both factors may have combined to give Milgram's experimenter the tremendous power that he had. Third, the fact that coercive power was ranked relatively high, as the third most likely explanation, is surprising, because it suggests that some of Milgram's original participants may have been reading things into the experimenter's words. Further, it leaves us with the gnawing possibility that many of his participants may have been reading other things into the experimenter's words that we don't know about, which may have figured importantly as determinants of their behavior. And, finally, this study affirms, as do other studies (Blass, 1990, 1995, 1996a; Collins & Brief, 1993; Guimond & Kwak, 1995; Miller, Gillen, Schenker, & Radlove, 1974; Pearson, 1992), the value of using person-perception and attributional methodologies to advance our understanding of obedience to authority.

DO PREDICTIONS OF THOSE UNFAMILIAR WITH THE EXPERIMENT UNDERESTIMATE THE ACTUAL OBEDIENCE RATES?

Milgram found that they did, vastly, and much of the revelatory power of the obedience work is based on this contrast between our expectations of very little obedience and the actual result that a majority of participants obeyed in Milgram's standard or baseline conditions. Milgram considered this finding so centrally important that, according to one of his students (Takooshian, 1993), he would become furious if a student suggested that it was all common sense, that if you thought about it you could have predicted the outcome. (Incidentally, this feature of the obedience studies was dramatized very effectively in 1976 in *The Tenth Level*, a made-for-TV movie starring William Shatner, which earned its writer, George Bellak, an honorable mention in the American Psychological Foundation's 1977 National Media Awards.) Specifically, Milgram (1963) found that a group of Yale seniors predicted an obedience rate of 1.2% whereas a group of psychiatrists predicted that only .125% of participants would be fully obedient. Here is how he described this latter finding in a letter to E. P. Hollander:

> Recently I asked a group of 40 Yale psychiatrists to predict the behavior of experimental subjects in a novel, though significant situation. The psychiatrists —although they expressed great certainty in the accuracy of their predictions—were wrong by a factor of 500. Indeed, I have little doubt that a group of charwomen would do as well. (September 24, 1962)

Although Milgram's powerful demonstration that normal individuals are much more willing to obey a legitimate authority's orders than one might have thought remains an enduring insight, subsequent studies suggest that it is in need of some qualification, because they show that greater accuracy in predicting the results of an obedience experiment is possible.

In studies using maximum voltages predicted on the 450-volt scale as the dependent variable, mean estimates of others' obedience levels have been as high as 276.75 (Miller, Gillen, Schenker, & Radlove, 1974), 225 (Maughan, 1981), and 216 (Maughan & Higbee, 1981) in specific conditions.

The gap between expected and obtained obedience narrows even more substantively when we consider studies that obtained predictions using obedience rates. Mixon (1971) read participants the Method section from Milgram (1963) and then asked them how "a hypothetical group of 100 American males" would behave. The percentage of participants predicted to be fully obedient ranged from an average of 33.52% (naive women's estimates) to 44.3% (estimates of a group of naive men). Kaufmann and Kooman (1967) gave participants descriptions based on Milgram's (1963) procedures and found 27% of them predicting that the "teacher" would continue to the end. A similar finding was obtained in a very recent study by Guimond, Kwak, and Langevin (1994) involving a group of Canadian officer candidates. After learning about a baseline obedience experiment (without the outcome) from a short videotape, 23.9% of them predicted full obedience by other Canadians. Furthermore, Mixon (1971) was able to get variations in predicted obedience by systematically modifying the details about the procedure read to participants. These variations ranged from 0% of the participants predicting complete obedience when the description they read clearly indicated that the learner was in danger of being harmed to 90% when indications of possible harm were minimized. Taken together, these findings point not only to greater accuracy in perceivers' predictions about obedience but also to a different way to understand underestimations of obedience.

An influential perspective on underestimations of obedience has been that of Ross (1977). According to his view, in attempting to predict obedience, people erroneously overlook the determining influence of the situation—the power of the authority—and place too much weight on the personal dispositions of the "teacher," exemplifying a tendency he labeled "the fundamental attribution error." Mixon's (1971) findings suggest, however, that the discrepancy between predictions and findings takes place not because people do not give enough weight to the immediate situation but because those who are asked to make predictions, on the one hand, and actual participants in an obedience experiment, on the other hand, may be responding to *different* situations: The descriptions given in prediction tasks may convey a procedure that is potentially more harmful for the learner than the real participant in an obedience experiment typically found it to be. Thus, for example, Bierbrauer (1974), in his doctoral dissertation, had participants learn about the obedience experiment by either watching, or serving as the "teacher" in, a reenactment of an experimental session that ends in complete obedience. Across two experiments and a number of conditions, their subsequent estimates of the percentage of participants who would give the 450-volt shock averaged 11.5%.[2] In introducing the reenactment, however, Bierbrauer (1974) told his participants that "Professor Milgram wanted to see whether subjects would obey an experimenter's instructions to deliver painful and *potentially dangerous* electric shocks to one of their peers" (p. 78; italics added). But, as Mixon (1976) has argued, both the scientific context and the experimenter's reassurances that the shocks may be painful but not dangerous probably led the actual participants in Milgram's experiments to anticipate that the "learner" would not be harmed.

In other words, Mixon's view of participants' behavior in the obedience experiment is a more benign one than Milgram's. If Mixon is right, then was Milgram wrong in referring to his obedient participants' actions as "destructive"? This is how Mixon sees it, and for a long time, I saw Milgram's and Mixon's approaches as conflicting and irreconcilable. But recently, in a review of Mixon's (1989) book, Lee Hamilton (1992) presented a persuasive and insightful perspective that brings the implications of Mixon's view closer to Milgram's:

> I believe ... that Milgram's work has a value beyond that accorded it in Mixon's account. True, perhaps Milgram's subjects suspended their doubts and disbeliefs in going along with experimental commands. Perhaps they did not really believe that damage and death could or should ensue from their actions. So what; they still did them. I see the actions of Milgram's subjects as more closely analogous to those of corporate employees who

---

[2]This number was computed by me by averaging across the condition means in Tables 2 and E-4 in Bierbrauer (1974).

produce unsafe products and believe that the company could not really be endangering consumers just to make a profit, than to the actions of a military subordinate ordered to shoot civilians. The fact remains that these employees—or Milgram's subjects—perform the deeds they are asked to perform. (p. 1313)

ARE THERE SEX DIFFERENCES IN OBEDIENCE?

Although almost all his participants were men, Milgram created one condition (Experiment 8, Milgram, 1974a) in which the participants were women. The result was exactly the same rate of obedience—65%—as for men in the comparable condition (Experiment 5). I found nine methodological replications in the literature that used both male and female participants. Consistent with Milgram's own findings, eight out of nine of these studies found no sex differences (see Table 4.2).

As can be seen in Table 4.2, the one exception is a study by Kilham and Mann (1974), conducted in Australia, in which the researchers found the obedience rate among men (40%) to be significantly higher than among women (16%). (The Kilham and Mann, 1974, study is also noteworthy for another reason: Its overall rate of obedience—28%— is the lowest reported in the literature for a standard obedience condition.)

It is also relevant to mention two other studies in this context, because they pose a challenge to understanding, although they were not included in Table 4.2: the first, because it lacked a comparison group of men and the second, because it used a real victim, an animal "learner." Ring, Wallston, and Corey (1970) conducted a voice-feedback replication using 57 female participants. Although the main focus of this study was the relative effectiveness of different debriefing methods, an important finding was that 91% of their participants were fully obedient, the highest rate for a standard condition reported in the obedience literature. Sheridan and King (1972) conducted a unique Milgram-type study using a puppy as the "learner." Even though the cute puppy was visible to the participants and enough actual shock was delivered to cause the puppy to yelp and jump in pain, 100% of the female participants were fully obedient, whereas only 54% of the males were obedient.

Milgram (1974a) had also reported that, although the level of obedience in women was the same as in men, the self-reported tension of the obedient women was higher than among 20 groups of obedient male participants. This result finds support in a study by Shanab and Yahya

48

TABLE 4.2

Studies Using the Milgram Paradigm That Have Compared Male and Female Participants on Level of Obedience

Author and Year	Country	Gender	N	Author's Name for or Description of Condition (When More Than One in Study)	Equivalent Milgram Condition(s)	% Fully Obedient	Gender of Experimenter	Participant Gender Differences Yes/No	Participant Gender Differences % Fully Obedient	Remarks
Milgram (1962)	United States	F	40	Experiment 8. Women as participants	N/A	65	Male	No	-	Compared with Milgram's Experiment 5 (same condition using 40 male participants) in which 65% were fully obedient. The data on women first appeared in Milgram (1974a), but all conditions were completed between the summer of 1961 and May 1962. The experiment using women was carried out in 1962. Thus the 1962 in the citation reflects the completion date, not the publication date.
Edwards et al. (1969)	South Africa	M F	10 6	-	Experiment 2. Voice feedback	87.5	Female	No	-	The experimenter, a 19-year-old female, as well as her two male "technician" assistants, were college students. See also the note about this experiment in the appendix.
Bock and Warren (1972)	United States	M F	17 13	-	Experiment 5. New baseline	?	Male	No	-	Percent of fully obedient participants not reported. The measure of obedience was maximum shock level given.
Bock (1972)	United States	M/F	25	Scientific authority	Experiment 5. New baseline	40	Male	No	-	Lack of participant gender differences reported only for total participant sample, i.e., across three conditions, of which the scientific-authority condition was one.
Kilham and Mann (1974)	Australia	M F	25 25	Executant	Experiment 2. Voice feedback	28	Male	Yes	M 40 F 16	Participants assumed role of executants taking orders to shock from confederate transmitters who they thought were also participants. Paired male executant with male learner and female executant with female learner.

Study	Country	Gender	N	Condition	Experiment	%	Experimenter			Notes
Costanzo (1976)	United States	M F	48 48	Retaliation and Non-retaliation conditions combined	Experiment 1. Remote	81	Female	No	'	Participant and learner paired in four conditions: M–M, M–F, F–M, F–F
Shanab and Yahya (1977)	Jordan	M F	48 48	Experimental	Experiments 1 and 2. Remote and Voice-feedback combination	73	Female	No	'	Participants were children aged 6–16. Participant and learner paired in two conditions: M–M, F–F
Shanab and Yahya (1978)	Jordan	M F	12 12	Experimental	Experiments 1 and 2. Remote and Voice-feedback combination	62.5	Female	No	'	Participant and learner paired in two conditions: M–M, F–F
Miranda, Caballero, Gomez, & Zamorano (1981)	Spain	M F	12 12	Not watching and Watching conditions combined	Experiment 2. Voice feedback Experiment 3. Proximity	50	Male and female	No	'	When participants were male, experimenter and learner were male. When participants were female, experimenter and learner were female. The dependent variable was highest shock given rather than percentage fully obedient. However, a graph in the report reveals indirectly that at least 50% were fully obedient.
Schurz (1985)	Austria	M F	24 32	—	Experiment 1. Remote	80	Female	No	'	Learner was female. Stimulus—"Ultrasound waves" supposedly damaging to skin at higher intensities.

(1977) involving Jordanian children and adolescents. They reported that females were more likely to show visible signs of tension than males.

Two consistencies emerge from the studies presented in this section. First, it is quite remarkable that 9 out of 10 comparisons (Table 4.2) showed no sex differences in obedience, despite the existence of between-experiment differences on such factors as country in which the experiment was conducted, gender of experimenter, gender of learner, and specific details of the experimental procedures. Eagly's (1978) seminal review of sex differences in influenceability showed that the widely held assumption that women are generally more influenceable than men was wrong. She found no sex differences in the majority of the studies she reviewed. A tendency for women to be more susceptible to influence than men showed up in only one domain—the Asch-type group-pressure conformity situation, in which 34% of the studies found women to be significantly more conforming than men. Her review, although mentioning the Milgram studies and two replications that looked at sex differences (Kilham & Mann, 1974; Sheridan & King, 1972), did not include a systematic review of studies of sex differences in the obedience paradigm. The findings reported here complement Eagly's (1978) review by identifying yet another social influence paradigm in which the majority of studies show no sex differences.

Second, the consistency of Milgram's findings on sex differences in self-reported tension is also quite noteworthy, with obedient women reporting greater tension than the obedient men in 20 conditions. These findings have wide-ranging implications beyond the question of sex differences. In particular, the fact that the same observable behaviors—identical rates of obedience (65%) in men and women in a baseline condition—were accompanied by different levels of nervousness should alert us to the importance of trying to identify the underlying processes involved in acts of obedience and defiance, whether they involve the Milgram paradigm or not.

HAVE OBEDIENCE RATES CHANGED OVER TIME?

One of the questions I have posed to my social psychology classes when presenting the obedience studies is what they thought the results would be if the research were conducted today. I collected systematic data relating to this and several other questions from students in 11 social psychology classes from 1983 to 1990. The results: 40% predicted less obedience today, 39% predicted the same amount, and only 11% predicted an increase in obedience (Blass & Krackow, 1991).

After completing this analysis, it occurred to me that it would be even more interesting to determine whether or not a change in obedience tendencies over time could be detected in the *actual* outcomes of obedience studies. So I took Milgram's standard or baseline conditions (i.e., in which the learner is physically separated from and not visible to the participant: Experiments 1, 2, 5, 6, 8, and 10 in Milgram, 1974a) and all the methodological replications of these experiments carried out by others (there were 14 of these) and correlated the rank order of the year of publication of the study with the rank order of its obedience rate. The studies spanned a period of 22 years, from 1963 to 1985, the year of publication of the last methodological replication that I have found (Schurz, 1985). Although levels of obedience across studies ranged from a low of 28% (Kilham & Mann, 1974) to a high of 91% (Ring, Wallston, & Corey, 1970), there was no systematic relationship between the year a study was conducted and the amount of obedience obtained: The Spearman rank-order correlation coefficient, r_s, came out to .002. A second correlation was performed, this time adding Milgram's proximity condition (Experiment #3) and three proximity-condition replications by other investigators (for a total of 24 conditions or studies). These had been excluded from the first correlation because the rate of obedience in Milgram's Experiment 3 was significantly lower than those of his Experiments 1, 2, 5, and 8 (see Blass, 1991), suggesting that methodologically and experientially they were distinct. However, as it turns out, the addition of the Proximity studies leaves the correlation virtually unchanged—$r_s = -.008$. (See the appendix for a listing of studies and findings that were used in the correlational analyses.)

An important implication of the findings of these correlational analyses is that they provide evidence—at least indirectly—against the operation of "enlightenment effects," which had been proposed by Gergen (1973). Gergen (1973) had argued that "sophistication as to psychological principles liberates one from their behavioral implications" (p. 313). If Gergen is right, the later studies should have found less obedience than the earlier ones, because with the longer passage of time the participants in the more recent studies would have had more of a chance to hear about Milgram's work and thereby become enlightened about, and liberated from, the unwanted demands of authority.

Two unpublished studies attempted to provide more direct tests regarding the operation of enlightenment effects using the Milgram paradigm—one a master's thesis by Brant (1978) and the other a doctoral dissertation by Shelton (1982). Brant chose college undergraduates who had first been familiarized with the obedience studies to participate in a "learning" experiment similar to Milgram's Experiment 11, in which they could choose any shock level on a 390-volt "shock" generator whenever the learner made an error. Brant reports that only 4 participants out of 44 refused to participate in the study after they heard the instructions—a finding that he interprets as "seriously call[ing] into question" (1978, p. 53) Gergen's thesis. However, the study suffers from a serious methodological flaw that precludes drawing any firm conclusions from it about enlightenment effects: It is not clear how many of the participants, if any, *actually* knew about the obedience studies prior to their own participation. The reason is that the attempt to inform them about it took the following form: "Prior to their participation, subjects had been assigned readings in their classes concerning the obedience research as well as other psychological findings in conjunction with their coursework. In addition, these students had been lectured to on topics relevant to this investigation" (Brant, 1978, p. 19). There was no attempt, however, to ascertain whether or not participants had actually read the assigned readings or attended the relevant lectures.

Shelton's (1982) attempt to determine the validity of Gergen's claim that the acquisition of psychological information can change a person's behavior was not only a methodological improvement over Brant's study but also was quite clever in its conception. First, she gave all her participants a detailed synopsis of the obedience experiment to read and then asked them a set of questions about what they had read. She then asked them to serve as experimenters in a similar "learning" experiment. Their job was to oversee a participant (the teacher) who was supposed to teach a verbal-learning task to another participant (the learner) by using increasing voltages of shock as punishment on each subsequent mistake. The participant (experimenter) was told that the learner was a confederate, but, unbeknownst to the experimenter, the teacher was also a confederate, who, as the shock levels and the learner's expressions of pain increased, "expressed uneasiness, then became quite anxious, angry, on the verge of tears; cursed, complained of stomach pains, asked for a glass of water, and pleaded with the experimenter to stop the session ... " (p. 31). In spite of this, 22 out of 24 participants continued to the end, commanding the teacher to keep increasing the shock to the maximum 450-volt level. Apparently, participants could not draw a parallel between their obedience to Shelton and the teacher's obedience to them.

How do we reconcile a finding like Shelton's with the life-changing testimonials of individuals who found the strength to resist the unwanted demands of authority after participating in, or otherwise learning about, the obedience experiments (e.g., appendix I in Milgram, 1974a)? One possibility is suggested in an insightful letter written to Milgram in April 1982 by a former participant in a Milgram-type experiment at the University of Minnesota in 1967. He wrote: "I'm writing to thank you for making a major contribution to my understanding of myself and of the meaning of the values I have." He wrote that he learned a number of things from his participation in the experiment, one of which was "that it is easier for me (although hardly simple) to recognize and avoid situations in which authority and obedience play significant roles (e.g., the military, many government and business organizations) than it is to defy authority within such situations." That is, contrary to what is implied by Gergen's "enlightenment effects" notion, knowledge does not or cannot always lead to action. Being enlightened about the unexpected power of authority may help a person stay away from an authority-dominated situation, but once he or she is *already* in such a situation, knowledge of the drastic degree of obedience authorities are capable of eliciting does not necessarily help free the individual from the grip of the forces operating in that concrete situation, (i.e., to defy the authority in charge).

SUMMARY AND CONCLUSIONS

In this chapter I set out to present a status report on four important questions and issues surrounding the obedience paradigm, grounded in systematic analysis—something that had heretofore not been done with these questions and issues. My analyses involved a variety of methods: literature reviews, a person-perception experiment, and correlational analyses. On the basis of these analyses, I believe the following conclusions are called for. First, in all likelihood, Milgram's experimental authority was perceived by participants as embodying a combination of legitimate authority and scientific expertise. Second, a review of prediction studies found that, although naive subjects generally underestimate actual obedience rates, the gap between estimated and actual obedience rates is often quite a bit smaller than what Milgram found. Third, with one exception, in all studies permitting a comparison between male and female participants, no sex differences in obedience have been found. And fourth, rates of obedience show no systematic change over time: Two correlational analyses between year of publication and obedience outcome showed no relationship whatsoever between when a study was conducted and how much obedience occurred. In each case, the wider implications of each of these findings were also discussed.

ACKNOWLEDGMENT

I want to express my thanks to Annamarie Krackow for her help with some of the analyses presented in this chapter.

REFERENCES

Ancona, L., & Pareyson, R. (1968). Contributo allo studio della aggressione: La dinamica della obbedienza distruttiva [Contribution to the study of aggression: The dynamics of destructive obedience]. *Archivio di Psicologia, Neurologia, e Psichiatria, 29,* 340–372.

Anderson, G. M., & Block, W. (1995). Procrastination, obedience and public policy: The irrelevance of salience. *American Journal of Economics and Sociology, 54,* 201–215.

Assiter, A. (1998). Communitarianism and obedience. In B. Brecher, J. Halliday, & K. Kolinska (Eds.), *Nationalism and racism in the liberal order.* Aldershot, U.K.: Ashgate.

Bierbrauer, G. A. (1974). *Attribution and perspective: Effects of time, set, and role on interpersonal inference. Dissertation Abstract International, 34,* 6232. (University Microfilms No. 74-13,602)

Blass, T. (1990, June 8). *Judgments about the Milgram obedience experiment support a cognitive view of defensive attribution.* Paper presented at the annual meeting of the American Psychological Society, Dallas, TX.

Blass, T. (1991). Understanding behavior in the Milgram obedience experiment: The role of personality, situations, and their interactions. *Journal of Personality and Social Psychology, 60,* 398–413.

Blass, T. (1992a, August 17). The nature of authority in Milgram's obedience paradigm. In H. C. Kelman (Chair), *Authority–crimes of obedience and disobedience.* Symposium conducted at the annual meeting of the American Psychological Association, Washington, DC.

Blass, T. (1992b). The social psychology of Stanley Milgram. In M. P. Zanna (Ed.), *Advances in experimental social psychology* (Vol. 25, pp. 227–329). San Diego, CA: Academic Press.

Blass, T. (1993). Psychological perspectives on the perpetrators of the Holocaust: The role of situational pressures, personal dispositions, and their interactions. *Holocaust and Genocide Studies, 7,* 30–50.

Blass, T. (1995). Right-wing authoritarianism and role as predictors of attributions about obedience to authority. *Personality and Individual Differences, 19,* 99–100.

Blass, T. (1996a). Attribution of responsibility and trust in the Milgram obedience experiment. *Journal of Applied Social Psychology, 26,* 1529–1535.

Blass, T. (1996b). Stanley Milgram: A life of inventiveness and controversy. In G. A. Kimble, C. A. Boneau, & M. Wertheimer (Eds.), *Portraits of pioneers in psychology* (Vol. 2, pp. 315–331). Washington, DC, & Hillsdale, NJ: American Psychological Association and Lawrence Erlbaum Associates.

Blass, T., & Krackow, A. (1991, June). *The Milgram obedience experiments: Students' views vs. scholarly perspectives and actual findings.* Paper presented at the annual meeting of the American Psychological Society, Washington, DC.

Bock, D. C. (1972). *Obedience: A response to authority and Christian commitment. Dissertation Abstracts International, 33,* 3276B–3279B (University Microfilms No. 72–31,651).

Bock, D. C., & Warren, N. C. (1972). Religious belief as a factor in obedience to destructive commands. *Review of Religious Research, 13,* 185–191.

Brant, W. D. (1978). *Situational pressure, racial stereotypes, and conformity in laboratory aggression.* Unpublished master's thesis, Oregon State University, Corvallis.

Browne, M. N., Kubasek, N. K., & Giampetro-Meyer, A. (1995/1996). The seductive danger of craft ethics for business organizations. *Review of Business, 17,* 23–28.

Browning, C. (1992). *Ordinary men: Reserve Police Battalion 101 and the Final Solution in Poland.* New York: HarperCollins.

CBS News (1979, March 31). Transcript of *Sixty Minutes* segment, "I was only following orders," pp. 2–8.

Collins, B. E., & Brief, D. E. (1993, August). *Using person perception methodologies to uncover the meanings of the Milgram obedience paradigm.* Paper presented at the annual meeting of the American Psychological Association, Toronto, Ontario, Canada.

Costanzo, E. M. (1976). *The effect of probable retaliation and sex related variables on obedience. Dissertation Abstracts International, 37,* 4214B (University Microfilms No. 77–3253)

Eagly, A. H. (1978). Sex differences in influenceability. *Psychological Bulletin, 85,* 86–116.

Edwards, D. M., Franks, P., Friedgood, D., Lobban, G., & Mackay, H. C. G. (1969). *An experiment on obedience.* Unpublished student report, University of the Witwatersrand, Johannesburg, South Africa.

Evans, R. I. (1976). [Interview with] Stanley Milgram. In R. I. Evans (Ed.), *The making of psychology: Discussions with creative contributors* (pp. 346–356). New York: Knopf.

Ferrell, O. C., & Gardiner, G. (1991). *In pursuit of ethics: Tough choices in the world of work.* Springfield, IL: Smith Collins.

Forsyth, D. (1987). *Social psychology.* Monterey, CA: Brooks/Cole.

French, J. R. P., Jr., & Raven, B. (1959). The bases of social power. In D. Cartwright (Ed.), *Studies in social power* (pp. 150–167). Ann Arbor, MI: Research Center for Group Dynamics, Institute for Social Research, University of Michigan.

French, S. (1997, May 21). Parents: Devil's seed. *The Guardian,* p. T14.

Gergen, K. J. (1973). Social psychology as history. *Journal of Personality and Social Psychology, 26,* 309–320.

Goldhagen, D. (1996). *Hitler's willing executioners: Ordinary Germans and the Holocaust.* New York: Knopf.

Green, M. J., Mitchell, G., Stocking, C. B., Cassel, C. K., & Siegler, M. (1996). Do actions reported by physicians in training conflict with consensus guidelines on ethics? *Archives of Internal Medicine, 156,* 298–304.

Greenwood, J. D. (1982). On the relation between laboratory experiments and social behavior: Causal explanation and generalization. *Journal for the Theory of Social Behavior, 12,* 225–250.

Guimond, S., & Kwak, K. (1995, June). *Learning about Milgram's experiments II: Effects on impressions of the "teacher" and the "learner."* Paper presented at the annual meeting of the Canadian Psychological Association, Charlottetown, Prince Edward Island.

Guimond, S., Kwak, K., & Langevin, P. (1994, June 30–July 2). *Obedience in the military: I. Psychological effects of learning about Milgram's experiments.* Paper presented at the annual meeting of the Canadian Psychological Association, Penticton, British Columbia.

Hamilton, V. L. (1992). Thoughts on obedience: A social structural view [Review of the book *Obedience and civilization: Authorized crime and the normality of evil*]. *Contemporary Psychology, 37,* 1313.

Helm, C., & Morelli, M. (1985). Obedience to authority in a laboratory setting: Generalizability and context dependency. *Political Studies, 33,* 610–627.

Holland, C. D. (1967). Sources of variance in the experimental investigation of behavioral obedience. *Dissertation Abstracts International, 29,* 2802A (University Microfilms No. 69-2146).

Katz, F. E. (1993). *Ordinary people and extraordinary evil.* Albany, NY: SUNY Press.

Kaufmann, H., & Kooman, A. (1967). Predicted compliance in obedience situations as a function of implied instructional variables. *Psychonomic Science, 7,* 205–206.

Kilham, W., & Mann, L. (1974). Level of destructive obedience as a function of transmitter and executant roles in the Milgram obedience paradigm. *Journal of Personality and Social Psychology, 29,* 696–702.

Koh, H. H. (1997). Why do nations obey international law? *Yale Law Journal, 106,* 2599–2659.

Laurent, J. (1987). Milgram's shocking experiments: A case in the social construction of "science." *Indian Journal of History of Science, 22,* 247–272.

MacLellan, C., & Dobson, J. (1997). Women, ethics, and MBAs. *Journal of Business Ethics, 16,* 1201–1209.

Mantell, D. M. (1971). The potential for violence in Germany. *Journal of Social Issues, 27*(4), 101–112.

Masters, B. (1996). *The evil that men do.* New York: Doubleday.

Maughan, M. R. C. (1981). *The effect of four methods of subject recruitment on subjects' estimated compliance for themselves and others in role-playing situations. Dissertation Abstracts International, 42,* 2134. (University Microfilms No. 8124785)

Maughan, M. R. C., & Higbee, K. L. (1981). Effect of subjects' incentives for participation on estimated compliance for self and others. *Psychological Reports, 49,* 119–122.

Milgram, S. (1963). Behavioral study of obedience. *Journal of Abnormal and Social Psychology, 67,* 371–378.

Milgram, S. (1965a). *Obedience* [film]. University Park, PA: Penn State Audio-Visual Services [distributor].

Milgram, S. (1965b). Some conditions of obedience and disobedience to authority. *Human Relations, 18,* 57–76.

Milgram, S. (1966). Einige Bedingungen von Autoritätsgehorsam und seiner Verweigerung [Some conditions of obedience to authority and its rejection]. *Zeitschrift für Experimentelle und Angewandte Psychologie, 13,* 433–463.

Milgram, S. (1967). Tnaim achadim shel tziut ve-itziut le-samchut [Some conditions of obedience and disobedience to authority]. *Megamot, 15,* 31–49.

Milgram, S. (1974a). *Obedience to authority: An experimental view.* New York: Harper & Row.

Milgram, S. (1974b, October 31). We are all obedient. *The Listener,* pp. 567–568.

Milgram, S. (1983). Reflections on Morelli's "Dilemma of obedience." *Metaphilosophy, 14,* 190–194.

Milgram, S. (1987a). Obedience. In R. J. Corsini (Ed.), *Concise encyclopedia of psychology* (pp. 773–774). New York: Wiley.

Milgram, S. (1987b). Obedience. In R. L. Gregory (Ed.), *Oxford companion to the mind* (pp. 566–568). New York: Oxford University Press.

Miller, A. G. (1986). *The obedience experiments: A case study of controversy in social science.* New York: Praeger.

Miller, A. G., Gillen, B., Schenker, C., & Radlove, S. (1974). The prediction and perception of obedience to authority. *Journal of Personality, 42,* 23–42.

Miller, F. D. (1975). *An experimental study of obedience to authorities of varying legitimacy.* Unpublished doctoral dissertation, Harvard University.

Miranda, F. S. B., Caballero, R. B., Gomez, M. N. G., & Zamorano, M. A. M. (1981). Obediencia a la autoridad [Obedience to authority]. *Psiquis, 2,* 212–221.

Mixon, D. (1971). *Further conditions of obedience and disobedience to authority. Dissertation Abstracts International, 32,* 4646B. (University Microfilms No. 72-6477)

Mixon, D. (1976). Studying feignable behavior. *Representative Research in Social Psychology, 7,* 89–104.

Mixon, D. (1989). *Obedience and civilization: Authorized crime and the normality of evil.* London: Pluto Press.

Morelli, M. (1983). Milgram's dilemma of obedience. *Metaphilosophy, 14,* 183–189.

Patten, S. C. (1977). Milgram's shocking experiments. *Philosophy, 52,* 425–440.

Pearson, K. N. (1992, May). *Assessing the obedient: Effects of behavioral extremity and information medium on observers' social judgments.* Paper presented at the annual meeting of the Western Psychological Association, Portland, OR.

Penner, L. A., Hawkins, H. L., Dertke, M. C., Spector, P., & Stone, A. (1973). Obedience as a function of experimenter competence. *Memory and Cognition, 1,* 241–245.

Podd, M. H. (1970). *The relationship between ego identity status and two measures of morality. Dissertation Abstracts International, 31,* 5634 (University Microfilms No. 71-6107)

Powers, P. C., & Geen, R. G. (1972). Effects of the behavior and the perceived arousal of a model on instrumental aggression. *Journal of Personality and Social Psychology, 23,* 175–183.

Raven, B. H. (1965). Social influence and power. In J. D. Steiner & M. Fishbein (Eds.), *Current studies in social psychology* (pp. 371–382). New York: Holt, Rinehart & Winston.

Raven, B. H. (1992). A power/interaction model of interpersonal influence: French and Raven thirty years later. *Journal of Social Behavior and Personality, 7,* 217–244.

Raven, B. H., & Rubin, J. Z. (1983). *Social psychology* (2nd ed.). New York: Wiley.

Ring, K., Wallston, K., & Corey, M. (1970). Mode of debriefing as a factor affecting subjective reactions to a Milgram-type obedience experiment: An ethical inquiry. *Representative Research in Social Psychology, 1,* 67–85.

Rogers, R. W. (1973). *Obedience to authority: Presence of authority and command strength.* Paper presented at the annual meeting of the Southeastern Psychological Association.

Rosenhan, D. (1969). Some origins of concern for others. In P. Mussen, J. Langer, & M. Covington (Eds.), *Trends and issues in developmental psychology* (pp. 134–153). New York: Holt, Rinehart, & Winston.

Ross, L. (1977). The intuitive psychologist and his shortcomings: Distortions in the attribution process. In L. Berkowitz (Ed.), *Advances in experimental social psychology* (Vol. 10, pp. 173–219). New York: Academic Press.

Schurz, G. (1985). Experimentelle Uberprüfung des Zusammenhangs zwischen Persönlichkeitsmerkmalen und der Bereitschaft zum destruktiven Gehorsam gegenüber Autoritäten [Experimental examination of the relationships between personality characteristics and the readiness for destructive obedience toward authority]. *Zeitschrift für Experimentelle und Angewandte Psychologie, 32,* 160–177.

Shalala, S. R. (1974). *A study of various communication settings which produce obedience by subordinates to unlawful superior orders. Dissertation Abstracts International, 36,* 979B (University Microfilms No. 75-17,675)

Shanab, M. E., & Yahya, K. A. (1977). A behavioral study of obedience in children. *Journal of Personality and Social Psychology, 35,* 530–536.

Shanab, M. E., & Yahya, K. A. (1978). A cross-cultural study of obedience. *Bulletin of the Psychonomic Society, 11,* 267–269.

Shelton, G. A. (1982). *The generalization of understanding to behavior: The role of perspective in enlightenment.* Unpublished doctoral dissertation, University of British Columbia, Vancouver, Canada.

Sheridan, C. L., & King, R. G. (1972). Obedience to authority with an authentic victim. *Proceedings of the eightieth annual convention of the American Psychological Association,* pp. 165–166.

Spector, B. J. (1978). *Military self-discipline: A motivational analysis.* Arlington, VA: CACI Inc.-Federal, Policy Sciences Division.

Takooshian, H. (1993). Interview by author. Fordham University at Lincoln Center, June 17.

Voronov, A. (1993, September 8–14). Provenyemost kak prestuplenya [Obedience as a crime] *Rossia,* p. 8.

APPENDIX

List of obedience studies and their findings (in obedience rates) used in the correlational analyses reported in the chapter.

The following should be noted:

1. Although the numbers designating Milgram's experiments are the ones he used in his book (Milgram, 1974a), all his obedience experiments (other than pilot work) were conducted between the summer of 1961 and the end of May 1962. In the correlational analyses, they were all designated by the year 1963, the year of the first publication of his obedience findings.

2. Studies preceded by an asterisk were included in the second, but not the first, correlation. (See the body of the chapter for an explanation.)

3. Some studies listed consisted of more than one condition. In such cases, the obedience rate reported is for the condition that represented the methodological replication of Milgram's standard or proximity conditions (i.e., Experiments 1, 2, 3, 5, 6, 8, or 10 in Milgram, 1974a).

4. The obedience rate found by Podd (1970) does not appear in his dissertation but was provided by him in a personal communication.

5. The study by Edwards, Frank, Friedgood, Lobban, & Mackay (1969) was conducted by 3rd-year psychology majors for a course in experimental social psychology at the University of the

Witwatersrand in Johannesburg, South Africa. Their instructor, L. Melamed, sent a copy of the report to Milgram on October 23, 1969. In his book, Milgram (1974a) mentions South Africa as one of the foreign countries where replications of the obedience experiments had been conducted but gave no reference for it. In searching the literature, I have not found any other South African obedience study; therefore, in all likelihood, this is the one that Milgram was referring to.

Study	Country	Obedience rate in %
Milgram (1963)	United States	
Exp. #1		65
Exp. #2		62.5
*Exp. #3		40
Exp. #5		65
Exp. #6		50
Exp. #8		65
Exp. #10		47.5
Holland (1967)	United States	75
*Ancona and Pareyson (1968)	Italy	85
Rosenhan (1969)	United States	85
*Podd (1969)	United States	31
Edwards et al. (1969)	South Africa	87.5
Ring, Wallston, and Corey (1970)	United States	91
Mantell (1971)	West Germany	85
Bock (1972)	United States	40
Powers and Geen (1972)	United States	83
Rogers (1973)	United States	37
Kilham and Mann (1974)	Australia	28
Shalala (1974)	United States	30
Costanzo (1976)	United States	81
Shanab and Yahya (1977)	Jordan	73
Shanab and Yahya (1978)	Jordan	62.5
*Miranda, Caballero, Gomez, & Zamorano (1981)	Spain	50
Schurz (1985)	Austria	80

5

Impression Management and Identity Construction in the Milgram Social System

Barry E. Collins
Laura Ma
University of California, Los Angeles

This chapter presents the most recent data and theoretical developments in a research program (Collins & Brief, 1995; Levy, Collins, & Brief, 1989) that explores impression-management and identity-management processes in the Milgram social system. Research participants view a videotaped reenactment of the baseline condition in the classic Milgram obedience experimental paradigm (Milgram, 1963, 1974). In the video reenactment (as in the classic Milgram paradigm), an experimenter instructs a "teacher" (the research participant in Milgram's original paradigm) to deliver electric shocks to a "learner" every time the learner makes a mistake. In the present person-perception paradigm, participants (who are told that the actors in the videotape were actual participants) complete a questionnaire asking them about the people and events they observed in the videotape. In Milgram's original paradigm, the dependent variable was the number of shocks delivered by the teacher to the learner. In the present research program, the dependent variables are the participants' interpretations of the people and events they have observed in the reenactment of the Milgram social system.

> Behavior in the Milgram paradigm is rich with meanings for the identities of all three interactants—experimenter, teacher, and learner. The desire to construct desirable self-images and social impressions is among the causal forces driving behavior in the Milgram paradigm. … [We] postulate that the teacher/subject's behaviors have symbolic meanings for the identities of all three of the actors/actresses in the script for the Milgram paradigm. (Collins and Brief, 1995, p. 89)

The key theoretical term in the present theory is *identity management*. By *identity* we mean the constellation of personality traits attributed to a particular person. When an actor forms an identity image of a target person (the typical methodology in a person-perception experiment), the resulting identity image has been classically labeled a social impression or just an *impression* (e.g., Asch, 1946). When actors form images of themselves, the process is most often labeled *self-concept development or self-perception*. The present theory speculates that the symbolic meaning of a particular behavior (e.g., delivering the 11th shock in the Milgram paradigm) will have similar implications for the personality of the actor—whether the person forming the image is the actor him- or herself or some third person. It is thus convenient to have one term, identity, that refers to both an actor's image of him- or herself and others' impressions of the actor. The target person for both images is the same, but the images are held in the minds of different people.

Others have also commented on the relevance of impression management in the Milgram paradigm. For instance, the "influence of the theater" was one of the themes Thomas Blass (1992) identified in his article, "The Social Psychology of Stanley Milgram": "The dramaturgical perspective of Goffman, suggesting that social behavior can be understood as performances staged to create a desired effect on others … " (p. 287). Using a person-perception, videotape-vignette methodology, Collins and Brief demonstrated that cues in the teacher's behavior lead observers to make inferences about the identity of the teacher. In other words, those behaviors have symbolic meaning for the identity of the teacher. In the first experiment with American participants (Collins & Brief, 1995; Levy, Collins, & Brief, 1989), research participants rated the teacher on a series of bipolar item scales representing the three classic factors in the semantic differential (Osgood, Suci, & Tannenbaum, 1957): General evaluation (e.g., good–bad), Activity (e.g., active–passive) and Potency (e.g., strong–weak). Disobedient teachers (teachers who did not deliver the

11th shock) were rated more favorably, as more active, and as stronger than obedient teachers.

Given that teacher behaviors in the Milgram scenario have symbolic meanings, at least four additional questions arise. First, what, more precisely, are the meanings that observers find in teacher behavior? The initial set of trait ratings used as dependent measures by Collins and Brief was small and limited to the three general semantic-differential scales. These three general, "one size fits all" scales may fail to capture some of the inferences observers make about the identity of the teacher. In other words, the participants may have reached conclusions about the teacher's personality that are not measured by this initial set of dependent variables. Second, which of the teacher's behaviors inform us about who the teacher is? There is an extensive script of teacher words and behaviors in the Milgram paradigm. Which specific teacher acts in this extensive set of behaviors inform us about his identity? In other words, what are the specific cues in teacher behavior that trigger the symbolic interpretations? Third, what is the structure of the cognitive system that is used to encode, store, and interpret teacher-behavior cues into a coherent image of the teacher's personality? Fourth, do teacher behaviors inform us narrowly about the personality only of the teacher (as in the Levy, Collins, and Brief, 1989, data) or will observers also learn something about the identities of the other actors in the Milgram social situation—the experimenter and/or the learner? Expert social psychological analyses (such as those in social psychology textbooks; Miller, 1995) interpret teacher behavior to inform us about the social system—the situation. Will lay observers also use the data provided by teacher behaviors to diagnose the structure of the role relationships among the three actors in the Milgram scenario?

THE CONSTRUCTION OF MEANING

Person-perception theories (e.g., Fiske & Taylor, 1991; Hastorf, Schneider, & Polefka, 1970; Jones, 1990) focus on the process by which an observer constructs an image of an actor (the other or target person). In other words, "How do I learn who you are?" Impression management (e.g., Baumeister, 1982; Leary, 1995; Schlenker, 1980, 1985; Schlenker & Trudeau, 1990; Schlenker & Weigold, 1992; Tedeschi, 1981) refers to the process by which actors modify their behavior in order to construct and edit their public identity—their social impressions. A social impression is an image of one person (the target) held in the mind of another (the observer).

The typical focus of person-perception and impression management theories is on how the actor's behavior edits an observer's impression of the actor. But some impression-management theorists acknowledge that the self is among the audiences that monitor our own behavior. Daryl Bem (1967, 1972) is often credited with the assertion that, in many ways, we learn about ourselves in much the same manner as others learn about us—by observing behavior. Others have sounded the same theme. Schlenker (1980), for instance, states that "Actions carry social meanings that affect the impressions others form of the actor, the way they treat the actor, and the way the actor views himself or herself" (p. 5). In a review of the relevant literature, Tice (1992) concludes that one's own behavior has implications for the construction of the self-image. Thus, teachers in the original Milgram experiments may have been concerned about how their behavior would affect the images they hold of themselves as well as how others might think about them.

IMPLICIT PERSONALITY THEORY

Central to both person-perception and impression-management theories is the assumption that a behavioral act has what Collins has labeled *symbolic meanings*. For example, a brief behavior vignette in which a man is observed to bump into a woman and the woman falls to the ground provides data that trigger inferences well beyond such simple, face-valid conclusions as "the man bumped the woman" and "the woman fell to the ground." When asked to write out descriptions of the event or to complete trait ratings of the man, many observers will infer that the man is awkward, mean, violent, a misogynist, and so forth. Such cues as gender (e.g., Branscombe & Smith, 1990; Deaux & LaFrance, 1998), ethnicity (Arroyo, 1996; Bell, Kuriloff, & Lottes, 1994; Foley, Adams, & Goodson, 1996; Foley, et al., 1995; Ford, 1997; Plater & Thomas, 1998), occupation (e.g., Lobel & Shavit, 1997), sexual orientation (e.g., Madon, 1997), and physical attractiveness (Dion, Berscheid, & Walster, 1972; Miller, Gillen, Schlenker, & Radlove, 1974; see review by Eagly, Ashmore, Makhijani, & Lango, 1991) lead to broad, sweeping generalizations about the identity of the target person. These phenomena comprise some of the most frequently replicated findings in social psychology.

The construction of the meaning of any stimulus event in general (and of behavioral acts in particular) will have both a top-down, schema-driven component and a bottom-up, data-driven component. The top-down component represents the biases and interpretations that are introduced as the behavioral data are encoded, elaborated, and stored by the observer's information-processing system. For example, observers infer that a physically attractive teacher will deliver fewer shocks than an unattractive teacher in the Milgram scenario (Miller et al., 1974). This inference follows from a theory about physical attractiveness ("What is beautiful is good"; Dion, Berscheid, & Walster, 1972) that is located in the mind of the observer. There is no evidence in the data provided by a single reenactment of the Milgram scenario suggesting the conclusion that the attractive people will be more defiant than their less attractive peers. So that inference must have come from inference rules or schemata in the mind of the observer.

According to implicit personality theory (Hastorf, Schneider, & Polefka, 1970; Schneider, 1973), the set of schemata or stereotypes that an observer uses to construct the meanings of behaviors in the Milgram social system can be measured by a set of intercorrelated adjectives (e.g., kind, strong, disobedient, supportive, etc.). These correlations can be viewed as a thesaurus of synonyms and antonyms that specifies the meanings and the overlap of meanings among the trait adjectives. One classic way to quantify schema-driven interpretations introduced by top-down processing is to compute the correlations among trait adjectives that observers use to describe the target person. This set of correlations is known as the observer's implicit personality theory (Hastorf, Schneider, & Polefka, 1970; Schneider, 1973). If observers who rate a target as high on "kind" also tend to rate the same target as low on "cruel," this correlation is evidence that the two words are antonyms in the observer's implicit personality theory.

What is the implicit theory that observers will use to find meanings in the behavior of the teacher in the Milgram scenario? Two questions about the implicit personality theory are interesting. First, how complex will the theory be? Will the implicit personality theory be full of simplifying, value-laden stereotypes, or will it be complex so as to capture many different nuances in the meaning of teacher behavior? The complexity of a set of correlations is reflected in the amount of variance that can be accounted for by a first common-theme factor and in the number of interpretable factors that can be rotated. The simplest cognitive structure possible would be represented by a single evaluative-halo factor structure among the trait ratings; in this extreme case no interpretable second factor could be identified. In an only slightly more complex cognitive structure, the classic three-factor structure of the semantic differential would collapse into a two-factor solution with a dominant first (General Evaluation) factor and a collapsed second factor combining the classic Activity and Potency factors; in this case, no interpretable third factor could be identified. Both of these relatively simple cognitive structures would imply that observers had functioned as cognitive misers (Taylor, 1981) and constructed highly simplified, stereotyped, and value-laden images of the teacher.

Second, what is the substantive content of the implicit personality theory? What is the content of (i.e., the particular traits in) the schemata or stereotypes used to construct meaning in the Milgram scenario? The factor structure of the correlations among the trait ratings can be regarded as a quantified projective test that taps the unconscious automatic processing typical of person-perception and impression formation (Bargh, 1997: Collins & Brief, 1995; Schneider & Shiffrin, 1977; Shiffrin & Schneider, 1977; Wegner & Bargh, 1998). Observers are asked to make judgments about the target person's likely personality, and the correlations among the trait ratings are computed and factor analyzed. Each correlation between two trait ratings (e.g., obedient and bad) is a measure of the functional equivalence of that pair of trait ratings. What, for instance, will be correlated with the trait rating "disobedient"? Perhaps observers (like many social psychological commentators on the Milgram paradigm) will see the teacher's response to the experimenter's demands as a struggle between good and evil. Thus most of the meaning they find in obedient versus disobedient behavior would be adequately represented by a single, good–bad, white hat–black hat dimension. If this hypothesis is true, good, kind, loyal, brave, active, stable, responsible, and so forth will all be synonyms of disobedient; and all of these trait ratings will be highly intercorrelated, and these correlations among all the trait ratings will be adequately represented by a single factor.

The small item set used Collins and his colleagues (Collins & Brief, 1995; Levy, Collins, & Brief, 1989) in their first study with an American sample was relatively small, and the scales were not factor analyzed. In a factor analysis based on a larger set of ratings of a version of our Milgram scenario video, with a Russian sample, Collins and Brief

(1995) reported a complex, five-factor implicit personality theory used by those observers to construct the teacher's identity.

1. *Positive Evaluation* (e.g. hostile–friendly, cruel–kind, bad–good, etc.), the largest factor, represents the classic General Evaluation factor.
2. *Disobedience* includes items (e.g., disobedient, dominant–submissive and leader–follower) that indicate that leadership was a s,nonym for disobedience among Russian observers. This factor includes both the classic Activity and Potency factors.
3. The third factor is probably specific to the Russian culture and expresses a sense of privileged class membership (e.g., likely to be optimistic–likely to be pessimistic, success–failure, and likely to be intelligent–unintelligent).
4. Emotional Stability (e.g., impulsive–controlled, emotionally unstable–emotionally stable, agitated–calm, and likely to quit easily on a task–likely to persevere on a task).
5. *Religiosity* (e.g., likely to believe in God–not likely to believe in God, likely to be religious–not likely to be religious, and delicate–rugged).

The factor analyses of an expanded set (see the appendix) of trait ratings reported in the following section reveal the implicit personality theory used by the present sample of American college students as they formed images of the actors in our video reenactment of the Milgram social system.

DISOBEDIENCE, DEFIANCE, AND TEACHER IDENTITY IN THE MILGRAM SOCIAL SYSTEM

Three of the four videotaped English-language vignettes used previously in this research program (Collins & Brief; 1995; Levy, Collins, & Brief, 1989) were used in the present study. These videotape reenactments of the Milgram obedience paradigm portray a putative participant (teacher) in the first 11 trials of the Milgram scenario. The first 10 trials are identical for all three vignettes. The teacher continues to deliver an electric shock after each of the first 10 learner errors, and the learner begins to protest. The teacher's behavior on the 11th trial was varied across the three experimental conditions in order to manipulate the independent variable in the present experiment. In the "obedient" condition, the teacher follows the experimenter's instructions and delivers the 11th shock after the 11th error—just as did the great majority of Milgram's baseline participants. In the other two vignettes, the teacher is disobedient; he does not deliver the 11th shock. This disobedience on the 11th trial would be unusual behavior on the part of a participant in Milgram's original paradigm, but the present vignette method allows us to explore the meanings of such behavior when it does occur. Thus the first of two behavior cues manipulated in this study is teacher *disobedience versus obedience*. The second behavioral cue is defined by the *style of disobedience*. In one of the two disobedient vignettes, the teacher politely demurs to deliver the 11th shock; in the other disobedient vignette, the refusal is adamant and defiant. What inferences about the teacher's personality will these two cues in the behavior of the experimenter trigger? What personality traits defining the teacher's identity will observers attribute to the teacher on the basis of these two cues in the behavior of the teacher?

Do the observers use these manipulated cues to make inferences about the identity of the teacher? Collins and Brief (1995) report that Russian observers interpreted teacher behavior in a manner very similar to that of professional social psychologists writing about the Milgram experiment: Teacher behavior tells us nothing about the personality of the individual who is assigned the teacher role in the Milgram scenario. The teacher's behavior is explained by the situation in which he is enmeshed. In other words, there were no differences among conditions on the General Evaluation scale. The Russian observers did perceive the obedient teacher as being more submissive and less of a leader than teachers in the disobedient conditions.

American observers in the prior study (Collins and Brief; 1995; Levy, Collins, & Brief, 1989), however, display the fundamental attribution error (Ross, 1977). In other words, they used the teacher's behavior in the Milgram scenario as data for reaching conclusions about the teacher's personality. Disobedient teachers (as compared to politely obedient teachers) were evaluated more favorably on the good–bad item, more active, stronger, less self-concerned, better adjusted, and more assertive. Defiant disobedience (as compared to polite disobedience) led observers to evaluate the teacher less favorably and to conclude that the defiantly disobedient teacher's personality was socially inappropriate, less predictable and emotionally volatile.

ATTRIBUTIONS OF RESPONSIBILITY
AND THE AGENTIC STATE

The phenomenology of perceived responsibility for the shocks administered by the teacher was a central (perhaps even *the* central) concept in
Milgram's own analysis of teacher behavior in the social system he created. "The most common adjustment of thought in the obedient subject is for him to see himself as not responsible for his own actions"
(Milgram, 1974, pp. 7–8). Perceived responsibility for delivering the
electric shocks was an important element in Milgram's (1974) discussion of his post-experimental interviews (Milgram, 1974, see examples
on pp. 46, 50, 51, 76, 77, 85, 87). Further, perceived responsibility is the
phenomenological component in Milgram's theory of the "agentic
state" (Milgram, 1974; see also review by Blass, 1992):

> I shall term this *the agentic state*, by which I mean the condition a person is
> in when he sees himself as an agent for carrying out another person's
> wishes. ... From a subjective standpoint, a person is in a state of agency
> when he identifies himself in a social situation in a manner that renders
> him open to regulation by a person of higher status. In this condition the
> individual no longer views himself as responsible for his own actions but
> defines himself as an instrument for carrying out the wishes of others. ...
> The most far-reaching consequence of the agentic shift is that a man feels
> responsible *to* the authority directing him but feels no responsibility *for* the
> content of the actions that the authority prescribes. (Milgram, 1974, pp.
> 133–134, 145–146)

The attribution of responsibility for a target's actions, of course, is also a
central tenet in attribution theory (see, for example, Weiner, 1995).

Milgram's focus on the phenomenology of responsibility in his
teacher-participants can be extended to the observer-participants in
the present research. The theory of the agentic state and most attribu-
tion-theory analyses would seem to imply that the observer's first task is
to decide whether or not the teacher was acting as an agent for the experimenter. To the extent that the teacher is perceived as an agent (and
thus not responsible for his actions), teacher behavior does not inform
us about the stable dispositions (personality, identity) of the teacher. In
other words, the observer must make an attribution of responsibility for
the shocks the teacher administers to the learner, and this attribution
of responsibility will play a central role in determining what meanings,
if any, the observer finds in the teacher's disobedience. Attribution and

agentic-state theories imply that observers will *not* make an attribution that the teacher is, say, cruel in particular if they make a situational attribution in general. If the teacher's behavior is understood as caused by factors in the situation (as most professional observers of the Milgram scenario believe), then that teacher behavior tells us nothing about the personality of the teacher. In other words, the attribution of a particular trait to the teacher on the basis of his or her behavior presumes an internal attribution—an assessment that the teacher is responsible for what he or she does. Structural-equation modeling was used to assess the role that attributions of responsibility play as mediators in the link between the manipulated behavioral cues and trait attributions.

Milgram used a "responsibility clock" to quantify perceptions of responsibility in his postexperimental interviews.

> Subjects in the first four experimental conditions were exposed to a "responsibility clock." This consisted of a disk which the subject divided into three segments by means of movable rods rotating from the center. The subject ... was asked to "cut slices of the pie" proportional to the responsibility of the three participants in the experiment (experimenter, subject [teacher], and victim). We asked, "how much is each of us responsible for the fact that this person was given electric shocks against his will?" (1974, p. 203)

In the questionnaire used in the present study, observers were asked, "To what degree were each of the following responsible for the 'LEARNER'S' getting shocked?" Participants could respond on an 8-point scale, ranging from 0 (*not at all*) to 8 (*totally*). Four versions of this question were included in the questionnaire, each asking, in turn, about responsibility attributed to "the TEACHER," to "the LEARNER," to "the EXPERIMENTER," and to "the SITUATION." This procedure substitutes questionnaire items for Milgram's "hands-on" responsibility-clock procedure. There are also two important conceptual differences between these questionnaire items and Milgram's responsibility clock. First, the present observers are allowed the option of attributing responsibility to "the situation." The decision to include a situation option follows from the common assertion in attribution theory that an observer must choose between a situational and dispositional attribution. Second, unlike Milgram's responsibility clock and the questionnaire items used previously in the Russian study (Collins & Brief, 1995), respondents are not required to divide up the responsibility among the various options. A respondent might decide that everybody was very responsible or that no one was particularly responsible. If the thinking behind Milgram's responsibility clock is accurate, of course, there will be high negative correlations among these measures. The responsibility clock logic implies, for instance, that the learner's and/or experimenter's perceived responsibility must increase in order for the teacher's perceived responsibility to decrease. The first data analyses for these four questions involved computing the correlations among these ratings.

INFERENCES ABOUT THE IDENTITY
OF THE EXPERIMENTER AND LEARNER

In the preceding discussion, we have focused on how the behavior of the teacher may inform us about his or her identity. Analogously, observers may learn something about the experimenter from the experimenter's behavior and about the learner from the learner's behavior. These are interesting questions. The experimenter uses four prods (e.g., "The experiment requires that you go on" and "The responsibility is mine") to pressure reluctant teachers. What, if anything, do we learn about the identity of the experimenter from his use of these prods? Further, the learner's protests in the Milgram scenario are also very distinctive. What do observers learn, if anything, from the learner's choice to protest in these particular ways? These are questions for future research, as only teacher behavior was manipulated in the present study.

There is another set of questions about the identities of the experimenter, teacher, and learner that can be addressed with the present independent variables that manipulate cues in the teacher's behavior. Systems theory (e.g., Powers, 1973) posits that the behavior of each person in the system is driven, in part, by the behavior of others in the system. Systems theory is best represented in the field of family therapy. According to a systems theory of family therapy, a child presenting for therapy is conceptualized as the "designated patient"—implying that the child's behavior is an indicator of family dynamics rather than an indicator of the personality of that particular child. Applying this metaphor to the Milgram social system, one could think of teacher behavior as an indicator of the nature of the teacher-learner-experimenter social system rather than an indicator of the personality of the teacher only. Further, theories about blaming the victim (Herbert & Dunkel-Schetter, 1992; Janoff-Bulman, 1992; Lerner, 1980), for instance, would focus on flaws in the learner as a cause of the shocks delivered by the teacher. Thus we can ask: "Do cues in the behavior of the *teacher* inform us about the identities of the *experimenter* and *learner?*"

INFERENCES ABOUT FUTURE PATTERNS
OF INTERACTION AMONG DYADS
(RELATIONSHIP IMAGES)

Continuing with the systems-theory perspective, we can also ask if cues in the teacher's behavior have implications for how the *social system* will function in the future. "Structure of the social system," in this case, refers to the stable properties of the dyadic relationships established among the three participants in the Milgram social system. In order to address this issue, the questionnaire included dependent-variable items that inquired about three potential dyads: teacher–learner, teacher–experimenter, and learner–experimenter. The literature on social inference has focused almost exclusively on inferences about individuals. However, it is also possible that role relationships, like individuals, have personalities in the sense that relationships might form a unit around which information is organized and about which stereotypes exist. Baldwin (1992) asserts that the construction of relationship schemas includes an interpersonal script that defines a sequence of behaviors that would occur between individuals within the relationship. Sedikides, Olsen, and Reis (1993) theorize that individuals may use relationships to form impressions of others and of themselves. They found that participants relied on categories of relationships in order to put together information regarding target individuals.

The context for the series of social interactions used as stimulus material in this study is, albeit dramatic, only a brief, one-time interaction with fellow participants in a psychology experiment. Compared to, say, a first-date interaction, the present vignettes have low potential as a foundation for future relationships. In other words, the present design does not maximize the probability that observers will use teacher behaviors to form schemas about teacher–learner, teacher–experimenter, and learner–experimenter relationships. Thus any such inferences that are detected here imply much stronger effects in such other contexts as first dates, job interviews, waiting around for a pickup basketball game, and so forth.

Two studies help define the adjective trait ratings that can be used to quantify relationships along a set of dimensions. Rands and Levinger (1979) investigated two dimensions, behavior and affective interdependence, whereas Wish and Kaplan (1977) investigated five dimensions—cooperation, intensity, dominance, formality, and task orientation. Our observers were told that we were:

> considering forming teams of subjects from these experiments like those you watched into two-person teams. Teams would help design modifications in the design of the experiment for future research. If the experimenter and the teacher were to form such a team, what would their relationship be like?

Similar items asked about the teacher–learner and the experimenter –learner dyads.

A VIGNETTE STUDY

Method

The basic procedure and videotape stimuli used have been described previously (Collins & Brief, 1995; Levy, Collins, & Brief, 1989). The participants in the present experiment were shown an instructional video that described the baseline condition in the classic Milgram experiment. Then they watched what was said to be a videotape of an actual experiment. Each participant then was shown one of the three versions of the experimental videotapes. All three videotapes were identical for the first 10 trials, and all teachers delivered the first 10 shocks as the learner made his first 10 errors. The experimental manipulation was the teacher behavior on the 11th trial. The teacher was either obedient, delivering the 11th shock; politely disobedient; or defiantly disobedient. The participants responded to a series of bipolar questionnaire items regarding, in turn, the teacher, the learner, the experimenter, the potential experimenter–teacher team, the potential learner–teacher team, and the potential experimenter–learner team. The set of bipolar items is included as an appendix. The script for the three different endings follows:

Condition 1: Politely Obedient Teacher

T: I don't mean to be disrespectful, sir, but can't we just check on him to see if he is OK?

E: You have no other choice, teacher.

T: Well, I understand that, sir. I really do. But the man does not want to go on.

E: If you don't continue, we're going to have to discontinue the experiment.

T: [After a pause] All right. It is up to you. [Into the microphone] Answer, please? [computer tone] That is incorrect. 165 volts. [Delivers shock.]

Condition 2: Politely Disobedient Teacher

T: I don't mean to be disrespectful, sir, but I have to find out if that guy in there is OK before we continue.

E: You have no other choice, teacher.

T: Well, I understand that sir. But, unless I find out, if, you know, he's OK in there, I am not going to continue.

E: If you don't continue, we're going to have to discontinue the experiment.

T: Well ... I hope I didn't ruin your experiment! [folds arms over chest], But I just ... I don't want to continue. [Pushes word lists away.] I'm sorry. [Folds arms over chest.]

Condition 3: Defiantly Disobedient Teacher

T: Well, that's crazy. You gotta be out of your mind if you think I'm going on with this.

E: You have no other choice, teacher.

T: Hey, forget this experiment! I'm not going to do it and that's it!

E: If you don't continue, we're going to have to discontinue the experiment.

T: Oh, well, that's just too bad. I don't need this garbage. See you around, jerk. [Throws papers at the experimenter and storms out of the room.]

Results and Discussion

What is the Implicit Personality Theory Used to Construct the Identity of the Teacher in the Milgram Scenario?

Twenty-five of the 26 bipolar items about individual target persons were combined into eight multi-item dependent-variable scales. The single item disobedient–obedient formed one additional single-item dependent variable. The nine dependent variables which focus on each of the three target persons are *general evaluation* (e.g., bad–good), *nurturing* (e.g., sympathetic–unsympathetic), *dominant* (e.g., assertive–unassertive), *leader* (e.g., leader–follower), *emotionally stable* (e.g., controlled–impulsive), *active* (e.g., enthusiastic–apathetic), *independent* (self-reliant–not self-reliant), and *strong* (e.g., forceful–meek). The single item *obedient–disobedient* was used as a ninth measure. The complete set of individual items, grouped into the eight multi-item scales, is presented in the first part of the appendix. The *general evaluation, active,* and *strong* scales are the classic three factors from the semantic-differential tradition (Osgood, Suci, & Tannenbaum, 1957). *Dominant* and *independent* are components of the Bem Sex Role Inventory (BSRI; S. Bem, 1974) measure of masculinity, and *nurturing* is drawn from the BSRI measure of femininity. *Leader* and *obedient* are aspects of personality measured here because they have face validity relevant to the construction of the identity of the actors in the Milgram scenario. Factor analyses of these nine measures were conducted separately for the teacher, experimenter, and learner ratings. These analyses consistently indicated that two pairs of these nine scales could be combined: *general evaluation–nurturing* and *dominant–leader*. These combinations resulted in a final list of seven trait attributes that are reliable for teacher, learner, and experimenter ratings and thus were used as the dependent variables.

The correlations among these seven variables for the teacher ratings are presented in Table 5.1. Several features of the correlations in Table 5.1 are interesting. First, with the exception of the active–strong–independent triad, the correlations are very low. These low correlations among all the scales reflect a complex, finely textured cognitive space into which the meanings of the observed behaviors are being mapped. A five-factor oblique-rotation solution of the correlations in Table 5.1 finds only one factor (the Active–Independent–Strong triad) on which two scales load above .40, and the highest correlation between any two factors is only .28. The first of the two questions raised earlier about the implicit personality theory used by observers concerned how *complex* the theory would be; these analyses demonstrate that the implicit personality theory is complex. The implicit personality theory does not reflect cognitive misers at work; observers did not reduce their cognitive load by employing simplifying, value-laden stereotypes.

The second question concerned the *substantive content* of the implicit personality theory used to construct the teacher's identity. Five features of the implicit personality theory quantified by the correlations in Table 5.1 are noteworthy:

1. *Active, independent,* and *strong* are synonyms; the three scales are highly correlated—the correlations among the three scales in the top three rows of Table 5.1 range from .54 to .74.

2. The dominant/leader dimension (e.g., forceful–not forceful and dominant–submissive) falls outside this triad of synonyms and has a unique meaning of its own that is orthogonal to the active–independent–strong triad.

3. Emotional stability also emerges as an additional dimension of meaning that is unique and separate from the other six.

4. The correlations of the general evaluation scale with the other six scales are, surprisingly, very low. Only two of five are even significant: the .21 ($p < .048$) with strong and the .23 with dominant–leader ($p < .023$). This pattern demonstrates that there is little or no evaluative halo in the other six scales. Interpreting teacher behavior is not simply a matter of locating the teacher along a single dimension defined by good and evil. The observers learn a great deal more about the teacher than how socially desirable he is.

Table 5.1

Correlations Among the Seven Teacher-Rating Scales

	Active	Independent	Strong	Dominant & Leader	Positive Evaluation	Emotionally Stable
Teacher is active						
Teacher is independent	.60***					
Teacher is strong	.74***	.54***				
Teacher is dominant and a leader	.20	.20	.20			
Teacher is positively evaluated ("good") and nurturing	.11	.00	.21*	.23*		
Teacher is emotionally stable	.15	.28**	.24*	.05	.16	
Teacher is disobedient	.25*	.28**	.18	.17	-.08	-.19

*$p < .05$; **$p < .01$; ***$p < .001$

5. The correlations with the disobedience item provide insight into what this word means to these observers in the context of the Milgram scenario. It is noteworthy that the correlations with the disobedience item are very low—only two (active and independent) of the six items reach the .05 level and no correlation is higher than .28 (accounting for only 8% of the variance). In the mind of these observers of the Milgram scenario, disobedience has a meaning of its own; to be disobedient is not simply a synonym of being strong, active, independent, assertive, emotionally stable, or good.

Are There Cues in the Behavior of the Milgram-Scenario Teachers That Inform Us About the Identity of the Teacher?

The two cues manipulated in this study are obedience versus disobedience (i.e., whether or not the teacher delivers the 11th shock to the learner) and polite versus defiant disobedience. Each of these two cues corresponds to one of the two orthogonal contrasts available in a three-cell design: the mean of the two disobedient conditions compared with the mean of the obedient condition and the mean of the politely disobedient condition compared with the mean of the defiantly disobedient condition (ignoring the obedient condition).

Obedience.   The obedient–disobedient contrast produced a significant difference on five of the seven dependent variables. The only two variables *not* driven by the obedience cue were emotional stability and general evaluation/nurturing. Disobedient teachers were perceived, of course, as more disobedient (4.0 vs. 2.9 on a scale that ranged from 1 to 7). The fact that the ratings of teachers who disobeyed on the 11th trial are a full 3 points lower than the maximum rating of 7 at the "disobedient" end of the scale probably reflects both the moderate variation on this item ($SD = 1.25$) and the fact that the teacher had been obedient on the prior 10 trials. This finding can be regarded as a manipulation check attesting to the efficacy of the obedience manipulation and the reliability of the bipolar item ratings. Disobedient teachers were also perceived to be relatively more active (5.0 vs. 3.9), independent (4.2 vs. 2.7), strong (5.0 vs. 3.6), and dominant (4.3 vs. 3.8).

The observers in this study did *not* evaluate the obedient and disobedient teachers differently on the general evaluation/nurturing scale. This finding fails to replicate the positive evaluation of the disobedient teacher found in a previous study that also used an American undergraduate sample and that used the same videotapes (Collins & Brief, 1995; Levy, Collins, & Brief, 1989). One possible reason for the discrepancy is that the individual items composing the general evaluation scale in the two studies are not identical. The three bipolar scales used in the first study were moral–amoral, fair–unfair, and kind–cruel. As can be seen in the appendix, only two of these bipolar items (moral–amoral and kind–cruel) are included among the four items used in the present general evaluation scale.

In order to explore the possibility that the discrepancy between the two studies might be due to the different individual items used in the general evaluation scale, separate ANOVAs were conducted for each of the four bipolar items that make up the general evaluation scale in the present data set. Only the moral–amoral item was associated with a significance level lower than .05. The omnibus 2 df F is significant at the .003 level, and the obedient–disobedient contrast is significant at the .001 level. Disobedient teachers are perceived to be relatively more moral (M = 5.9) than their obedient counterparts (M = 5.0). Thus the prior finding in which disobedient teachers were more positively evaluated than obedient teachers was replicated for the moral item but not for the other three items. This different between-condition pattern for the moral item is surprising, because the moral item is substantially correlated with the other three items in the present general evaluation scale: hostile–friendly ($r = .42$), cruel–kind ($r = .37$), and good–bad ($r = .67$). In fact, the .67 correlation between the moral–amoral and good–bad individual items is noticeably higher than the next highest correlation (.53) in the matrix of correlations among the four items. Nevertheless, there is unique meaning in the moral–amoral item, and that unique meaning is attributed to the disobedient teachers to a greater extent than it is attributed to the obedient one.

In summary, the cues in teacher behavior produced a significant univariate F test for five of the seven dependent variables. But how independent are these five univariate findings? Given the pattern of generally low correlations among the scale scores (save only the substantial correlations among the active–independent–strong triad), one might expect that many of these findings represent inferences that are unique to the meaning of that scale and capture an aspect of the teacher's personality that does not overlap with any of the other six traits. The most conservative test of this uniqueness hypothesis is a set of seven ANCOVAs in which the other six scales are entered in turn as co-variates in each of the seven analyses. For example, the two contrasts and the six other scales are entered as predictors in the ANCOVA for the disobedient item. The two orthogonal contrasts and the six other trait attributes will be significantly associated with the disobedient item only to the extent to which one of those eight (two contrasts and six covariates) adds predictive power with respect to the disobedient item; that predictive power must be unique to that variable and independent of all the other seven predictors that have been entered in the equation. Table 5.2 contains the results of these seven analyses of covariance. The disobedience item continues to be significant even when the overlap between disobedience and the other six scales is carved away. In fact, of the five scales that were significant in the univariate analyses of variance, it is only the active scale that fails to add its own unique meaning when discriminating the personalities of obedient and disobedient teachers. (Interestingly enough, with the smaller error term, the obedient–disobedient contrast for emotionally stable is significant in the analysis in Table 5.2.)

Polite versus defiant dissent.   Only one of the seven scale scores yielded a significant difference between the polite and defiant styles of disobedience in the univariate analyses: defiantly disobedient teachers were perceived to be less emotionally stable (4.4 vs. 5.2, $p < .004$) than their polite counterparts. Thus both styles of dissent were perceived as comparably disobedient (about 4.0). The two behavioral cues clearly lead to different inferences. Obedience had impact on five scales, and the polite–defiant style had impact on a different, sixth, scale. Of the two cues, obedience–disobedience was clearly more pregnant with meaning. In the analysis of covariance in Table 5.2, there are three significant effects for polite–defiant. First, polite teachers are rated as more emotionally stable (as was the case in the univariate analyses). Second, because of the smaller error term in the covariance analyses, the polite teacher is also rated significantly less dominant and more obedient.

Do Attributions of Responsibility Mediate the Trait Attributions?

The data do not support the expectation that the four (teacher, learner, experimenter, and the situation) responsibility ratings would be negatively intercorrelated. In fact, the only significant correlation among these four ratings is a *positive* correlation of .30 ($p < .005$) between teacher responsibility and experimenter responsibility. Observers who

Table 5.2

Analyses of Covariance for the Seven Dimensions of Teacher Identity, Controlling Each Dimension for the Other Six

Dependent Variables	F	p
Teacher is disobedient		
Unique Obedient–Disobedient	15.53	.002
Unique Polite–Defiant	6.94	.030
Teacher is good/nurturing		
Unique Obedient–Disobedient	.50	ns
Unique Polite–Defiant	.55	ns
Teacher is emotionally stable		
Unique Obedient–Disobedient	5.24	.025
Unique Polite–Defiant	11.97	.001
Teacher is Dominant/Leader		
Unique Obedient–Disobedient	6.83	.011
Unique Polite–Defiant	6.12	.016
Teacher is Strong		
Unique Obedient–Disobedient	3.22	.033
Unique Polite–Defiant	1.82	ns
Teacher is Active		
Unique Obedient–Disobedient	.01	ns
Unique Polite–Defiant	.33	ns
Teacher is Independent		
Unique Obedient–Disobedient	10.86	.001
Unique Polite–Defiant	.26	ns

thought the teacher was responsible also thought the experimenter was responsible. Rather than dividing up the responsibility between the teacher and experimenter, observers indicated a mildly stable bias toward dispositional attributions to both the teacher and experimenter. To perceive responsibility in one was associated with seeing responsibility in the other. Although there is a significant effect of the obedience manipulation on teacher responsibility in a structural equations analysis to be presented subsequently, none of the effects of either disobedience or style of obedience even approaches significance in the univariate analyses of these four responsibility ratings.

A series of small structural equation models were run using the EQS (Bentler, 1989) statistical program. One of these, presented in Figure 5.1, examines the relationships among three variables: the obedient–disobedient manipulation contrast, ratings of teacher responsibility for the learner's shocks, and perceptions that the teacher was independent. The numbers on the lines in Figure 5.1 are standardized; thus they can range from values of -1.0 to $+1.0$, and a value of 0.0 indicates no relationship between the two variables. Both components of the mediation link in Figure 5.1 are significant. Manipulated obedience is associated with higher ratings of teacher responsibility ($.20, p < .05$), and teacher responsibility is linked to ratings of teacher independence ($.31, p < .01$). But the mediation link through teacher responsibility does not account for all of the correlation between manipulated obedience and perceptions that the teacher was independent; the direct link between manipulated obedience and the teacher's independence ratings is also significant and notably larger than the variance accounted for by the mediation link ($.63, p < .001$). A similar pattern to that seen in Figure 5.1 holds for the relationships among manipulated obedience, teacher respon-

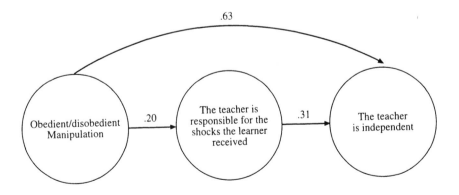

FIG. 5.1. Weak mediation of perceived responsibility. This is the only significant mediational effect.

sibility, and perceptions that the teacher is active—although the link between manipulated obedience and teacher responsibility is only marginally significant in that case.

The pattern in Figure 5.1, however, is *not* repeated for any of the other six teacher trait ratings. This is not surprising in the case of the general evaluation–nurturing rating because the general evaluation–nurturing rating is not affected by the obedience manipulation. However, manipulated obedience did have a significant impact on ratings of disobedience, dominance, and strength in the univariate analyses. But there can be no significant mediational link because the second component of that link (the correlation between ratings of teacher responsibility and the ratings of disobedience, dominance, and strength) is not significant for any of those three scales.

It is surprising that trait ratings (e.g., dominant) associated with teacher disobedience are unrelated to perceptions that the teacher was responsible for the shocks the learner received. We know both measures are reliable because they have significant relationships to other variables—just not with each other. Others (e.g., Blass, 1992) have seen problems with Milgram's theory of the agentic state, in which Milgram theorizes that teachers are obedient because they do not feel responsible for the consequences of their actions, and the present data also fail to confirm a rather direct implication of that theory.

Once forced to think about the link between disobedience and the teacher's responsibility more carefully, one becomes aware that participants in the Milgram paradigm are not simply obedient or disobedient. Very, very few participants refused to deliver the first shock in Milgram's original experiments. Most "disobedient" participants terminated their participation after they had delivered some of the milder shocks and after the learner had begun to protest. They are thus responsible for the shocks they did administer, even if they refused to participate at some point. In the present experiment, observers saw the "disobedient" teachers administer 10 shocks on the first 10 trials. This fact may have muddled the meaning of their ratings of the extent to which the teacher was responsible for the shocks the learner received.

The only significant impact of the polite–defiant independent variable in the univariate analyses—its impact on emotional stability—was not mediated by ratings of teacher responsibility.

These findings do not support any theory in which perceptions of responsibility for the shocks received by the learner play a central role.

Are There Cues in the Behavior of the Milgram-Scenario Teachers That Inform Us About the Identity of the Experimenter or Learner?

With respect to the experimenter, the answer to this question is no. Neither the teacher's disobedience per se nor his style of disobedience had any impact on any of the seven measures of the experimenter's personality. But in spite of the fact that the learner's behavior was identical in the two conditions, disobedient *teacher* behavior led observers to conclude that the *learner* was more active ($p < .001$) and more dominant ($p < .057$). The two effects are not independent from each other; the key element of meaning for the identity of learners paired with disobedient teachers is in the active scale. The disobedient–obedient contrast is significant for the active scale when dominance is controlled ($p < .001$), but not vice versa. This is a version of blaming the victim for the shocks the learner received; observers appear to have reasoned that the teacher must have delivered the shocks in part because the learner was not sufficiently active.

Are There Cues in the Behavior of the Milgram-scenario Teachers That Inform Us About the Structure of the Role Relationships Among the Three Actors?

When Milgram wrote about his scenario, he most often focused on the structure of the teacher–experimenter role relationship—the hierarchical, authority relationship between them. Do the observers in the present experiment also build models of the structure of the Milgram social situation as they encode teacher behaviors? Observers in the present study were asked to imagine that the teacher and experimenter might form a team to work on a task in the future and to rate the nature of their interactions in that hypothetical team. Factor analyses of these team ratings suggested that two of Wish and Kaplan's (1977) five dimensions for dyads could be combined in this data set (see the second part of the appendix). Formality (e.g., very formal–very informal) and task-orientation (e.g., very task-oriented–not at all task-oriented) items were combined into an index of formality–productiveness. The other three dimensions are competitiveness, intensity (e.g., completely engrossed–uninterested and uninvolved), and democracy (one totally dominates the other–each treats the other as an equal and very autocratic–very democratic). The disobedience manipulation influenced only the democracy dimension and the polite–defiant manipulation impacted only the intensity dimension. There were no effects for the ratings of either learner–teacher or learner–experimenter relationships.

Teachers who were observed to disobey on the 11th trial were seen as likely to have more democratic structure to their role relationships with the experimenter in any future interactions than were teachers who obeyed (5.1 vs. 4.3 on a scale where 1 represented the autocratic relationship extreme and 7 represented the democratic relationship extreme). The obedient–disobedient contrast was significant at the .002 level, and Bonferroni post hoc tests indicated that both disobedient conditions were different from the obedient condition ($ps < .021$ and .025). Thus the dimension of the teacher–experimenter role relationship onto which the present observers mapped the meaning of teacher behaviors was the same dimension Milgram intended to establish with his design of the Milgram scenario—hierarchical or authoritative. But Milgram would probably have argued that the situation was equally hierarchical for all participants—both those who obeyed and those who, at some point, did not.

There are at least two ways to look at this difference on the democracy scale. If we assume that ratings of the structure of a future teacher–experimenter interaction would reiterate the structure of the observed interaction in the Milgram scenario, then this finding implies that observers constructed different situations for obedient and disobedient teachers. (e.g., "The disobedient teachers must have not been in a very hierarchical relationship with the experimenter.") This interpretation could be tested in future studies by asking observers to rate the role relationship between the experimenter and teacher that they actually observed in the videotape rather than to predict some future interaction. Alternatively, the present observers may have reasoned that the disobedience per se would cause any future teacher–experimenter relationship to be more egalitarian (e.g., "The teacher's disobedience changed the role relationship to make it more egalitarian. Anybody who refuses to deliver a shock after the experimenter said that the experiment required it will be hard to boss around in the future.")

When the style of the teacher's disobedience was defiant (vs. polite), the present observers anticipated that future teacher–experimenter interactions would be more intense (3.1 vs. 4.0, $p < .006$). This is probably what most of us would have guessed. If we assumed that observers would use teacher behavior as a cue to infer the structure of the relationship, then his outrageous, defiant style would seem to imply an intense (vs. superficial) relationship. Thus, although the content of the interpretation is not surprising, the fact that cues in teacher behavior would be used to make inferences about the structure of the teacher–experimenter role relationship is less obvious.

CONCLUSION

Returning to the questions with which we started, the implicit personality theory used to construct meaning in the Milgram scenario is complex and contains at least four dimensions in addition to general evaluation. The word "disobedient" has a unique meaning of its own in this context and cannot be reduced to a combination of such other dimensions as dominant, active, or strong. Teacher behavior was used as a cue for making inferences about the teacher's identity and also about the identity of the learner. Seeing that the teacher was disobedient led observers to infer that the learner was active. Attributions of responsibility do not play a mediating role. Observers do make inferences regarding the structure of the situation (the stable dyadic relationships among the three participants) on the basis of teacher behavior. Seeing that the teacher was disobedient led observers to infer that any future teacher-experimenter interactions would be structured more democratically than would future interactions between an experimenter and an obedient teacher.

Overall, the results of this experiment strongly support the speculations with which we started:

Behavior in the Milgram paradigm is rich with meanings for the identities of all three interactants—experimenter, teacher, and learner. The desire to construct desirable self-images and social impressions is among the causal forces driving behavior in the Milgram paradigm. ... [We] postulate that the teacher–subject's behaviors have symbolic meanings for the identities of all three of the actors/actresses in the script for the Milgram paradigm. (Collins & Brief, 1995, p. 89)

Most theories of person perception in contemporary social cognition posit that the observer's inferences linking concrete behavioral cues to the symbolic meanings of those cues are unconscious or automatic (see, for instance, Levy, Collins, & Nail, 1999). This theoretical assumption implies that we cannot look to introspection or the phenomenological interview (Milgram's choice of method) as a sole source of insight into the meanings of teacher behavior. The methodologies of social cognition, including the vignette person-perception methodology, may be required to uncover all the meanings of "obedient" behavior—just as these same methodologies have proven necessary to uncover the full meaning of being, say, physically attractive, physically disabled, Jewish, or female.

Contemporary social cognition focuses on the content-free cognitive processes (e.g., priming and bias) that intervene between objective data and cognitive interpretation. One implication of the present study is that these techniques can also uncover the substantive content in the symbolic meanings of socially important behaviors. The present data imply that a disobedient act would make some concepts (e.g., strong and dominant) more accessible and thus more likely to be used in the interpretation of subsequent behaviors. These social-cognition paradigms are projective methodologies; we learn about people from the manner in which they bias the interpretation of incoming data. These projective methodologies can be used to write the dictionary that catalogues the symbolic meaning of specific behaviors. It is the symbolic meanings that specify how a particular behavior, such as delivering the 11th shock in the Milgram paradigm, will drive the impressions others form of the teacher.

To broaden the question, we might ask how adding impression management and self-concept development to the mix of psychological processes at work in the Milgram scenario casts light on behavior outside the laboratory to which the Milgram paradigm has been applied by analogy. How might we rethink the Holocaust, for instance, in light of the controversial analogy between the Milgram laboratory findings and the actions of the Nazis during World War II? Milgram's use of an obedience metaphor has led social scientists to focus on the anti-Semitism of German leaders at the *top* of the organizational hierarchy. The implication that the impetus for the destruction of Jews came from the top is central in these analyses.

Adding identity management to the set of metaphors applied to the Holocaust (an admittedly highly speculative activity) leads one to focus on how the murder of Jews might have expressed and augmented the (anti-Semitic) identity of the individual German. If one were anti-Semitic and proud of it, would there be a more effective way for the person on the street to express that identity than by personal participation in the Holocaust? This analysis goes beyond thinking of anti- Semitism as an internal personality trait correlated with behavior. Participation in, say, *Kristallnacht* may have served the function of reaffirming and expressing the ordinary individual's sense of identity. This analysis is compatible with the assertion that the anti-Semitism of the person on the street caused the Holocaust (e.g., Goldhagen, 1996).

The inclusion of self-perception theory (i.e., how our behaviors feed back into our own identities) in the present analysis also leads one to turn that (anti-Semitism caused the Holocaust casual sequence) around. Self-perception theory, unlike Milgram's theory of the agentic state, would postulate that an individual would need to feel choice or responsibility for each anti-Semitic act in order for that act to feed back into an anti-Semitic self-view and public image. In other words, it may have been the cumulation of the concrete, behavioral minutiae of the Holocaust and its prolegomena that, in part, intensified the anti-Semitism of the perpetrators.

REFERENCES

Arroyo, J. A. (1996). Psychotherapist bias with Hispanics: An analog study. *Hispanic Journal of Behavioral Sciences, 18,* 21–28.

Asch, S. E. (1946). Forming impressions of personality. *Journal of Abnormal and Social Psychology, 41,* 258–290.

Baldwin, M. W. (1992). Relational schemas and the processing of social information. *Psychological Bulletin, 112,* 461–484.

Bargh, J. A. (1997). The automaticity of everyday life. In R. W. Wyer (Ed.), *Advances in social cognition* (Vol. 10, pp. 1–61). Mahwah, NJ: Lawrence Erlbaum Associates.

Baumeister, Roy F. (1982). A self-presentational view of social phenomena. *Psychological Bulletin, 91,* 3–26.

Bell, S. T., Kuriloff, P. J., & Lottes, I. (1994). Understanding attributions of blame in stranger rape and date rape situations: An examination of gender, race, identification, and students' social perceptions of rape victims. *Journal of Applied Social Psychology, 24,* 1719–1734

Bem, D. J. (1967). Self-perception: An alternative interpretation of cognitive dissonance phenomena. *Psychological Review, 74,* 183–200.

Bem, D. J. (1972). Self-perception theory. In L. Berkowitz (Ed.), *Advances in experimental social psychology* (Vol. 6, pp. 1–62). New York: Academic Press.

Bem, S. L. (1974). The measurement of psychological androgyny. *Journal of Consulting and Clinical Psychology, 42,* 155–162.

Bentler, P. M. (1989). *EQS structural equations program manual.* Los Angeles: BMDP Statistical Software.

Blass, T. (1992). The social psychology of Stanley Milgram. In M. P. Zanna (Ed.), *Advances in experimental social psychology* (Vol. 25, pp. 277–329). San Diego, CA: Academic Press.

Branscombe, N. R., & Smith, E. R. (1990). Gender and racial stereotypes in impression formation and social decision-making processes. *Sex Roles, 22,* 9–10.

Collins, B. E., & Brief, D. E. (1995). Using person-perception vignette methodologies to uncover the symbolic meanings of teacher behavior in the Milgram paradigm. *Journal of Social Issues, 51*(3), 89–106.

Deaux, K., & LaFrance, M. (1998). Gender. In D. T. Gilbert, S. T. Fiske, & G. Lindzey (Eds.), *The handbook of social psychology* (4th ed., Vol. 2, pp. 788–827). Boston: McGraw-Hill.

Dion, K., Berscheid, E., & Walster, E. (1972). What is beautiful is good. *Journal of Personality and Social Psychology, 24,* 285–290.

Eagly, A. H., Ashmore, R. D., Makhijani, M. G., & Longo, L. C. (1991). What is beautiful is good, but … : A meta-analytic review of research on the physical attractiveness stereotype. *Psychological Bulletin, 110,* 109–126.

Fiske, S. T., & Taylor, S. E. (1991). *Social cognition.* Reading: Addison-Wesley.

Foley, L. A., Adams, A. M., & Goodson, J. L., Jr. (1996). The effect of race on decisions by judges and other officers of the court. *Journal of Applied Social Psychology, 26,* 1190–1212.

Foley, L. A., Evancic, C., Karnik, K., King, J., and others. (1995). Date rape: Effects of race of assailant and victim and gender of subjects on perceptions. *Journal of Black Psychology, 21,* 6–18.

Ford, T. E. (1997). Effects of stereotypical television portrayals of African-Americans on person perception. *Social Psychology Quarterly, 60,* 266–275.

Goldhagen, D. J. (1996). *Hitler's willing executioners: Ordinary Germans and the Holocaust.* New York: Knopf.

Hastorf, H. C., Schneider, D. J., & Polefka, J. (1970). *Person perception.* Reading, MA: Addison-Wesley.

Herbert, T., & Dunkel-Schetter, C. (1992). Negative social reactions to victims: An overview of responses and their determinants. In L. Montada, F. Sigrun-Heide, & M. Learner (Eds.), *Life crises and experiences of loss in adulthood* (pp. 497–518). Hillsdale, NJ: Lawrence Erlbaum Associates.

Janoff-Bulman, R. (1992). *Shattered assumptions: Towards a new psychology of trauma.* New York: The Free Press.

Jones, E. E. (1990). *Interpersonal perception.* New York: Freeman.

Leary, M. R. (1995). *Self-presentation: Impression management and interpersonal behavior.* Madison, WI: Brown & Benchmark.

Lerner, M. J. (1980). *The belief in a just world.* New York: Plenum Press.

Levy, D. A., Collins, B. E., & Brief, D. E. (1989, April). *Perception of responses to malevolent authority.* Paper presented at the annual meeting of the Western Psychological Association, Reno, NV.

Levy, D. A., Collins, B. E., & Nail, P. R. (1998). A new model of interpersonal influence characteristics. *Journal of Social Behavior and Personality, 13,* 715–733.

Lobel, T. E., & Shavit, T. (1997). Targets' and perceivers' occupation and gender as determinants of social judgments. *Social Behavior and Personality, 25,* 339–343.

Madon, S. (1997). What do people believe about gay males? A study of stereotype content and strength. *Sex Roles, 37,* 663–685.

Milgram, S. (1963). Behavioral study of obedience. *Journal of Abnormal and Social Psychology, 67,* 371–378.

Milgram, S. (1974). *Obedience to authority: An experimental view.* New York: Harper & Row.

Miller, A. G. (1995). Constructions of the obedience experiments: A focus upon domains of relevance. *Journal of Social Issues, 51*(3), 33–53.

Miller, A. G., Gillen, B., Schlenker, C., & Radlove, S. (1974). The prediction and perception of obedience to authority. *Journal of Personality, 42,* 23–42.

Osgood, C. E., Suci, G. J., & Tannenbaum, P. H. (1957). *The measurement of meaning.* Urbana: University of Illinois Press.

Plater, M. A., & Thomas, R. E. (1998). The impact of job performance, gender, and ethnicity on the managerial review of sexual harassment allegations. *Journal of Applied Social Psychology, 28,* 52–70.

Powers, W. T. (1973). *Behavior: The control of perception.* Chicago, IL: Aldine.

Rands, M., & Levinger, G. (1979). Implicit theories of relationship: An intergenerational study. *Journal of Personality and Social Psychology, 37,* 645–661.

Ross, L. (1977). The intuitive psychologist and his shortcomings: Distortions in the attribution process. In L. Berkowitz (Ed.), *Advances in experimental social psychology* (Vol. 10, pp. 173–219). New York: Academic Press.

Schlenker, B. R. (1980). *Impression management: The self-concept, social identity, and interpersonal relations.* Monterey, CA: Brooks/Cole.

Schlenker, B. R. (1985). *The self and social life.* New York: McGraw-Hill.

Schlenker, B. R., & Trudeau, J. V. (1990). Impact of self-presentations on private self-beliefs: Effects of prior self-beliefs and misattribution. *Journal of Personality and Social Psychology, 58,* 22–32

Schlenker, B. R., & Weigold, M. F. (1992). Interpersonal processes involving impression regulation and management. *Annual Review of Psychology, 43,* 133–168.

Schneider, D. J. (1973). Implicit personality theory: A review. *Psychological Bulletin, 9,* 294–309.

Schneider, W., & Shiffrin, R. M. (1977). Controlled and automatic human information processing: I. Detection, search, and attention. *Psychological Review, 84,* 1–66.

Sedikides, C., Olsen, N., & Reis, H. T. (1993). Relationships as nature categories. *Journal of Personality & Social Psychology, 64,* 71–82.

Shiffrin, R. M., & Schneider, W. (1977). Controlled and automatic human information processing: II. Perceptual learning, automatic attending and a general theory. *Psychological Review, 84,* 127–190.

Taylor, S. E. (1981). The interface of cognitive and social psychology. In J. Harvey (Ed.), *Cognition, social behavior, and the environment* (pp. 189–211). Hillsdale, NJ: Lawrence Erlbaum Associates.

Tedeschi, J. T. (Ed.). (1981). *Impression management theory and social psychological research.* New York: Academic Press.

Tice, D. M. (1992). Self-concept and self-presentation: The looking glass self is also a magnifying glass. *Journal of Personality and Social Psychology, 63,* 435–451.

Wegner, D. M., & Bargh, J. A. (1998). Control and automaticity in social life. In D. T Gilbert, S. T. Fiske, & G. Lindzey (Eds.), *The handbook of social psychology* (4th ed., Vol. 2, pp. 446–496). Boston: McGraw-Hill,.

Weiner, B. (1995). *Judgments of responsibility: A foundation for a theory of social conduct.* New York: Guilford.

Wish, M., & Kaplan, S. J. (1977). Toward an implicit theory of interpersonal communication. *Sociometry, 40,* 234–246.

Appendix:
Items in Rating Scales for Individuals and Dyads

Rating Scale Items for Individuals

1. General Evaluation
   Hostile–Friendly
   Cruel–Kind
   Bad–Good
   Amoral–Moral
2. Nurturing
   Sensitive to the needs of others–Not sensitive to the needs of others

Gentle–Not gentle
Sympathetic–Unsympathetic
Eager to soothe hurt feelings–Not eager to soothe hurt feelings
3. Dominant
   Assertive–Unassertive
   Competitive–Uncompetitive
   Dominant–Not Dominant
   Forceful–Not forceful
   Intimidating–Not intimidating
4. Leader
   Dominant–Submissive
   Leader–Follower
5. Emotionally Stable
   Controlled–Impulsive
   Emotionally Unstable–Emotionally Stable
   Likely to persevere on a task–Likely to quit easily on a task
6. Active
   Active–Passive
   Enthusiastic–Apathetic
7. Independent
   Self-reliant–Not self-reliant
   Self-sufficient–Not Self-sufficient
8. Strong
   Forceful–Meek
   Strong–Cowardly
9. Obedient–disobedient [single–item dependent variable]

Rating Scale Items for Structure of Role Relationship in Dyads

1. Competitiveness
   Very competitive–Very cooperative
   Very hostile–Very friendly
   Constant conflict–No conflict
2. Intensity
   Very intense–Very superficial
   Completely engrossed–Uninterested and uninvolved
   Very emotional–Very unemotional
   Very personal–Very impersonal
3. Democracy
   Each treats the other as an equal–One totally dominates the other
   Very democratic–Very autocratic
4. Formality
   Very informal–Very formal
   Very frank and open–Very reserved and cautious
5. Productiveness
   Very task-oriented–Not at all task-oriented
   Very production–Very unproductive

6

Captain Paul Grueninger: The Chief of Police Who Saved Jewish Refugees by Refusing to Do His Duty

François Rochat
Andre Modigliani
University of Michigan

On April 3, 1939, Paul Grueninger, the chief of police of the canton of Sankt Gallen, Switzerland, was suspended from his job and charged with helping refugees enter Switzerland illegally. These refugees were fleeing the persecution of the Nazis, but by assisting them Grueninger had defied the explicit instructions given by the Swiss federal authorities to all the police chiefs of cantons located along the Swiss border. Thus Captain Grueninger stood accused of disobeying legitimate orders, as well as of violating federal law. He was summarily tried and convicted in 1940 and, at the age of 48, was stripped of both his job and his pension. These actions committed him to a life of poverty until his death in 1972 at the age of 80. Paul Grueninger was officially exonerated of all wrongdoing in 1995, but only after a long legal struggle waged by his daughter.

In this chapter we address the following question: How did Grueninger come to play such a notable role in saving refugees' lives at a time when he was under strict orders to turn them back and, more generally, to insure that the Swiss border remained firmly closed to all foreigners who lacked proper entry visas? Thanks to the recent historical work of Stefan Keller (1993), we know reasonably well what Grueninger did and what led the authorities to punish him for doing so. Yet knowing the facts about Grueninger's deeds leaves us with a deeper motivational question: Why did he choose to disobey the law in order to help refugees find sanctuary in Switzerland? And related to this question there is yet another: Why did so few others try to do what he did?

Grueninger's resistance to the orders of federal authorities, which directed him to show no compassion for those fleeing the persecution of the Third Reich, is reminiscent of the Milgram experiment on obedience to authority. In particular, it reminds us of the defiant minority of participants who successfully opposed the experimenter's orders to continue inflicting severe pain on a fellow participant (Milgram, 1974). Although there are many differences between the simulated authority situation designed by Milgram and the very real circumstances in which Grueninger came to oppose the orders he was given, there are also some noteworthy commonalities between Grueninger's behavior and the behavior of defiant participants in the Milgram experiment. These commonalities are all the more striking when we consider that Milgram's participants believed they were taking part in a scientific study on memory and learning, whereas Grueninger knew he was dealing with the brutal circumstances surrounding the Nazis' rise to power in Germany and Austria. Nonetheless, there is a pathway connecting Grueninger's setting to Milgram's scenario, and it is a two-way path— for not only do Milgram's findings help to explicate certain features of Grueninger's behavior, but Grueninger's actions are also an impressive example of the difficult process of shifting from cooperation with authority to defiance of it.

Grueninger's acts of disobedience occurred in the late 1930s following the Anschluss (the annexation of Austria to the Third Reich). This was a time when the attitude of the Swiss government toward the refugees was not shared by the Swiss population. For the most part, the people of Switzerland were more in tune with a long-standing tradition that viewed their country as a safe haven for those being persecuted because of their religious faith or political ideas (Haesler, 1967). Furthermore, the Nazis were perceived by most of the Swiss population as extremists and quite possibly as a danger to Switzerland (Graf, 1996;

Lasserre, 1995). This rather negative perception of the Nazis was often associated with a feeling of sympathy for the refugees fleeing terrorism. This was especially true among the Swiss living near the borders of Germany and Austria, who regularly observed these refugees in a state of great agitation, severely affected by the horrors they had witnessed being inflicted by the Nazis.

NAZI PERSECUTION AND SWISS REFUGE AFTER THE ANSCHLUSS

On March 10, 1938, Hitler's troops marched into Austria, thereby annexing it to the Third Reich. The annexation immediately opened the door to a brutal persecution of Jews living in Austria, causing many of them to try to flee the country. In point of fact, however, there were not many places where they could go: Czechoslovakia had closed its Austrian border, and Italy was under Fascist rule. The only readily accessible country was Switzerland. As a consequence, soon after the Nazis took over, many persecuted people sought to cross the Swiss border. But these refugees were not welcome in Switzerland—indeed, the attitude of the Swiss government toward the refugees was fear and rejection. Their official policy stressed the risks associated with having an "overload" of foreigners who would have difficulty integrating into the indigenous Swiss population. This fear of foreign "overpopulation" in a small country such as Switzerland was expressed quite overtly a couple of years later by government officials who publicly repeated a particular slogan: As far as refugees were concerned, "the boat is full" (Haesler, 1967).

It did not begin that way. The first refugees from the Nazis crossed the Swiss border without much difficulty just after Hitler marched into Austria—they were allowed to enter provided they had identification papers with them. But within a few days, in order to keep Switzerland from becoming overloaded with refugees, the Swiss government instructed the border guards at the Austrian frontier to order refugees to return from wherever they had come. At first these harsh new instructions (which had been issued in the Swiss capital far from the border) had little impact on the border guards, who could see for themselves the extreme misery and fear of the arriving refugees. Then on April 1, 1938, the Swiss government decided that Austrian citizens who wished to cross the border would need an entry visa, which meant that all refugees who lacked such a document had to be turned back by the border guards. This was a cruel decision, for it meant that even those who had been allowed by Third Reich authorities to leave the country provided that another country was willing to take them in would not be accepted by Switzerland. In effect, the Swiss government refused to grant such persons the status of "political refugee," and, to make things worse, they refused to do so even if these persons could establish that they were Jewish. However, at the actual Austrian border, matters did not go quite as the Swiss government had intended that they should: In fact, it appears that during the spring and summer of 1938 very few refugees who reached the border crossing commanded by Captain Paul Grueninger were forced to turn back.

It may be helpful to understand the difficulties facing Jewish refugees during this period. In July 1938, at the initiative of President Franklin D. Roosevelt, representatives of 36 nations convened in Evian, France, in an effort to help Jews fleeing the Third Reich find safe havens from the Nazi persecutions. At the conference, President Roosevelt ruled out the possibility of increasing the United States' immigration quota for Jews. As it turned out, the other countries followed suit, refusing to show any real generosity toward the Jewish refugees (Lasserre, 1995). As a result, those countries immediately bordering the Third Reich became even more wary of the "dangers" of being flooded by refugees from Germany and Austria.

In August 1938 the Nazis sharply escalated their persecution of the Jews, forcing them to flee wherever they could, typically leaving behind all their possessions. Many fled to the Swiss border, so that, suddenly, there were many more people asking to be taken in. At about the same time racial persecutions began in Italy under the Fascist regime of Benito Mussolini. Also at this time, Third Reich authorities delivered German passports to all its newly annexed Austrian citizens, which meant that these citizens no longer needed entry visas to go into Switzerland, for they were, technically speaking, German citizens. These turns of events so alarmed Swiss authorities that the federal police called a special meeting of the chiefs of police of all cantons to discuss the refugee problem. Captain Grueninger attended this meeting and expressed his point of view on the matter. According to historian Stefan Keller, the minutes of this meeting were the first document that recorded Grueninger's stance on asylum (Keller, 1993). The record shows that Grueninger made the following statement: "Turn them [the refugees] back? How could this be done when they are arriving fifty at a time? This is physically impossible, let alone from a humanitarian standpoint. What is happening at the border is heartbreaking! And many of them tell us they are political refugees. We must let in many of them" (Keller, 1993, p. 49).

Grueninger was not the only police chief who felt this way and spoke up at the meeting. But in spite of these protests, 2 days later, on August 18, 1938, the Swiss federal authorities decided to close the border. They ordered the border police to turn back anyone still holding Austrian passports who did not also have an entry visa for Switzerland. In addition, they decreed that all refugees who managed to enter the country illegally be returned to the border and sent back. Captain Grueninger never fully obeyed these orders. Instead of carrying out the federal decree, he improvised methods for letting in the refugees—for instance, he backdated the dates of their arrival at the Swiss border to make it legal for the refugees to remain in Switzerland. With practice, Grueninger became quite adept at undermining the Swiss border policy, so that by the time he was suspended from his job on April 3, 1939, he had helped to admit some 3,000 illegal refugees (Dindo, 1997).

HOW GRUENINGER BECAME A RESCUER

It is unlikely that anyone could have predicted that Paul Grueninger would become one of the very few Swiss police officers who would come to defy the authority of the federal government in order to help refugees fleeing the persecutions of the Nazis. Captain Grueninger was an elementary school teacher by training. After teaching for several years with success, he applied for a better paying job with the police in 1919. The position had come to his attention through a friend of his parents; the salary the position promised meant a good deal during the difficult days of the 1920s. The fact that Grueninger was an officer in the Swiss army certainly helped to get him the job. In 1925, he was promoted to the rank of captain of police, that is, chief of police, of the canton of Sankt Gallen (Keller, 1993).

Grueninger was especially fond of soccer and was quite good at it, having once played on a team that won the Swiss National Championship. For several years, while serving as chief of police, he coached a soccer team and spent a great deal of his time organizing games and training players. A variety of people played for the team: blue-collar workers, owners of small businesses, state employees, conservatives, right-wing extremists, socialists, and even some members of the Jewish community. As coach of the team, Grueninger was widely respected and very well liked; he provided financial assistance to those in need and was generally recognized as being a kind and helpful person (Keller, 1993).

Prior to the Anschluss, Grueninger had never had any encounters with refugees. Soon after the beginning of the Spanish civil war in 1936 his main concern with respect to the Swiss border was trying to stop the flow of volunteers going to Spain to fight with the Republicans against Generalissimo Franco's army, which was trying to overthrow the democratically elected government. In his efforts to stop this illegal stream of volunteers, Grueninger managed to gain a reputation for honesty, civility, and kindness among the volunteers (Keller, 1993). This was perhaps an antecedent to the humaneness he showed toward refugees a couple of years later, although in the case of the volunteers there was no humanitarian motive behind his attitude, nor was there an ideological one. Grueninger was kind to these people not because they were on their way to battle Franco's army but because they were largely young and poor and because they had had the misfortune of getting caught—of being thwarted in their desire to reach Spain.

When the Swiss border was closed by the federal authorities in August of 1938, Grueninger initially did cooperate with them by trying to stop Austrian refugees from illegally crossing the Swiss border. However, he soon became convinced that they needed his help. He was struck by the tragic misfortune of the refugees, as were many Swiss people living near the border. His own direct superior in the canton government of Sankt Gallen was in agreement with him on this matter; he himself had witnessed the distressing events at the border and fully supported his subordinate's generous inclinations.

Grueninger used both legal and illegal means to prevent refugees from being sent back to the territory of the Third Reich. The manner in which he acted was fully in accord with a long-standing tradition of the Swiss people—a tradition that regarded their country as a safe haven for people persecuted for their religious or political beliefs. Grueninger's actions were also in accord with the feelings of many of the Swiss in another respect. People knew about the horrendous events unfolding on the other side of their borders; they knew, for example, about the concentration camp at Dachau through newspaper reports and the testimonies of former inmates. And they were convinced that Switzerland was a place where refugees should be able to find protection and a sanctuary from the brutality they were being subjected to by the Nazis.

Both this image of Switzerland and these feelings toward the refugees were in sharp opposition to the views held by their federal government, which, instead, was much more tuned to what was happening in Germany and several other countries. In these countries a strong emphasis was beginning to be placed on the term *New Order*—a catch phrase that was intended to rally people to a new social or political order but that was, in fact, a code word for more authoritarian regimes, if not dictatorships. Furthermore, the refugees were increasingly being depicted as rejects, as the dregs of society. They were welcome nowhere and would often be turned away entirely. The Swiss federal authorities could not entirely escape this view of the refugees. They did not want them freely entering Switzerland just as Germany, Austria, and others were throwing them out. Because the refugees were considered "unfit" for the New Order and because, at that time this form of government seemed to the Swiss authorities to be a likely future for Europe, the authorities feared that the presence of refugees would be taken as evidence that the Swiss government was deficient—lacking in a modern and "orderly" orientation. In a way, then, Grueninger was attempting to uphold an old tradition of sympathy and sanctuary for victims of misfortune and persecution, whereas the federal authorities were looking to the changes being brought about throughout Europe by the rise of fascism and, therefore, were far readier to compromise their country's basic humanitarian principles.

WHAT GRUENINGER DID

A careful examination of what Grueninger did to protect refugees from the Nazi persecutions reveals an impressive list of wonderfully clever actions that included backdating refugees' day of arrival at the border to make their entry "legal"; sending the administrators of the Dachau concentration camp instructions and entry visas that directed certain prisoners to leave the camp and enter Switzerland; travelling to the Austrian side of the border to pick up refugees in his own car, thus insuring that, when he returned, no one at the border would ask Captain Grueninger about his passengers; and writing a letter to the Swiss Consulate in Italy asking that entry visas be issued to the family members of a refugee who was already in Switzerland. Yet another example of his creativity was a subpoena he dispatched to the authorities in Vienna requesting that the parents of a refugee be sent to Switzerland so they could testify at a legal proceeding; when they arrived, he authorized them to remain. He lied to Third Reich authorities who were trying to arrest a refugee whom Grueninger was convinced was merely a target of Nazi persecution. When recently arrived refugees called him on the phone to ask for help in getting other refugees into the country, he told them what they needed to do and where they should go. Then he would devise ways of getting these other refugees over the border. In addition, he even collected money to help refugees, many of whom were in dire need because everything they owned had been appropriated by Third Reich authorities before they left German territory (Keller, 1993).

The account provided by Harry Weinreb of his arrival at the Swiss border in August 1938 perhaps typifies the sort of techniques used by Grueninger to get refugees through the border crossing (Butler & Nada, 1993; Keller, 1993). Weinreb came to the Swiss border with two of his friends. All three attempted to cross into Switzerland illegally and were caught by a Swiss border guard, who ordered them to return to Austrian territory. They refused to do so and, after a lengthy period of pleading and arguing, the guard suddenly changed his tone. He told the youths he was going to call the chief of police (Grueninger) and that when the chief arrived, he (the guard) would warn them that, "You have to go back where you came from or we will be forced to shoot you." He assured them that, of course, the chief would not have them shot but that they should respond to the warning by saying, "No, we refuse to go back because, if we do, we will be shot anyway." When Grueninger arrived, the border guard threatened them in exactly the manner he had told them he would. The youths then delivered their lines, as instructed. At this point Grueninger furrowed his brow, as if giving the situation a great deal of thought, and then responded, "Well, if your life would be endangered by being sent back, then in that case you can remain in Switzerland" (Keller, 1993, p. 33).

Although Grueninger was the person who usually made the official decisions about how to handle refugees, many of his subordinates cooperated with him and shared his attitude. Even his superior in the canton's government fully supported his activities—although he did not want to know the details of just how Grueninger managed to rescue refugees. In contrast, knowledge of the details was an important feature of Grueninger's efforts: As chief of police he was in charge of the Swiss border and felt responsible for what was happening to refugees. He visited the border on a regular basis to see for himself exactly what was going on and just who the refugees were. He talked to his subordinates

about the situation, and many of them worked closely with him in helping people flee the Third Reich. Grueninger was convinced that the
Swiss people shared his belief to the effect that Switzerland was a land
of refuge. Furthermore, as he stated on more than one occasion, it was
plain common sense that one had to give aid to victims who were terri-
fied of being persecuted and of being imprisoned in concentration
camps and ultimately killed. In January 1939, Grueninger wrote the following in a note to his superior:

> In this matter [of assisting refugees], we have been open to the needs of
> refugees for strictly humanitarian reasons. After the influx of November
> 10, we did not have the heart purely and simply to send the refugees back
> and, who knows, perhaps even to condemn to death people who had been
> mistreated in the most shameful way in Germany, and who had succeeded
> in reaching Switzerland only after an exhausting trip. In doing so, we were
> guided also by the opinion of a large portion of the Swiss people, of the
> press, and of the political parties. (Cited in Keller, 1993, p. 146)

In many ways, Grueninger was not so different from other chiefs of police who were in charge of portions of the Swiss border, and we know
that initially several of them were in favor of adopting a generous attitude toward the refugees. However, whereas most of the others gradually began to implement the policies established by the federal
authorities, Grueninger did not. Instead he held on to his belief that
Switzerland was a land of refuge. It appears that he never could comprehend the federal authorities' decisions, which he felt amounted to returning people to their torturers. It was as if the law no longer made any
sense to him compared to what he could see at the border. And, as noted
earlier, Grueninger was the type of police chief who personally visited
the border to meet with refugees instead of staying in his office and
making decisions at a distance. One might say that Grueninger used his
authority to bend the law to the reality of the refugees' ordeal. He never
doubted that the refugees had a right of asylum and that Switzerland
could provide them with the sanctuary they sought.

WHY DID HE DO IT?

When one tries to understand the values and motives that led
Grueninger to disobey the law, one cannot fail to see that he was not a
heroic type, not a fighter, not someone working for a cause, not a rebel
confronting the government in a defiant manner. As depicted by many

people who knew him, he was an exceptionally accommodating person whose objective was not that of opposing an adversary, least of all the federal authorities. Rather, it was to help the refugees. Grueninger was deeply moved by their condition and their potential fate, and for him people came first and the law came second. Looking back at the period during which Grueninger was helping refugees, one cannot fail to notice that very few of the other police chiefs were providing such assistance, and that none were helping to the extent that he was. However, it appears that Grueninger was not aware that he was in the minority, and quite possibly a minority of one. This was because what he was doing seemed perfectly natural to him; it was simple common sense, obviously right.

Even after being fired, tried, and deprived of his pension and all other benefits associated with his position as a state employee, he never sought to justify or explain what he had done. In his old age he answered questions and even participated in a documentary film about his case (Vitali, 1971), but even on these occasions he did not attack anybody or try to make a case that the Swiss authorities had treated him unjustly. He never acted like a victim despite the poverty that he and his family had to suffer after he lost his job. In effect, he never seemed to feel that the burden of proof was on his shoulders. Surely he had nothing to prove, for the virtue of his course of action was transparently obvious. He only wished that the Swiss authorities would acknowledge this, thereby giving him credit for having upheld one of his country's finest traditions.

What is striking about Grueninger's deeds is that he never altered his values to suit the government. The refugees whose lives were in danger took priority over the legitimate orders of the administration. In the face of the Nazi persecutions, the right of asylum seemed self-evident. There would always be ways of finding food and shelter for the refugees once they had been allowed into the country. Grueninger never spoke or wrote about moral values or moral principles. He made his decisions on the spot and seemed not to deliberate much about the rightness of his course of action. Indeed, he objected immediately when the federal authorities introduced, at the special meeting of chiefs of police, the possibility of closing the Swiss border. There is a remarkably straightforward quality to Grueninger's behavior that actually has led some people to maintain that he simply lacked the courage to turn back refugees, something he really should have done far more than he did (Butler &

Nada, 1993). For such people, Grueninger might well have lacked the personal qualities needed to be an effective chief of police. In effect, he was far too soft-hearted. It is, of course, true that some people may be constitutionally unable to implement rules that they really should be enforcing, but it is also true that stealth, subterfuge, sabotage, and other softer forms of resistance can be exceptionally effective ways of deliberately defying powerful authorities.

A COMPARISON WITH DEFIANT PARTICIPANTS IN THE MILGRAM EXPERIMENTS

Another way to gain insight into Grueninger's surprising deeds is to compare his actions with those of defiant participants in the Milgram experiments. Part of the rationale for such a comparison lies in the fact that, just as Grueninger's defiance was not predictable from his initial reactions to the requests of his superiors, so disobedience in the Milgram experiments was almost impossible to predict from participants' behavior at the beginning of the experiment. In Milgram's experimental procedure all participants were assigned the task of punishing a fellow participant with increasingly powerful electric shocks each time the latter made another error on a learning task. At the very start of the session virtually every participant began by cooperating with the experimenter and carrying out this task. Similarly, virtually all of them were quite surprised and distressed when they heard their fellow participant complaining of serious pain and asking to be "let out" of the experiment.

Once the experimental procedure was under way, however, participants who wished to stop inflicting pain necessarily had to end their cooperation with the experimenter, for he continued persistently to press them to carry on with their teaching task despite the rising intensity of the victim's cries of pain and protest. One might think that every participant who objected to the way in which the experimental procedure was unfolding—who was distressed by the brutal manner in which the experimenter seemed to be placing his own research agenda ahead of the well-being of participants—would take a firm stand against continuing with the experiment. For instance, it would seem reasonable to expect that some of them would leave their seats, go into the next room (where the victim had been strapped into a chair), and set him free, thereby rescuing him from the experimenter.

Such events simply did not occur in Milgram's experiments. No participant ever attempted to unstrap the learner; none even opened the door to the room he was in. Yet in Milgram's standard conditions, a substantial minority (about one third) of participants did disobey the experimenter's authority to the extent of managing to stop the experimental procedure. The demeanor of these participants was not that of rugged heroes or inspired crusaders nor of militants in the service of a cause. The manner in which they defied the experimenter's authority and rescued their fellow participant was quite different. Yet in a number of ways it closely resembled Captain Paul Grueninger's relatively soft and noncombative way of disobeying the authorities of the Swiss federal police.

Many defiant participants seemed to oppose the experimenter's commands out of sympathy for their fellow participant, even though he was a complete stranger to them. The way in which such participants behaved during the experimental session is perhaps best conveyed through excerpts taken from their own verbal responses to the experimenter's demands that they continue. The following person, for example, said to the experimenter, who was insisting that he go on:[1]

> I don't think I ought to force him to do it, much as I'd like to cooperate. But … you're asking me to help administer punishment and I don't think I should.

Another participant responded as follows:

> I don't want to get into any altercation here. I'm willing to cooperate, but if the man doesn't want to, I don't want to. I don't know this man. I don't want to injure him and he doesn't want the shocks.

Yet another reacted in the following manner:

> I won't. The man … I can't, sir. It's against my wishes now. I don't like this myself this much. I don't believe in it this much. I can't, I'm sorry. I picture myself in his place. I wouldn't take it myself.

Another was even more explicit:

> I can't do it to him. It's hurting him. I can't. How can I do it to him? If he doesn't want it, how can I do it? Hey, would you punish your children like this? I wouldn't do it to my own. I have a choice. I can walk out of here. I can't hurt this man. He's a human being like I am. I wouldn't want it done to myself.

---

[1]All of the quotations from participants are taken from Milgram's manuscripts in the Yale University Library.

It would seem that these disobedient participants were made markedly uncomfortable by their fellow participant's expressions of pain and anguish. They felt compassion for him—a man whom they had never previously met—simply because he was already suffering and might soon receive more severe electric shocks. Their attitude was not so different from what Grueninger's might have been as he met with refugees arriving at the Swiss border. Their fear and suffering was obvious to him, and, being unable to make sense of the federal authorities' insistence that they be turned back, he tried to help them enter Switzerland to the extent possible.

We know that Grueninger was sensitive to the refugees' suffering, but we also know that this attitude was not new. A few years earlier he had shown a decidedly sympathetic attitude toward the military volunteers who were seeking to reach Spain to fight in the civil war. Even though by doing his duty he prevented them from attaining their political objectives, most of them viewed him as a kind man because of the respectful and sympathetic manner in which he treated them. Some years before this, he had shown sympathy and generosity toward those on his soccer team who were short of funds. Using his own personal resources, he provided loans to those in need, and he did so without regard to their social backgrounds, which were quite diverse with respect to religion, class, and even political ideology (Keller, 1993). In general, it would seem that Grueninger utterly disliked the sight of people who were facing difficult circumstances or who were visibly suffering and that he would react by trying to provide them with assistance. This attitude toward human torment was not unlike that of many defiant participants in Milgram's experiment.

Although Grueninger's sensitivity to suffering very likely played a key role in motivating his behavior, it is also true that the dedicated manner in which he fulfilled his duties as chief of police, through frequent visits to the border, may well have further increased his empathic response to refugees. This can best be appreciated by considering another of Milgram's experimental conditions—a variation on the one we have thus far been considering. In this variant, instead of placing the fellow participant in a room adjacent to the one in which the participant and experimenter were located, Milgram placed him in the very same room as the other two. Thus, in addition to being audible to the participant, the victim was now fully visible as well. In this condition, nearly twice as many participants disobeyed the experimenter as compared to the condition in which the victim was in an adjacent room. As Milgram explains:

> It is probable that the visual cues associated with the victim's suffering trigger empathic responses in the [participant] and give him a more complete grasp of the victim's experience. ... [Moreover,] the actions of the [participant] now come under scrutiny by the victim. Possibly, it is easier to [fail to help] a person when he is unable to observe our actions than when he can see what we are doing. (Milgram, 1974, p. 38).

These considerations suggest that Grueninger's conscientious habit of regularly visiting the border and meeting face-to-face with refugees may well have had two important effects: (a) it increased his sympathetic response by allowing him actually to observe their fear, exhaustion, and suffering; (b) it made it more difficult for him to turn down their requests, because they could watch him as he pondered whether to allow them to remain in Switzerland.

Nevertheless, it should be kept firmly in mind that no matter how much a person may empathize with mistreated victims, taking decisive action on the basis of this sympathy is no easy matter, particularly when this requires defying authority and thereby disrupting the implicit expectations that underlie the smooth functioning of any authority–subordinate relationship. In the Milgram experiment, for example, participants had been paid to complete their task as defined by the experimenter, and he, in turn, was counting on their assistance to carry out his research project. Thus participants had their role clearly defined: They had an obligation to follow the experimenter's directions. They knew that violating these obligations by refusing to continue would likely upset the experimenter a good deal. Moreover, they sensed that, due to the face-to-face nature of the situation, refusing to go on would precipitate a highly awkward confrontation.

In many respects the same sort of social structure was in place for Grueninger as well. The federal police were counting on him to implement the decisions of the Swiss government. He too was paid to do his job well, and he too was in a subordinate relationship with the federal authorities. His own personal sympathy for the refugees was, of course, wholly irrelevant to these authorities. In a parallel manner, Milgram's experimenter did not care about the participants' compassion for their fellow participant. Expressions of concern about the learner's suffering would typically draw the following callous responses from the experimenter: "Whether the learner likes it or not, we must go on until he's learned all the word-pairs correctly." Or, "Although the shocks may be painful, there is no permanent tissue damage, so please go on" (Milgram, 1974, p. 21).

One significant difference between the two situations is that Grueninger was very likely not under the direct scrutiny of the authorities while he was in the process of taking disobedient actions. Thus his acts of defiance, although clearly a violation of his duty toward these authorities, presumably did not precipitate an awkward face-to-face confrontation of the sort that faced Milgram's participants. In this respect Grueninger's task was somewhat easier, though, of course, he faced infinitely greater sanctions if he were to get caught, as he eventually did. As it happens, Milgram conducted yet another version of his experiment, one in which the experimenter was not in the same room as the participant. Instead, he gave his orders by telephone, which meant that he was not in a position to maintain surveillance of the participant. As might be expected, Milgram found that when the experimenter was not in the same room as the participant, the number of defiant participants approximately doubled. Thus it seems very likely that lack of direct surveillance was one factor that helped Grueninger achieve his remarkable record of defiance. More specifically, it made it possible for him to employ schemes whose implementation depended on being able to use the powers of his office without being observed—for example, his stratagems for bringing into Switzerland refugees who were being detained in foreign countries, including those in concentration camps.

The technique, described earlier, that Grueninger used to get the three youths across the border (in which his subordinate instructed them on what they should say to him) is similar to a subterfuge used by some participants in the Milgram experiments. During the experimental procedure, participants were required to read a series of multiple-choice test items to their fellow participant. The items were read one at a time, and, after each one, the fellow participant had to select the correct choice out of the four that were offered. Each incorrect choice was punished by an electric shock. Milgram describes the subterfuge as follows: "Some [participants] could be observed signaling the correct answer to the victim by stressing it vocally as they read the multiple-choice words aloud. That is, they attempted to prompt the victim and thus prevent his receiving shocks" (Milgram, 1974, p. 159).

Other participants could be heard blurting out the first syllable of the correct answer as they waited for their fellow participant to answer. The parallels to Grueninger's far more theatrical ploy are clear. In both cases, the subordinate in charge of administering punishments prompts or shapes the victim's responses in such a way that he can then say, "That's fine. You have given the response that legitimately allows me to avoid punishing you."

GRUENINGER AND THE SWISS TRADITION OF SANCTUARY

One final quotation from a defiant participant is useful in understanding Grueninger's orientation and behavior, because it relates to his vision of Switzerland as a sanctuary. In response to the experimenter's prod, "Whether the learner likes it or not, you must go on until he's learned all the word pairs correctly," this participant responded:

> What sort of business is this, "whether he likes it or not." I don't understand why the experiment is placed above his personal life. If he doesn't want to continue, I'm taking orders from him. I refuse to go on. If this were Russia maybe, but not in America.

In a different yet similar way, Grueninger believed that the refugees' lives ought to be placed above federal decrees regarding who should or should not be allowed into Switzerland. Note also how, in this quotation, the participant makes a distinction between a country in which an ordinary individual's life would hardly matter to an authority and one in which each life is accorded dignity and value: In America one does not impose suffering on a person "whether he likes it or not." Grueninger fully believed in Switzerland's long-standing humanitarian tradition—a tradition that called for taking care of people whose lives were in danger. In his own mind, those refugees who came to the Swiss border had done the right thing, for Switzerland was meant to be a safe haven. On one occasion when Grueninger was at the border crossing, he noticed a young girl crying in fear at the sight of his uniform and boots. He bent down toward her and said in a protective tone, "Cheer up little girl, you are in Switzerland now" (Keller, 1993, p. 126).

There was a touch of patriotism in the way Grueninger viewed his country. He seemed convinced that the Swiss people felt bad for the refugees—that they felt a sense of responsibility toward them, as they had previously when other persecuted peoples had needed assistance. To an

even greater extent, Grueninger was convinced that the refugees conceived of Switzerland as a safe haven and, hence, that they shared with
him the same shining image of his country. Perhaps it is not too
far-fetched to suggest that, partly for this reason, he felt they were his
friends. In any case, he did not want to disappoint the refugees; he felt
certain that they deserved to be protected and that it was his overriding
duty as a police officer to provide them with such protection.

Breaking the law was never Grueninger's objective; he did so only
because the law seemed cruel and he was unwilling to inflict such cruelty on the refugees. However official and legitimate it might be, the
law had to be ignored. Grueninger had no apparent interest in politics,
nor for that matter did he have an affinity for any ideology. As we saw
earlier, he was not a political person. Consistent with this orientation, it
seems that Grueninger paid little or no attention to the political concerns of federal authorities, although he was very attentive to his re-
sponsibilities as chief of police, especially his duty to protect people
against crime. In a way, protecting the refugees from their persecutors
was an extension of this understanding of his duties. What he was doing
at the Swiss border, to the extent possible, was protecting refugees from
the criminal acts of their persecutors.

CONCLUSIONS

Some might think that because there were so few people like Paul
Grueninger, his case is not particularly significant. Far more important
were the decisions of the federal authorities, which had such terrible
consequences for the lives of thousands of refugees. Yet the fact that
someone like Grueninger did exist makes a tremendous difference, for
it shows us that there were ways of defying the orders of the federal authorities, and this fact changes both the meaning of what actually happened to the refugees and the domain of what realistically could have
happened to them. Knowing how nearly everyone behaved in a given
situation may tell us a great deal about the relative strength of the social
pressures at work, but it cannot tell us about the realm of the possible—about what might have happened.

Holocaust rescuers, too, were few in number compared to the millions who did nothing to help the victims of the Nazis and their collabo-
rators. Being so few, they were hardly in a position to stop the Nazis, nor
were they able to save very many of the victims. Yet their deeds have
meaning, not merely for those whose lives they managed to save but for

all of us. The deeds of Grueninger and the Holocaust rescuers are significant because they show that it was possible to go against that stream of destruction that swept across Europe from the 1930s until the collapse of the Third Reich in 1945. Had there had been more rescuers, the history of the Nazi occupation would no doubt have been different. More important, if we believe that ordinary people—people such as ourselves or Paul Grueninger—can act counter to such streams of destruction, then every one of us may be able to mitigate the harmful consequences of some future malevolent regime. We, too, may be capable of disobeying authorities and saving lives. We do not lack the requisite abilities.

It is difficult to draw general conclusions based on Grueninger's rescue efforts, not only because one must be cautious when working from single historical cases for which the data are incomplete but also because the thoughts and motives behind his deeds may forever remain only partially understood. Nevertheless, the following points can be made by way of summarizing his orientation and his actions.

1. Despite being in many ways a very ordinary person, Grueninger nevertheless managed to accomplish deeds that were extraordinary (Dindo, 1997; Paldiel, 1996; Salvi & Aubert, 1998), and he did so without ever conceiving of himself as having exceptional qualities. He did not possess the characteristics popularly associated with heroes. Certainly, he was no John Wayne. In this respect, he was very much like the other rescuers we have studied (Rochat & Modigliani, 1995, 1998).

2. Grueninger went from being a popular elementary school teacher to a respected police officer to a distinguished chief of police to a disgraced ex-chief of police to an impoverished citizen. His punishment was extremely harsh, especially when one considers that it was inflicted on him for no other reason than the generosity he extended to refugees—a generosity that led him to disobey authorities.

3. There are indications that Grueninger had always been a compassionate person who responded generously to those in need (see Fogelman, 1998, for an analysis of the rescuer's self). Nonetheless, his penchant for caring and responsibility reached remarkable heights when he responded to the refugees, whose suffering he observed at the Swiss border, by developing a deep sense of obligation toward those persecuted people. There is a great difference between loaning money to needy friends and defying one's superiors to save lives. Yet we do not know whether this difference in his behavior cor-

responded to a real growth in his capacity to think and act morally. He may have been much the same principled person throughout his life.

4. Grueninger had an extraordinary flair for devising schemes that enabled him to bring refugees into Switzerland. From using the powers of his office to snatch prisoners from concentration camps to staging performances in which refugees were given the lines that entitled them to legitimate entry, Grueninger was able to save lives by subverting the law in ways that largely escaped the attention of the authorities. That he was finally caught and punished reflects less on his ingenuity and more on his inability to believe that those above him were serious about wanting to send the refugees back—an inability that led him to be dangerously open about his true attitudes and, perhaps, about his behavior.

5. Grueninger's conduct never showed any signs of rebellion against his superiors. This was so not only because his immediate superior supported his efforts and several of his subordinates cooperated with him but also because he was not ideological, not political, not able to understand that "the boat was full." For him, what was occurring at the border was purely a humanitarian emergency. He was convinced that breaking the law under these circumstances was in no way criminal; he understood that a life was more precious than a law. It is no wonder, then, that he never could grasp why the federal authorities, even long after the war, were unwilling to reconsider his case. He could not comprehend why they steadfastly refused to acknowledge that his actions had not only helped people in dire need but also had promoted the image of Switzerland and its humanitarian tradition.

REFERENCES

Butler, A., & Nada, L. (Directors). (1993). *Paul Grueninger: Puni pour avoir sauvé des juifs.* [Paul Grueninger: Punished for having saved Jews]. [Film]. Genève: Télévision Suisse (TSR).

Dindo, R. (Director). (1997). *L'Affaire Paul Grueninger.* [The case of Paul Grueninger]. [Film]. Lea Production, Zurich: Télévision Suisse (SF-DRS).

Fogelman, E. (1998). The rescuer's self. In M. Berenbaum & A. J. Peck (Eds.). *The Holocaust and history: The known, the unknown, the disputed, and the reexamined.* Washington, DC: United States Holocaust Memorial Museum; Bloomington: Indiana University Press.

Graf, C. (Ed.). (1996). La Suisse et les réfugiés. [Switzerland and the refugees]. *Revue des Archives Fédérales Suisses. Etudes et Sources.* Berne, Switzerland: Verlag Paul Haupt.

Haesler, A. (1967). *Das Boot ist voll. Die Schweiz und die Fluechtlinge, 1933–1945.* [The boat is full. Switzerland and the refugees, 1933–1945]. Zurich, Switzerland: Ex Libris Verlag.

Keller, S. (1993). *Grueningers Fall: Geschichten von Flucht und Hilfe*. [The case of Paul Grueninger: Stories of flight and rescue]. Zurich, Switzerland: Rotpunkverlag.

Lasserre, A. (1995). *Frontières et camps: Le refuge en Suisse de 1933 à 1945*. [Borders and refugee camps: Safe haven in Switzerland from 1933 to 1945]. Lausanne, Switzerland: Editions Payot.

Milgram, S. (1974). *Obedience to authority: An experimental view*. New York: Harper & Row.

Paldiel, M. (1996). *Sheltering the Jews: Stories of holocaust rescuers*. Minneapolis: Fortress Press.

Rochat, F., & Modigliani, A. (1995). The ordinary quality of resistance: From Milgram's laboratory to the village of Le Chambon. *Journal of Social Issues, 51(3)*, 195–210.

Rochat, F., & Modigliani, A. (1998). The ordinariness of goodness. *Clio's Psyche, 4*, 115–116.

Salvi, M., & Aubert, R. (1998). *Ces justes qui sont l'honneur de la Suisse*. [These righteous who are the honor of Switzerland]. Lausanne, Switzerland: RSR (Radio Suisse Romande).

Vitali, F. (Director). (1971). *Paul Grueninger* [Film]. Zurich: Télévision Suisse (DRS).

7

Self-Destructive Obedience in the Airplane Cockpit and the Concept of Obedience Optimization

Eugen Tarnow
Avalon Business Systems, Inc.

The Milgram obedience experiments demonstrate that the willingness of individuals in our society to obey authority figures regardless of the consequences is surprisingly strong. One context for this obedience dynamic is the airplane cockpit. The situation of a captain with too much authority who is in error can have disastrous consequences. Dangerously high levels of obedience to erring captains have been noted by the National Transportation Safety Board (NTSB). In fact, as will be discussed later, a review of airplane accidents in the United States by the NTSB indirectly suggests that destructive obedience causes up to 25% of all plane crashes.

This chapter has four goals. First, I analyze the sources of the captain's authority in a commercial airplane. Second, I demonstrate how and why the obedience dynamic identified by Milgram is at work in the relationship between the captain and the first officer (copilot) of the airplane. Then I use the findings of the NTSB review of 37 airplane accidents to estimate how often excessive obedience results in accidents. Finally, I suggest ways to achieve the proper balance of obedience and dissent by use of a simple "obedience optimization" technique that may lower the airplane accident rate by as much as 25%.

THE SOURCES OF THE CAPTAIN'S AUTHORITY IN THE COMMERCIAL AIRPLANE COCKPIT

In a typical commercial airplane cockpit there are a captain, a first officer, and sometimes a flight engineer. In this chapter I limit myself to considering the relationship between the captain and the first officer. There are several reasons why the captain's authority may tower over the first officer.

One source of authority is the Code of Federal Regulations (CFR) that states that a captain is the final authority on the airplane, a code that gives him or her considerable power. The CFR also sets differential requirements for captains and first officers. For a captain it requires about 1500 hours of flight time, whereas for a first officer the requirement is only 200 hours of flight time.

Once a first officer fulfills the CFR requirement to become a captain, he or she must also fulfill the stricter captaincy requirements of the particular airline. Personnel policies differ by airline, and they are proprietary information. Some of those policies provide thresholds for both overall flight hours and flight hours in the particular aircraft. It typically takes on the order of a decade or two to become a captain on a large airplane. There are large variations, however. For example, Singapore Airlines makes first officers into captains 7 to 9 years faster than is typical (Mecham, 1994). There are also personnel policies related to the training of the captain and first officer, and these also vary with the airline.

An additional airline requirement for captaincy is to have attained seniority on the pilot union list for the particular airline. The specifications of such a list can be found in the contracts between the airline owners and the pilot unions. When the stability of this list becomes threatened, the pilots may reject the contract (a news search shows that conflicts involving this seniority clause have recently included pilots from several major airlines). The seniority position is lost if a pilot switches airlines, and a transferring captain would become a first officer again.

Due to the personnel and contract policies, captains typically have more flight hours behind them than do first officers. Indeed, in the NTSB's accident review sample, captains typically had three to four times more experience than their first officers, whether measured by total flying time (median times of 14,000 vs. 5,100 hours or—using a translation of 800 hours as a typical flight year—18 vs. 6 years) or by amount of experience in the type of aircraft involved in the accident (median times of 3,300 vs. 880 hours or about 4 years vs. 1 year). (NTSB, 1994b)

The strength of the authority of the aircraft captain is also enforced by aviation organizational norms, such as the norm of individualistic thinking that developed in the historical period of single-pilot planes. Thus the institution of the first officer is "not fully developed," and the latter plays a "distinctly secondary role" (Helmreich & Foushee, 1993, p. 4). Indeed, "in 1952 the guidelines for proficiency checks at one major airline categorically stated that the first officer should not correct errors made by the captain" (pp. 4–5).

Military values enter commercial airlines when pilots who are military veterans enter the civilian workforce. These values include "respect for rank, for leaders who take charge and act decisively, and for subordinates who understand that it is usually not appropriate to question the decisions of their superiors" (Birnbach & Longridge, 1993, p. 265).

The abundance of rules further enhances the strength of authority. Some flight rules have been given the force of law, as in the case of the rule of the Federal Aviation Administration (FAA) just mentioned that states, "the pilot in command of an aircraft is directly responsible for, and is the final authority as to, the operation of that aircraft" (1996 CFR, Paragraph 91.3). But whether these rules put more emphasis on obedience than on avoiding catastrophes remains to be understood. Indeed, this delicate balance is also codified: the same CFR Paragraph 91.3 also states that, "in an in-flight emergency requiring immediate action, the pilot in command may deviate from any rule of this part to the extent required to meet that emergency."

Additionally, the values of a hierarchical corporate culture contribute to strong authority relationships. For example, in a New York Times article, the strength of the authority of the chief executive officer (CEO) of a particular airline was indicated by the CEO's staying power in conjunction with seemingly extreme incompetence. He would "doze off" in meetings and call the company officers, and even the airline, by the wrong name (Bryant, 1994, p. 17N).

Note that there are considerable variations across cultures in how the authority relationship is perceived among aircraft crews. An investigation by Merritt and Helmreich (1996) regarding the cultural component points to significant differences between stated opinions of flight crews in different countries. The statement, "Senior staff deserves extra benefits and privileges," elicited positions from neutrality to slight disagreement among captains and first officers from four American airlines, but those from a Brazilian airline agreed with it. The statement, "Crew members should not question the decisions or actions of the captain except when they threaten the safety of the flight," elicited variations in agreement between 15% and 93% among pilots in different countries, and the statement, "If I perceive a problem with the flight, I will speak up, regardless of who might be affected," elicited variations in agreement between 36% and 98% among pilots from different countries. Finally, the statement, "The organization's rules should not be broken—even when the employee thinks it is in the company's best interests," elicited variations in agreement between 22% and 76% among pilots in different countries. That these statements carry over to actual differences in behavior seems reasonable. Milgram (1961) quantified national differences in behavioral conformity in his Asch-like conformity experiments in Norway and France. He found an important difference in actual behavior (63% vs. 49% conformity, averaged across different experimental conditions, among Norwegian and French participants, respectively). Similarly, variations exist also in cross-cultural replications of the Milgram obedience experiment (see Miller, 1986, and Blass, 1998, for reviews).

In terms of a phase-transition model of conformity in large groups (Tarnow, 1996), such differences may be crucial in determining whether employees of a large corporation will undergo large-scale conformity transformations, leading them to act in concert as if they were a single mind. Such a single-minded group allows authority to rule more easily.

CORRESPONDENCE BETWEEN THE MILGRAM FINDINGS AND BEHAVIOR IN THE AIRPLANE COCKPIT

Excessively obedient behavior in the presence of a psychology experimenter was found in the laboratory by Stanley Milgram over 35 years ago (Milgram, 1974). In these experiments, a participant, the teacher, is asked by the experimenter to give electrical shocks to a confederate, the learner. The stated purpose of the experiment is to understand how punishment affects memory recall. The learner first fakes discomfort, and as the fake electrical shocks increase to dangerous levels, he suddenly becomes quiet. Four of Milgram's findings can help shed light on excessive obedience in the airplane cockpit:

1. *Excessive obedience.* Milgram found (at least in his standard conditions) that most people can be made to inflict intense pain on, seriously injure, or even possibly kill other people by verbal orders.[1]

2. *Hesitant communications.* The teacher's objections to giving the learner electrical shocks were often hesitant and easily overruled by the experimenter's replies, such as telling the teacher that "the experiment requires that you continue."

3. *Accepting the authority's definition of the situation.* The teacher accepts the authority's definition of the situation, which does not include the choice of disobedience but only the necessity of continued obedience. Indeed, in the Milgram experiment, not one out of almost one thousand teacher-participants came up with an interpretation leading them to call the police or free the learner (Zimbardo, 1974).

4. *Closeness effect.* The strength of the authority of the experimenter was found to be higher the closer the teacher was to the experimenter.

There are similarities between the Milgram experimental situation and behavior in the cockpit as a plane is in distress. We make a simple correspondence between the Milgram experiment and the cockpit dynamics: the role of the experimenter is taken by the captain, the teacher's role belongs to the first officer, and the harm to the learner is the airplane crashing.[2] When the plane goes down, the consequences involve many lost lives with ensuing lawsuits, negative media coverage, and loss of business. One accident brought ValuJet Airlines from a very good financial position to the verge of bankruptcy, after which it changed its name.

---

[1] It is somewhat unclear to the teachers what actually happens to the learner. Mantell (1971) conducted a replication of the Milgram experiment in Germany and interviewed the participants after the experiment. Many claimed that they believed the learner had been dead or at least unconscious.

[2] One could argue that an airplane crash would be a case of a self-inflicted injury, which is different from the original Milgram experiment and may make it easier to dissent. However, the captain is also risking his life, giving him more credibility, which may make it more difficult to dissent. Note also that a Milgram-like experiment that supposedly caused a self-inflicted hearing loss (Martin, Lobb, Chapman, & Spillane, 1976) found obedience rates similar to the original Milgram experiment.

Observers of behavior in the aviation field have noted the tendency of the captain–first officer relationship to be too authoritarian in many instances. Ginnett (1993) writes about the tendency of the first officer not to question the captain (here, and later in other examples, I have inserted the applicable findings of Milgram, mentioned previously, in square brackets):

> The authority dynamic surrounding the role of the captain must be extremely powerful ... [and] has resulted in crewmembers not speaking up when necessary [hesitant communications]. ... This inclination may also result in excessive psychological dependence on the captain as leader to the extent that individual contributions to problem-solving are neither voiced nor attempted [accepting the authority's definition of the situation]. For example, one captain with whom I flew made a particularly poor approach ... setting off numerous alarms. In reviewing crew members' inactions afterward, the young second officer (who literally said nothing during the final approach) admitted that he had never seen an approach quite like that, but figured "the captain must know what he's doing" [accepting the authority's definition of the situation] (Ginnett, 1993, pp. 88–89).

A first officer also comments on how difficult it was for him to convince the captain that an error was being made:

> I was the first officer on an airline flight into Chicago O'Hare. The captain was flying. ... On our approach, Approach Control told us to slow to 180 knots. I acknowledged and waited for the captain to slow down. He did nothing, so I figured he didn't hear the clearance. So I repeated, "Approach said slow to 180," and his reply was something to the effect of, "I'll do what I want." I told him at least twice more and received the same kind of answer [hesitant communications].[3] ... [Approach Control] then asked us to turn east. I told them we would rather not because of the weather and we were given present heading and to maintain 3000 ft. The captain descended to 3000 ft. and kept going to 2500 ft. even though I told him our altitude was 3000 ft. His comment was, "You just look out the damn window." (from a confidential report submitted to the NASA/FAA Aviation Safety Reporting System; quoted in Ginnett, 1993, p. 74).

Two researchers write similarly about the difficulty a first officer has in alerting the captain that an error is being made, referring to "a co-pilot,

---

[3]Although it may seem that repeating the assertion twice is not being hesitant, in the context of this dangerous situation one would expect a much more vigorous protest.

concerned that take-off thrust was not properly set during a departure in a snow storm, failing to get the attention of the captain [hesitant communications] with the aircraft stalling and crashing into the Potomac River" (Helmreich & Foushee, 1993, p. 6).

Wiener, Kanki, and Helmreich (1993) have classified typical crew errors. If we investigate this classification, we find that several are related to aforementioned elements of the Milgram experiment. Three of these errors may be related to the element *accepting the authority's definition of the situation*: failure to set priorities, inadequate monitoring, and failure to utilize available data. A fourth error is related to *hesitant communications*: failure to communicate intent and plans. (Wiener et al., 1993, p. xvii).

A PLANE CRASH CONTAINING ELEMENTS OF THE MILGRAM EXPERIMENT: A CASE STUDY WITH A COCKPIT VOICE RECORDING

On December 1, 1993, Express II Airlines, Inc./Northwest Airlink Flight 5719 descended too quickly and crashed before it hit the runway in Hibbing, Minnesota. All sixteen people on board died. According to the NTSB (National Transportation Safety Board, 1994a), the crash was caused by several factors: The captain flew the airplane inappropriately and did not "exercise proper crew coordination"; the first officer did not properly monitor and alert the captain of the problematic descent [accepting the authority's definition of the situation]; the captain intimidated his first officer; the airline failed to adequately supervise the captain, who had a history of intimidating his first officers; and the FAA did not provide adequate surveillance of the airline.

That the captain's authority was strong in the cockpit can be deduced as follows. The captain intimidated five out of six first officers interviewed. He had actually struck one of them for mistakenly leaving the intercom on, and this fact had been passed on to the first officer of the flight that crashed. His first officers never reported that the captain did not fly by the book or violated company policies on sexual harassment, sleeping in flight, and flying with mechanical irregularities.

The flight's first officer, on the other hand, was a new probationary employee who "had just spent $8,500 of his own money to be trained for a job that provided an annual earning potential of $18,000." Such a high stake may have made it less likely that such a first officer would challenge a captain who could have a detrimental effect on his career.

The Cockpit Voice Recorder (CVR) transcript showed that "most of the captain's communication with the first officer was either to correct him or to tell him what to do." Other captains testified afterward that the first officer had not needed these directions during their flights. Some of these instructions were even absurd. Further, according to the NTSB, "the statements of the first officer on the CVR suggest a tense and almost reserved attitude toward the captain. Information provided by the first officer to the captain was couched in a questioning manner rather than as an assertion" [hesitant communications] (1994a).

Finally, the airline provided only a single approach chart, which both captain and first officer had to use. This vital piece of information could only be shared by making the interpersonal distance minimal, thus further increasing the captain's authority [closeness effect].

Here are some excerpts from the CVR transcript provided in the NTSB (1994a) report. We begin as the captain and the first officer discuss where they are going to stay that night, a passage that seems to imply a rather large power difference between them:

First Officer: It's not the Radisson or anything?
Captain: Yeah right.
First Officer: No are you serious with this thing ... travel?
Captain: No I'm kidding it's the Holiday Inn.
First Officer: They have a Holiday Inn in ... in ah l' Falls?
    so then I assume they have a bus?
Captain: They have a van.
First Officer: And they ah don't care if it's a four o'clock ah—
Captain: Nope because they're also taking our people to the airport besides us.
First Officer: Ah (that's right). Do we get our own room?
Captain: No you're going to have to room with me and it's only a single
    bed so there's a little carpet at the base of my bed and you can curl up
    at the base of my bed ... course you get your own room ... you're under
    contract now ... this is ALPA [Air Line Pilots Association] contract.

The captain then asks about the time:

Captain: What time were we out of the gate?
First Officer: Fifty-two
Captain: Okay. According to your watch or according to the clock?
First Officer: Ah well it's the same.
Captain: Oh okay.
First Officer: I think I'm showing the same ... yeah.

The time issue suggests that the first officer is somewhat deferentially checking whether his watch and the airplane clock show the same time.

The first officer keeps asking the pilot questions as if the pilot is his teacher: How long it takes to go between different locations, if there are jet stream routes, where they are at the moment, what the control tower said, what approach they can take to the airport, and so forth.

First Officer: Okay ... what's the ah see that falling star?
Captain: Either that or a falling Cessna.

The first officer's questions keep coming. He fails to make standard call-outs for lowered altitudes, and, according to the NTSB, fails to call out the need to execute a missed approach. The captain did not fly the approach according to the stated plan but remains at a high altitude too long, suggesting that the landing is going to be very steep. The first officer makes one attempt to challenge it:

First Officer: Just ... you just gonna stay up here as long as you can?
Captain: Yes. Guard the hor- I mean an speeds one hundred.

When the pilot asks the first officer whether Hibbing's control tower gave him the weather, the first officer affirms it after a pause, even though this did not happen.

According to the NTSB, at the time of the approach, the pilot should have made clear to the first officer what his duties were. The consequence of his failure is indicated by a variety of distracting orders given during the approach. At the point the plane is scraping the trees, the following dialogue occurs:

Captain: Did you ah click the ah airport lights ... make sure the co-common traffic advisory frequency is set. [sound of seven microphone clicks]. Click it seven times?
First Officer: Yup yeah I got it now. [momentary sound of scrape lasting for .1 secs]

The plane crashes.

ESTIMATING THE CONSEQUENCES OF EXCESSIVE OBEDIENCE

Accident information is routinely collected and made available to the public by the NTSB. Recently the NTSB (1994b) reviewed all serious airplane accidents between 1978 and 1990 subject to the conditions that (1) a voice recorder was required on the plane, (2) the NTSB had conducted a major investigation (limiting the number of accidents to 75), and (3) the flight crew's actions were a causal or contributing factor (limiting the number of accidents further to 37). Twenty-three of the 37 accidents resulted in fatalities.

The NTSB found that after procedural errors, errors of the type called "monitoring/challenging" were the most common, occurring in 80% of the accident sample. These were errors in which the nonflying crew member (the first officer in 81% of the cases) did not properly monitor and challenge the flying crew member when errors were committed. Usually the primary errors that should have been monitored or challenged were listed as causal or as contributing to the accident.

How many accidents are related to excessive obedience? According to the NTSB, in 19 of the 37 accidents a monitoring/challenging error followed a primary error. A monitoring/challenging event could have prevented the accident. Because the initial pool consisted of 75 accidents, we can estimate that approximately 25% of all accidents could have been prevented by monitoring/challenging events. If we assume that both monitoring and challenging errors are due to excessive obedience, we conclude that excessive obedience may cause as many as 25% of all airplane accidents.

Line-oriented flight training (LOFT) is real-time simulation of real flight scenarios (with accident transcripts) that allows for experiential practice and feedback. Videos are made of the simulation hours, and the crew can review the cockpit behavior (see, for example, Hackman, 1993). The NTSB's discussion of human errors included the need for practicing monitoring/challenging behavior in LOFT scenarios and emphasizing monitoring/challenging errors in the LOFT debriefings. In particular, the NTSB felt that an important avenue would be the

> intentional introduction of a procedural or decisional error by the flying pilot in the LOFT scenario. This technique would make certain that the non-flying pilot is confronted with the opportunity to detect and challenge the error made by the flying pilot. (NTSB, 1994b, p. 63)

This leads us, next, to propose obedience optimization as a technique.

OBEDIENCE SHOULD BE OPTIMIZED

The costs incurred during faulty pilot decisions can be high. It is evident for the sake of error correction that the degree of obedience is a parameter that should be modified to some best value between 0 and 100%. The intelligence and experience of the first officer should be utilized, but at the same time a structure of order and accountability needs to be present.

How can we measure the obedience level? Role-playing versions of the obedience experiments have yielded levels of obedience remarkably similar to those of the original experiments (Blass, 1991, Meeus and Raijmakers, 1995). It seems reasonable that the obedience level in the LOFT situation, an active form of role-playing, should be similar to the obedience level during an actual flight. Using the NTSB's recommendation, we introduce intentional errors on the captain's part. These errors vary on a scale from small to large. Some of the decisions, whether erroneous or not, will be challenged by the first officer and others will not. Each challenge will subtract a value from the overall obedience score of the captain–first officer relationship, whereas each error not challenged will add a value to the overall obedience score.

The obedience score can now be used in two ways:

First, the captain and first officer can be informed about their scores. If the score was too high, the first officer can be asked to practice challenging the captain according to a script, and the captain can be asked to respond to those challenges in amenable ways. If the score was too low, the first officer has to be told that the captain is in charge of the plane and cannot be challenged excessively, and the captain should be taught how to deal more effectively with challenges to his or her authority.

Second, one can use this data to probe the correlation between the obedience score and the corresponding error rate (intentional or not) during the simulation. The expected result would be a strong correlation of the obedience rate with the error rate. If so, the obedience rate can be used as a *predictor* of the error rate. A high obedience rate before an actual take-off, perhaps measured by obedience testing in the checklist procedure, may then be used to prevent the particular crew combination from taking off. In any case, the regular use of obedience optimization will serve to create a norm for orders that can be given and to encourage critical evaluations of future orders.

If one accepts the estimate that 25% of all airplane accidents are due to excessive obedience, optimizing the authority level of the captain could lower the total number of serious airplane accidents by as much as 25%.

In their review of airplane accidents (see the previous discussion), the NTSB noticed that although, typically, airplanes are flown roughly half the time by the captain and half the time by the first officer, in their accident sample the captain was flying 85% of the time. Suggestions have been made that the first officer should fly the plane more often. The captain should have much less difficulty correcting the first officer than vice versa. This is another way to attempt to optimize the obedience rate.

CONCLUSIONS

In this chapter, I related the captain–first officer relationship in the airplane cockpit to the obedience studies of Milgram. Many of the factors leading to human errors in the cockpit are similar to ones in the Milgram obedience experiments.

The amount of obedience has an optimal value, and this value should be sought after. Obedience optimization is an application of the Milgram experiment that measures the crew's obedience level through LOFT on a scale from too low to too high. Feedback into the social system includes crew debriefing. Organizational feedback includes using obedience levels as predictors of expected error rates and setting up an organizational norm for obedience optimization. Obedience optimization may prevent up to 25% of all aircraft accidents.

Finally, I may note that there are many other potential areas of society in which obedience optimization could be used, especially in social systems that handle large risks, such as financial trading floors.

ACKNOWLEDGMENTS

I thank Thomas Blass, Wim Meeus, Barbara Smith, Helena Tarnow, and Phil Zimbardo for critical readings of the manuscript and Michelle Fine, my wife, without whom the manuscript would not have been published. Eugen Tarnow can be reached at etarnow@avabiz.com, or www.avabiz.com.

REFERENCES

Birnbach, R., & Longridge, T. (1993). The regulatory perspective. In E. Wiener, B. Kanki, & R. Helmreich (Eds.), *Cockpit resource management* (pp. 263–281). San Diego, CA: Academic Press.

Blass, T. (1991). Understanding behavior in the Milgram obedience experiment: The role of personality, situations, and their interactions. *Journal of Personality and Social Psychology, 60,* 398–413.

Blass, T. (1998, August 16). *A cross-cultural comparison of studies of obedience using the Milgram paradigm.* Paper presented at the annual meeting of the American Psychological Association, San Francisco.

Bryant, A. (1994, November 19). Chastened, T.W.A. tries again; business plan built on hope is revised. *The New York Times,* p. 17N.

Ginnett, R. (1993). Crews as groups: Their formation and their leadership. In E. Wiener, B. Kanki, & R. Helmreich (Eds.), *Cockpit resource management* (pp. 71–98). San Diego, CA: Academic Press.

Hackman, J. (1993). Teams, leaders, and organizations: New directions for crew-oriented flight training. In E. Wiener, B. Kanki, & R. Helmreich (Eds.), *Cockpit resource management* (pp. 47–69). San Diego, CA: Academic Press.

Helmreich, R., & Foushee, H. (1993). Why crew resource management? Empirical and theoretical bases of human factors training in aviation. In E. Wiener, B. Kanki, & R. Helmreich (Eds.), *Cockpit resource management* (pp. 3–45). San Diego, CA: Academic Press.

Mantell, D. (1971). The potential for violence in Germany. *Journal of Social Issues, 28,* 101–112.

Martin, J., Lobb, B., Chapman, G., & Spillane, R. (1976). Obedience under conditions demanding self-immolation. *Human Relations, 29,* p. 345–356.

Mecham, M. (1994). SIA remakes pilot training program with Learjet 31s. *Aviation Week & Space Technology, 140,* 40–41.

Meeus, W., & Raaijmakers, Q. (1995). Obedience in modern society: The Utrecht studies. *Journal of Social Issues, 51*(3), 155–176.

Merritt, A., & Helmreich, R. (1996). Human factors on the flight deck: The influence of national culture. *Journal of Cross-Cultural Psychology, 27,* 5–24.

Milgram, S. (1961, December). Nationality and conformity. *Scientific American,* pp. 45–51.

Milgram, S. (1974). *Obedience to authority: An experimental view.* New York: Harper & Row.

Miller, A. G. (1986). *The obedience experiment: A case study of controversy in social science.* New York: Praeger.

National Transportation Safety Board (1994a). *Controlled collision with terrain: Northwest Airlink Flight 5719, Hibbing, Minnesota, December 1, 1993.* Washington, DC: Author.

National Transportation Safety Board (1994b). *A review of flight crew-involved major accidents of U.S. air carriers, 1978 through 1990.* Washington, DC: Author.

Tarnow, E. (1996). Like water and vapor—conformity and independence in the large group. *Behavioral Science, 41,* 136–151.

Wiener, E., Kanki, B., & Helmreich, R. (1993). *Cockpit resource management.* San Diego, CA: Academic Press.

Zimbardo, P. G. (1974). On "obedience to authority." *American Psychologist, 29,* 566–567.

8

The Role of the Obedience Experiments in Holocaust Studies: The Case for Renewed Visibility

Ann L. Saltzman
Drew University

Stanley Milgram's experiments on obedience to authority remain one of the most visible and controversial set of studies in the history of psychology. Miller's (1995) survey of 50 texts in social psychology, introductory psychology, and sociology published since 1990 documents a disproportionate number of pages devoted to this one series of experiments. Elsewhere, Miller, Collins, and Brief (1995) state that "the Milgram experiments ... have stimulated thought as has perhaps no other single research program" (p. 2). Initiated the same year as the daring capture of Adolf Eichmann by Israeli agents and first published in the same year (Milgram, 1963) as Hannah Arendt's *Eichmann in Jerusalem: A Report on the Banality of Evil*, Milgram's work on obedience has been associated with the Holocaust from the beginning. Indeed, Miller's survey also reveals that most texts (86%) make explicit reference to Nazi Germany in their discussion of the Milgram studies; 19% specifically mention Eichmann. These findings were supported by my own informal survey of introductory and social psychology texts that were displayed at the 1996 meeting of the Eastern Psychological Association.

In contrast, a strong association between the obedience studies and the Holocaust is not evident in Holocaust studies curricula. Indeed, despite Dawidowicz's (1990) and Lipstadt's (1995) searing criticisms of these curricula that imply that the obedience research dominates the world of Holocaust education, Milgram's work is conspicuous mainly by its absence. As a former student of Stanley Milgram and a social psychologist who believes that his work still has a place in illuminating certain aspects of the Holocaust and who incorporates the obedience studies into her Holocaust curriculum, I find this absence regrettable. In this chapter, then, I will make the case for renewed visibility of Milgram's research on destructive obedience within Holocaust studies. First, I will document its invisibility within this arena, analyzing the reasons for its absence. Second, I will raise the question of whether the obedience studies actually tell us about the Holocaust, reviewing both the critiques of Milgram's findings vis-à-vis the Holocaust and research that suggests that they do, indeed, have something to tell us. Finally, I will describe how I incorporate the obedience studies into my curriculum.

THE OBEDIENCE STUDIES AND HOLOCAUST CURRICULA: A LOUD ABSENCE

Middle School and High School Curricula

In her 1990 article, Lucy Dawidowicz, a historian of the Holocaust, reports on a review of 25 Holocaust curricula. She states that they "undertake to do two things: first to give pupils basic information and, second, to provide moral education" (p. 26). Further, she disagrees with their approaches, which, she says "focus on 'individual responsibility' as against 'obedience to authority' as keys to moral behavior" (p. 27). Given this conclusion, one would expect an extensive discussion of Milgram's work on obedience in these curricula. However, a review of 13 of those curricula originally critiqued by Dawidowicz does not confirm this expectation; only 5 include any reference to the obedience studies.[1] These 13 are a subset of a larger sample of 134 middle school and high school curricula that I reviewed at the Resource Center of the United States Holocaust Memorial Museum or obtained from member

---

[1]I was unable to obtain all 25 curricula reviewed by Dawidowicz; many were printed as early as 1979 and are no longer available.

organizations of the Association of Holocaust Organizations;[2] they range from curricula produced by state departments of education to those created by large organizations or Holocaust centers (e.g., *You can change the world: March of the Living Study Guide*) to those written by local school districts or individual teachers. Only 20 of the 134 curricula (15%) include any reference to Milgram's work, and, for some, this reference is merely a bibliographic or videographic entry with little actual discussion of the studies in the text.[3]

In contrast, Facing History and Ourselves highlights the research on obedience to authority and its implications for the Holocaust. Its most recent resource book, *Holocaust and Human Behavior* (1994), begins its 42-page chapter titled "Conformity and Obedience" with a 4-page review of Milgram's work, including a discussion of approximately half of Milgram's experimental variations. The chapter then refers back to the research in its discussion of the massacre of the Jews at Jozefow by Reserve Police Battalion 101 and its analysis of the role of clerks, administrators, guards, and other employees of the Third Reich in implementing the "final solution." Indeed, this prominent role assigned to the phenomenon of obedience is one of the attributes of the Facing History and Ourselves curriculum that Dawidowicz finds so objectionable: "But anyone knows who has studied totalitarian societies, the critical ingredient of these societies is not obedience but terror. It is terror that elicits obedience under duress, even to unjust laws" (p. 30).

---

[2]To my knowledge, this is the most complete set of Holocaust curricula available. The Resource Center of the Museum and the Association of Holocaust Organizations represent two of the most widely used reference services. Others include the Simon Wiesenthal Center, the Anti-Defamation League of B'nai Brith, and Yad Vashem, Jerusalem. Each of these, however, houses only its own curricula, which are included in the current sample.

[3]It is difficult to assess what this statistic means. It is possible that the 15% figure actually underestimates the actual exposure students get to Milgram in Holocaust curricula if the ones that mention him are more widely used than others. For example, Facing History and Ourselves, one of the most popular Holocaust curricula, highlights Milgram's work. According to Marc Skversky, national program director of Facing History and Ourselves (1998), "over 12,000 teachers have participated in Facing History institutes and workshops in the United States and Europe. Together they reach 900,000 students" (p. 5). However, in a follow-up phone conversation with Mr. Skversky, I learned that, because most teachers do not have the time to implement the entire Facing History curriculum, teachers choose what portion of the curriculum they will actually cover. This may or may not include Milgram's work. Thus it is difficult to estimate exactly how many students are actually exposed to Milgram's work even when the Facing History and Ourselves curriculum is the base one used (M. Skversky, personal communication, June 19, 1998). Further, the Anti-Defamation League, whose Holocaust curriculum does not mention Milgram, claims that it has trained 350,000 teachers and administrators and more than 21 million youth (L. Skop, personal communication, June 22, 1998).

It is interesting to note that Milgram's work is less visible in Holocaust curricula printed since 1990, the year of Dawidowicz's article.[4] Of the 134 curricula in my sample, only 71 are dated. Thirty-seven were printed before 1990; 34 since. Ten of the pre-1990 curricula (27%) include references to Milgram, whereas only three of the later ones do (9%). This finding is statistically significant ($x^2 = 3.94$, $df = 1$, $p < .05$).

College Curricula

The Milgram studies are even less visible in college curricula. Crouch (1996) surveyed colleges in the middle states area (Delaware, Pennsylvania, New York, New Jersey, Maryland, and Washington, D.C.); according to college course catalogues, 26% offer courses on the Holocaust, amounting to a total of 90 courses. Over one third are history courses, another third are Jewish Studies courses, and close to one fifth focus on religious or theological implications of the Holocaust. None of these incorporate the Milgram studies into their syllabi. Crouch's data included only one psychology course that is no longer offered and none in sociology or the other social sciences. Unfortunately, her survey did not include courses which are taught as part of a "floating topics" structure, such as my own, that is subsumed under the title of Seminar in Social Issues Psychology in the college catalogue.

I also surveyed 140 college syllabi housed at the Resource Center of the United States Holocaust Memorial Museum or obtained from colleagues in the Association of Holocaust Organizations. Although Milgram's work is more prevalent in these course outlines than in Crouch's data, the results are still surprising: Only 9 out of the 140 (6%) incorporate the obedience studies. Six of the seven psychology syllabi do reference Milgram's work, yielding the same 86% representation rate as found by Miller (1995) in his survey of psychology texts.

WHAT EXPLAINS THE INVISIBILITY OF MILGRAM'S WORK IN HOLOCAUST CURRICULA?

A general lack of psychology citations

The lack of attention paid to the Milgram studies within Holocaust curricula is symptomatic of the larger absence of psychology per se. Consis-

---

[4]I am not arguing that Dawidowicz's criticism actually caused the declining presence of Milgram's work, merely making an observation. Other criticisms of the relevance of obligation-based obedience to genocide have been rendered since 1990.

tent with Dawidowicz's (1990) observation, most middle school or high school curricula "plunge right into the story of Hitler's Germany; a few provide some background on the Weimar Republic, presumably to explain Hitler's rise to power .... All curricula discuss Nazi anti-semitism, preferring generic terms like 'racism' and 'prejudice'" (p. 26). Relatively few, then, attempt to explore the psychological underpinnings of behavior and how that behavior is shaped by either a hierarchical social–political context or the intergroup structure of society. If any psychology reference is included, it is most likely Gordon Allport's (1954) classic work on prejudice.

When viewed in light of the limited time allocated to Holocaust education in most school districts, the current emphasis is understandable. What can one teach in 1 to 5 hours a semester? The review of syllabi suggests that the answers are: Holocaust chronology, something about anti-Semitism (or more broadly, as Dawidowicz observed, prejudice), and victim/survivor stories. Indeed, a few curricula tell the story of the Holocaust through a particular victim's (or group of victims') experience (e.g., Shawn, 1989). Although feedback from teachers provides anecdotal evidence that survivor testimony *is* probably the most potent and engaging way of telling students about the Holocaust, this approach also makes the psychology of perpetrators irrelevant to the story. Similarly, a less frequent but still prevalent focus on rescuers[5] shifts attention away from the vast majority of people who were passive before the forces of tyranny, complicit with them, or—as Goldhagen's recent (1996) analysis suggests—eager participants.

Curricula designed for 6 to 8-week courses of study are more expansive, including units on all four groups of Holocaust actors (perpetrators, victims/survivors, bystanders, and rescuers). Some even encompass post-Holocaust issues such as responsibility (i.e., the War Crimes Tribunals), the need to remember, and Holocaust denial. These curricula also tend to include units on "The Nature of Human Nature" or human rights abuses. When included, this is where one finds reference to Milgram's work. It is interesting to note that some curricula that do not cite Milgram still include a discussion of the Nuremberg trials and the stated defense, "I was only following orders"; teachers are even instructed to initiate lessons on "when should you obey?" or "what are the limits of obedience?" Yet the empirical research is ignored.

---

[5]Approximately 43% of all middle and high school curricula that I surveyed include a unit on rescuers. For 5 of the 34 produced since 1990 this is the exclusive focus.

At the college level, Holocaust education is even less informed by psychological theory and findings. Despite the proliferation of a psychology literature relevant to the Holocaust,[6] this work has not entered the classroom—or crossed disciplinary boundaries. Assuming that—with time—this situation is remedied, that more psychology courses are developed or that more non-psychology courses and/or curricula outside of psychology incorporate psychological knowledge, is Milgram's research relevant to understanding the Holocaust?

As the following review indicates, some have answered "No" to this question.

NAYSAYERS: OBEDIENCE TO AUTHORITY *DOES NOT* EXPLAIN THE HOLOCAUST

There are many conceptual differences between Milgram's laboratory study of destructive obedience and the Holocaust. Milgram himself recognized the time disparity: "The laboratory experiment takes an hour; the Nazi calamity unfolded over more than a decade" (1974, p. 175). Further, as Blass (1992) points out, there is a crucial distinction in perpetrators' perceptions of harm-doing. Nazis clearly knew that they were killing. However, Milgram's participants put their trust in the authority when they were told that the electric shocks would not cause permanent tissue damage. Still further, each of Milgram's participants took part in only one experiment, unlike Nazi perpetrators who continued to inflict harm "trial after trial," day after day. Even with these differences, the obedience studies would have much to tell us about the Holocaust *if* one agrees with Milgram that both his laboratory studies and the Holocaust reveal a *common psychological process*—the process by which people in subordinate-superordinate relationships cede personal autonomy in favor of meeting higher order needs, even if this entails violating their own moral beliefs. By so doing, therefore, they relinquish responsibility for their actions and become agents for someone else's will; that is, they enter what Milgram refers to as the "agentic state." This analysis is akin to Arendt's "banality of evil" thesis, which Milgram heartily endorsed.

However, historical critiques have not supported Arendt's thesis. As early as 1965, Robinson disputed her contention that Eichmann was

---

[6]A December 1997 PsycLIT review revealed 342 articles and 210 books and book chapters related to the Holocaust published since 1987.

"merely a passive receiver of orders" (p. 21): It was Eichmann who suggested to Rudolf Höss that exhaust gases in trucks be used to kill people (p. 21); it was Eichmann who tried to dissuade Hitler from allowing Jews to emigrate to Palestine at the end of the war (p. 32); it was Eichmann who hunted down individual Jews in the face of opposition from both the Reich's ally, the Italian government, and the Reich Foreign Office itself (pp. 46–47). As Yaacov Lozowick, director of the Yad Vashem archives, concludes in his 1995 dissertation:

> The historical data ... cut the ground from beneath Hannah Arendt's thesis. Eichmann and his cohorts knew very well what they were doing, ... ideology played a central role. They wished to create a new world order, and they wished to have no Jews in it. (p. 7)

In a similar way, Goldhagen emphasizes ideology in his 1996 work, *Hitler's Willing Executioners: Ordinary Germans and the Holocaust*. Indeed, Goldhagen identifies radical "eliminationist anti-Semitism"—and not obedience—as the primary motivation for perpetrators' actions: "Germans routinely took initiative in killing Jews, both by customarily carrying out their orders with dedication and inventiveness and, frequently, by taking it upon themselves to kill Jews even when they had no orders to do so ... "(p. 376). Nazi officers even disobeyed orders (those not focused on killing Jews) when they disagreed with them (p. 382). Further, according to Goldhagen, belief in eliminationist anti-Semitism made it unlikely that Germans would take advantage of opportunities to exit the killing institutions or specific activities within these institutions or even to voice dissent with the institutional policies. Still further, perpetrators reveled in killing. He highlights:

> their celebrations, their willingness to have their wives live among them as they slaughtered Jews by the thousands, their eagerness to preserve the memories of their genocidal deeds by means of photographs which they took and posed for with evident pride and willingly exhibited and made available to their comrades, not to mention the boasting of cruelties. (p. 378)

Clearly these types of behaviors cannot be seen as originating from obligation-based obedience; that is, obedience predicated on the felt duty to follow orders given by a perceived legitimate authority. In fact, these data would seem to render Milgram's research totally irrelevant to explaining the Holocaust. And yet, Browning (1992) notes that "many of Milgram's insights find graphic confirmation in the behavior and testimony of the men in Reserve Police Battalion 101" (p. 174). For exam-

ple, Browning reports that "direct proximity to the horror of killing significantly increased the number of men who would no longer comply"
(pp. 175–176). Milgram obtained similar findings in his Experiments 1
through 4 (Milgram, 1974): As he brought the victim closer, obedience
dropped significantly. Browning also makes a direct connection between Milgram's Experiment 7 (experimenter absent) and the situation in which the police battalion reservists were not directly
supervised (p. 176). Further, in yet another analysis of a German Order
Police Battalion, Matthaus (1996) concludes that from the perpetrators' perspective:

> it mattered little what was done as long as certain legitimizing methods
> were applied ... The impulse for mass murder seems to have come from a
> variety of factors more closely linked to *specific surrounding circumstances*
> than to an antisemitic grand design. (pp. 144–145, emphasis added)

Matthaus also emphasizes the importance of "the traditions of obedience and identification with the state, which characterized German
culture at least since the late nineteenth century" (p. 145). Similarly,
Staub (1993) has identified "a strong respect for authority and a pre-
dominant tendency to obey authority"(p. 319) as an important antecedent—among others—to genocide. And, of course, Milgram
includes "socialization for obedience" (pp. 135–137) as one of the general antecedent conditions that facilitate entry into the agentic state in
which a person "no longer views himself as acting out of his own purposes but rather comes to see himself as an agent for executing the
wishes of another person" (Milgram, 1974, p. 133). However, whether
people make this shift is also dependent on the "specific surrounding
circumstances." Within the Milgram paradigm, these circumstances
translate into his experimental conditions. Accordingly, we now turn
to look at some of the social forces operating in his laboratory and how
they cast light on certain aspects of the Holocaust.

SOCIAL FORCES IN THE LABORATORY/
SOCIAL FORCES DURING THE HOLOCAUST

Situational definition and ideology

In his analysis of why people obey, Milgram states, "every situation ...
possesses a kind of ideology, which we call the 'definition of the situation,' and which is the interpretation of the meaning of a social occa-

sion" (1974, p. 145). Milgram further asserts that "there is a propensity for people to accept definitions of action provided by legitimate authority" (p. 145). However, his own data indicate that this is not always the case; at times, the situation is so constructed that the authority's command is overridden (e.g., in experiment 17, in which peer confederates break off the experiment). In this condition, a new definition of the situation has been fostered.

During the Holocaust, however, few people offered an alternate definition of the situation; those who did were sent to Dachau for political reeducation, killed, forced into submission, or—if they were lucky—emigrated. Further, as Staub points out, during difficult life circumstances, people who have been trained for obedience tend not to look elsewhere for an interpretation of the situation. This tendency was made even stronger by a massive propaganda campaign to convince the populace that the Nazis' definition of the situation was the only definition.

In his analysis, Milgram likens the concept "definition of the situation" to ideology in that both exert cognitive control over how an individual understands a situation. He proposes that if you can get people to accept an authority's definition of the situation, they will willingly act:

> That is why ideology, an attempt to interpret the condition of man, is always a prominent feature of revolutions, wars, and other circumstances in which individuals are called upon to perform extraordinary action. Governments invest heavily in propaganda, which constitutes the official manner of interpreting events (1974, p. 145).

As has been amply documented, the Third Reich employed a two-pronged approach to propaganda. First, there was propaganda that likened Hitler to a god. For example, in Leni Riefenstahl's (1934) masterful propaganda film, *Triumph of the Will*, Hitler descends from the skies to an adoring crowd. Nazi dignitaries inform the attendees at a party rally (and the viewers) that industry is booming, a network of superhighways has been built, Germany is headed toward a glorious future, and all is due to the Führer. The point of the film is to capture the hearts of the people, which is exactly what we hear Joseph Goebbels, the Reich's Propaganda Minister and one of the Nazi dignitaries, say: "Guns are nice but to win the hearts of the people is better."

The second type of propaganda was virulently anti-Semitic. Jews were variously depicted as exploitative usurers, power-seeking capitalists, godless communists, sexually perverse threats to Aryan women and children, and demons bent on destroying Germany (Balmore et al., 1991). As depicted in the Nazi film *Der Ewige Jude* (*The Eternal Jew*; 1938), the most insidious attribute of the Jews is the ability to camouflage themselves as normal Germans. Thus, an all-out war against the Jews was necessary; one always had to be alert, vigilant in uncovering the Jewish "pestilence" before it spread. And, of course, only the Nazi way of life could ensure German safety and purity.

Taken together, these two types of propaganda shaped the way people thought and felt. In addition to the cognitive function of propaganda that Milgram describes, Goebbels emphasized the emotional function; one must win the people's hearts. Once that is accomplished, people willingly, joyfully act on behalf of the authority—even if the authority is not actually there, and even if it means committing murder. In the case of the Holocaust, the concept of murder itself was redefined to mean something positive. As Bandura (1990) indicates, morally reconstructing the value of killing makes it a highly lauded activity: "People see themselves as fighting ruthless oppressors who have an unquenchable appetite for conquest, or protecting their cherished values and way of life ... saving humanity from subjugation to an evil ideology, or honoring their country's international commitments" (p. 29).

But what of those whose hearts and minds are not completely won over? What of those who do not "buy" the official definition of the situation but who find themselves unable to extract themselves from it? In his analysis, Milgram proposes three factors that maintain participants in the agentic state despite their apparent desire not to go on: sequential nature of the action, situational etiquette, and anxiety. With regard to the latter two, he theorizes that, in order to break off, the participant would have to violate his own felt belief that authorities deserve respect. The issue becomes how to extract oneself from the situation without appearing "arrogant, untoward, and rude" (Milgram, 1974, p. 150). More recent work by Collins and Brief (1995) suggests that, indeed, the desire to maintain a positive self-image and to disengage oneself from the teacher role in a socially appropriate way are operating in the Milgram paradigm. Do these forces also apply to behavior during the Holocaust?

On the one hand, to say that, in the midst of a regime built on terror, people were concerned with politeness seems absurd. Yet, on the other hand, the regime was built on "winning people's hearts." The Nazis brilliantly used the principles of mass psychology:

The choreography of mass meetings and demonstrations ... created a sense of power and belonging. ... The isolated individual [was] drawn into a mood of intoxication at well-organized mass meetings by feeling himself for the first time to be part of a larger community. (Wistrich, 1996, p. 43)

People were swept along by the pageantry and perception of good times that were craftily constructed and nurtured by Nazi propaganda. The whole enterprise aimed at emotional complicity by the German people. To disengage from this enterprise, then, was to confront normative pressures similar to those that operated in Milgram's laboratory.[7]

In addition, the Nazis revealed their genocidal plan in a piecemeal manner. The first official boycott of Jewish shops occurred in April 1933; it was not until September 1935 that the Nuremberg Laws, which stripped Jews of citizenship, prohibited them from marrying "Aryans," and defined them as a separate and distinct "race," were passed; it was yet another 3 years before Kristallnacht was to occur. Even most Jews did not foresee the end result of the Nazi plan. As the German people complied—each step along the way—it became increasingly more difficult to break free psychologically. This is exactly how Milgram describes the dilemmas of his participants; he identifies the "sequential nature of the task" as a potent binding force.

Sequential nature of the task, routinization, and bureaucracy

Milgram describes how his "subject is implicated into the destructive behavior in a piecemeal fashion" (1974, p. 149). Participants don't hear the first "ugh" of protest from the learner until they have already pressed the 5th lever (75 volts); it is not until the 10th (150 volts) that the learner first demands to be released, and not until the 22nd (330 volts) that he falls silent. In order to disengage oneself from the destructive enterprise once the "big picture" is realized, respondents need to justify their previous actions. Unable to find that justification, they remain bound to the situation.

This piecemeal structure of the task is akin to Kelman's (1973) concept of routinization, the process whereby tasks are structured so that their purpose is disconnected from their enactment. As Kelman

---

[7]In his 1995 article, "When is 'obedience' obedience?," Neil Lutsky proposes that these normative forces are actually a better explanation for Milgram's findings than the felt obligation to obey authority.

states, routines "reduce the necessity of making decisions ... [they] make it easier to avoid the implications of one's actions ... and [they] create a shared illusion that one is engaged in a legitimate task" (pp. 46–47). These dynamics are illustrated in a film clip of Walter Stier, former head of Reich Railway Department 33, as shown in Claude Lanzmann's (1985a) film *Shoah*. Stier's work involved preparing time-tables and coordinating the movement of "resettlement" trains. In this film clip, he describes how he was strictly a bureaucrat who was merely following orders, who knew nothing, and who was "glued to his desk" (Lanzmann, 1985b, p. 126). In a second excerpt from *Shoah*, Holocaust historian Raul Hilberg decodes the symbols on a Reich Railway schedule for a train destined for Treblinka, the same type of schedule Stier would have prepared. Hilberg concludes: "We may be talking about ten thousand dead Jews on this one *Fahrplananordnung* here" (Lanzmann, 1985b, p. 131).

Elsewhere, Hilberg has suggested that Holocaust functionaries coped "by not varying their routine and not restructuring their organization, not changing a thing in their correspondence or mode of communication" (1978, p. 274). One could almost add Milgram's words to those of Hilberg:

> [It] is an unfolding process in which each action influences the next. The ... act is perseverative; after the initial instructions, the experimenter does not command the subject to initiate a new act but simply to continue doing what he is doing. (Milgram, 1974, p. 149)

An additional process, identified by a number of writers (Bandura, 1990; Hilberg, 1978; Kelman, 1973; Staub, 1989, 1993), that supports the power of routinization is the use of euphemistic labels: call the activities you are doing something else that further obscures the true purpose of the task and legitimizes it at the same time. One can hear many examples of euphemisms in the film *Shoah*: Stier talks about the "resettlement" trains that carried "criminals"; Lanzmann reads a memo that requests changes to the "special vehicles now in service at Kulmhof" (read "gas vans at Chelmno"). In it, people are variously referred to as "the load," "number of pieces," and "merchandise" (Lanzmann, 1985b, pp. 92–93). Applying this analysis to the Milgram study, one can think of the experimental cover story ("This is an experiment on learning and memory") as a kind of euphemism.

Displacement of responsibility

All the aforementioned factors foster the displacement of responsibility from self onto others (see, for example, Bandura, 1990; Kelman, 1973). This, of course, is one of the main features of Milgram's (1974) agentic-state concept. In his "responsibility clock" data (p. 203), he finds that obedient participants assumed less responsibility for their actions than did defiant ones.[8] Further, in order to defy the experimenter, "those who disobey [must] accept responsibility for destruction of the experiment" (p. 164). We turn next to look at some theoretical similarities between disobedience in the Milgram studies and resistance during the Holocaust.

Dissent, disobedience, and resistance

Modigliani and Rochat's (1995) analysis of the Milgram paradigm focuses on the fact that participants' behaviors are not actually under experimental control and thus their random comments have the potential to alter the definition of the situation. More specifically, when participants' unplanned, unsolicited comments of concern about the learner are met by an indifferent experimenter, a new situation arises if:

> subordinates escalate their resistance to a level of questioning or objecting, they make manifest and obvious the authority's attitude of indifference toward their concerns. ... Questions and objections demand a response that addresses their content. ... Since authorities' prods typically disregard the content of a question or objection, this tends to make increasingly clear to resistant subordinates that their concerns are not being addressed. (1995, p. 114)

In other words, the situation is now one in which the experimenter is unresponsive to both the learner and the naive participant; the experimenter's disregard stimulates mutual disregard by the participant, erodes any rationalization for continuing, and facilitates the partici-

---

[8]It must be noted that Milgram's "responsibility clock" data only partially support his concept of the agentic state. Although obedient participants do assume less responsibility for their actions than do defiant participants, they do not project more responsibility onto the authority than defiants do. Rather, they transfer more responsibility to the victims, a form of victim blaming, yet another psychological process associated with genocide (see, for example, Bandura, 1990; Kelman, 1973; Staub, 1989, 1993). However, as Blass (1992) indicates, victim blaming "is not intrinsic to the agentic-shift process" (p. 303).

pant's exit from the situation. According to Modigliani and Rochat, the earlier in the experiment dissent begins, the more likely the participant will be defiant; "it all depends on timing—on the extent to which subjects have not yet constructed justifications for continuing that work to counterargue their own natural proclivities toward discontinuing" (p. 120). In another article, they note the similarities between Milgram's early dissenters and the citizens of Le Chambon, a town in southern France that resisted Vichy edicts to persecute Jews and—as a result—saved five thousand Jews (Rochat & Modigliani, 1995).

In closing this section, I would like to share an anecdote that supports the ecological validity of Milgram's work with regard to disobedience. After Stanley Milgram's death in 1984, there were several memorial services and gatherings held at the City University Graduate Center, where I was a student and he had been Distinguished Professor of Psychology. At the gathering specifically for students and faculty affiliated with the Social-Personality Psychology program, a former student—who until recently had been living in a Latin American country—spoke. He told how those engaged in resisting dictatorial governments embraced Milgram's work. It gave them courage to resist; it illustrated that people could disengage themselves from tyranny. In short, the speaker re-framed the discussion, making disobedience—and not obedience—the significant focus of the studies. I think that Stanley would have approved.

HOW I INCORPORATE MILGRAM'S RESEARCH ON OBEDIENCE INTO MY HOLOCAUST CURRICULUM

I teach a semester-long, 13 week, upper-level course in the Psychology of the Holocaust that focuses on four groups of questions. Only the first set is relevant to the present discussion:[9] How could the Holocaust have happened? Who were the perpetrators: Were they mad or ordinary people subjected to extreme but still common social forces? Are some people more predisposed to perform genocidal behaviors than others? How do people change as they move along what Staub (1989) calls the "continuum of destruction"?

I approach these questions from a historical perspective. After two class sessions in which the history of the Holocaust is reviewed, we turn

---

[9]The other sets of questions focus on victim/survivor behaviors, intergenerational transmission of trauma in both survivor and perpetrator families, and research on bystanders and rescuers.

to dispositional explanations for perpetrator behavior, including: the psychiatric research on the Nuremberg War Crimes defendants (Borofsky & Brand, 1980; Zillmer, Harrower, Ritzler, & Archer, 1995); the work of Adorno, Frenkel-Brunswik, Levinson, and Sanford (1950) on the authoritarian personality; an excerpt from Alice Miller's (1990) book *For Your Own Good*; and a review of the dispositional theories as found in Blass's (1993) article on the psychology of perpetrators. Class discussion centers on how satisfactory these theories are: What do they explain? What do they not explain? What unanswered questions remain? Students' questions usually serve as a natural segue into situational hypotheses and Milgram's work on obedience, the first situational theory of perpetrator behavior.

Most students have already been exposed to the obedience studies many times: first, in an introductory psychology course in which they see the film (Milgram, 1965); second, in a course on research methods in which the main focus is the ethics of Milgram's research; and third, in a social psychology course where the various experimental conditions are reviewed, the theory of the agentic state is first presented, and methodological and theoretical critiques are offered. However, this is the first time students are asked to critique Milgram's studies vis-à-vis the Holocaust. Which perpetrator behaviors do his studies explain? Which do they not explain? To assist us in answering these questions, we read Arthur Miller's (1986) discussion of genocide from the perspective of the obedience experiments and Blass's (1991, 1993) review articles on situation–personality interaction explanations for both Milgram's findings and perpetrator behaviors.

In the following class session we read additional social psychological formulations of perpetrator behavior (i.e., those of Bandura, Kelman, Lutsky, and Staub). Here I find it useful to structure the discussion around Milgram's theoretical analysis of obedience. Thus we look at a variety of antecedent forces operating on participants/perpetrators: social influence processes, devaluation of the victim via propaganda, and difficult life circumstances, as well as those Milgram specifically mentions (socialization for obedience, overarching ideology, perception of the legitimacy of the authority). Similarly, we look at a multiplicity of binding factors: the piecemeal nature of the task, routines, normative pressures, self-justification. Film excerpts (from *Der Ewige Jude, Heil Hitler: Confessions of a Hitler Youth, Shoah*, and *Triumph of the Will*) are used to ground the discussion in the Holocaust.

The next class session is devoted to exploring the psychological consequences of being bound to a malevolent system. We compare Milgram's concept of the agentic state to Lifton's theory of doubling, "the division of the self into two functioning wholes, so that a part-self acts as an entire self" (1990, p. 180). Lifton further describes the dialectic between the part-selves (the Auschwitz self and the humane physician/husband/father self) that occurs on an unconscious level and that protects the personality from guilt. These "divided self" theories of evildoing, as Waller (1996) labels them, are then contrasted to his "unitary-self perspective [which] asserts that the primary, and only, self or psychological constellation is fundamentally altered as a result of the power of potent social forces generated by the situation or organization" (p. 16). This theory is further compared with Staub's (1989) theory of "learning by doing" and Kelman's (1973) thesis that victimizers themselves become dehumanized in the process.

In sum, Stanley Milgram's work on obedience to authority is the chronological center of my teaching approach to the psychology of perpetrators. We move from a focus on personality to a focus on the situation (Milgram) to a focus on interaction and change in the self-system of perpetrators. Further, Milgram's work actually serves as a linchpin holding all the various theories together as we continually return to evaluate it vis-a-vis more recent ones. As the first psychologist to propose a situational theory of perpetrator behavior and as one who withstood worldwide criticism in so doing, I believe that this is Stanley Milgram's rightful place in any discussion of the psychology of the Holocaust.

CONCLUSION

Surveys of middle school, high school, and college Holocaust curricula indicate that the discipline of psychology is woefully absent. This deficiency is remarkable in view of the fact that, at its core, the Holocaust comprised hundreds of thousands of behavioral acts performed by thousands of people. Clearly, a more complete understanding of the horror that engulfed Europe from 1933 to 1945 cannot be acquired without consulting psychological theory and knowledge. And within that corpus of information, Stanley Milgram's work on obedience to authority still has much to tell us. True, it does not explain many things about the Holocaust. Yet, as I have demonstrated earlier, Milgram's research *is* more relevant than his critics would have us think. Further, as the first situational theory of perpetrator behavior, it is the stimulus to which subsequent theorizing has responded. All the authors who have dealt with perpetrator behavior whom I have cited in this paper have in turn cited Milgram in their work. It is laudatory that psychological theory of state-sanctioned evildoing has evolved over the five decades since the Holocaust, and, in so doing, has moved beyond "obedience to authority" as the sole explanation for perpetrators' behaviors. However, to ignore this first theory is analogous to ignoring Sigmund Freud in a discussion of theories of personality and psychological dysfunction. Understanding of the Holocaust will not progress without incorporating psychological theory and research. And, as I have proposed, Stanley Milgram's work surely deserves its place, along with that of Gordon Allport, Albert Bandura, Herbert Kelman, Robert Jay Lifton, Ervin Staub, and others.

REFERENCES

Adorno, T. W., Frenkel-Brunswik, E., Levinson, D. J., & Sanford, R. N. (1950). *The authoritarian personality.* New York: Harper & Row.

Allport, G. (1954). *The nature of prejudice.* Reading, MA: Addison-Wesley.

Arendt, H. (1963). *Eichmann in Jerusalem: A report on the banality of evil.* New York: Viking Press.

Balmore, S., Dlin, E., Imbar, S., Rokhsar, J., Silberklang, D., & Yaron, M. (1991). *The Jew in Nazi ideology.* Jerusalem, Israel: Yad Vashem.

Bandura, A. (1990). Selective activation and disengagement of moral control. *Journal of Social Issues, 46* (1), 27–46.

Blass, T. (1991). Understanding behavior in the Milgram obedience experiment: The role of personality, situations, and their interactions. *Journal of Personality and Social Psychology, 60,* 398–413.

Blass, T. (1992). The social psychology of Stanley Milgram. In M. P. Zanna (Ed.), *Advances in experimental social psychology* (Vol. 25, pp. 277–329). San Diego, CA: Academic Press.

Blass, T. (1993). Psychological perspectives on the perpetrators of the Holocaust: The role of situational pressures, personal dispositions, and their interactions. *Holocaust and Genocide Studies, 7,* 30–50.

Borofsky, G. L., & Brand, D. J. (1980). Personality organization and psychological functioning of the Nuremberg War Criminals: The Rorschach data. In J. Dimsdale (Ed.), *Survivors, victims and perpetrators: Essays on the Nazi Holocaust* (pp. 359–403). New York: Hemisphere Publishing.

Browning, C. (1992). *Ordinary men: Reserve Police Battalion 101 and the final solution in Poland.* New York: HarperCollins.

Collins, B., & Brief, D. (1995). Using person-perception vignette methodologies to uncover the symbolic meanings of teacher behaviors in the Milgram paradigm. *Journal of Social Issues, 51* (3), 89–106.

Crouch, M. (1996, March 3). *The Holocaust in undergraduate education.* Paper presented at the Annual Scholars' Conference on the Holocaust and the Churches, Minneapolis, Minnesota.

Dawidowicz, L. (1990, December). How they teach the Holocaust. *Commentary*, pp. 25–32.

Der Ewige Jude (1938). [Film]. Deutsche Filmherstellungs and Vertriebs; directed by Fritz Hippler. (Available from International Historic Films, Chicago.)

Facing History and Ourselves: Holocaust and Human Behavior. (1994). Brookline, MA: Facing History and Ourselves National Foundation.

Goldhagen, D. J. (1996). *Hitler's willing executioners: Ordinary Germans and the Holocaust*. New York: Knopf.

Heil Hitler: Confessions of a Hitler Youth. (1991). [Film]. Home Box Office (HBO), producer. (Available from Zenger Video, Culver City, California).

Hilberg, R. (1978, April). Confronting the moral implications of the Holocaust. *Social Education*, 272–276.

Kelman, H. C. (1973). Violence without moral restraint: Reflections on the dehumanization of victims and victimizers. *Journal of Social Issues*, 29 (4), 25–49.

Lanzmann, C. (Producer & Director). (1985a). *Shoah* [Film]. (Available from the Simon Wiesenthal Center, Los Angeles.)

Lanzmann, C. (1985b). *Shoah: The complete text of the acclaimed Holocaust film*. New York: DaCapo Press.

Lifton, R. J. (1990). Doubling: The Faustian bargain. In R. Gottlieb (Ed.), *Thinking the unthinkable: Meanings of the Holocaust* (pp. 180–195). New York: Paulist Press.

Lipstadt, D. (1995, March 6). Not facing history: How not to teach the Holocaust. *The New Republic*, 26–29.

Lozowick, Y. (1995). *Malicious clerks* [Abstract]. Unpublished doctoral dissertation, Hebrew University, Jerusalem.

Lutsky, N. (1995). When is "obedience" obedience? Conceptual and historical commentary. *Journal of Social Issues*, 51 (3), 55–65.

Matthaus, J. (1996). What about the "ordinary men"?: The German Order Police and the Holocaust in the occupied Soviet Union. *Holocaust and Genocide Studies*, 10, 134–150.

Milgram, S. (1963). Behavioral study of obedience. *Journal of Abnormal and Social Psychology*, 67, 371–378.

Milgram, S. (1965). *Obedience* [Film]. (Available from the Pennsylvania State University Audiovisual Services.)

Milgram, S. (1974). *Obedience to authority: An experimental view*. New York: Harper & Row.

Miller, A. (1990). Adolf Hitler's childhood: From hidden to manifest horror. In R. Gottlieb (Ed.), *Thinking the unthinkable: Meanings of the Holocaust* (pp. 88–106). New York: Paulist Press.

Miller, A. G. (1986). *The obedience experiments: A case study of controversy in social science*. New York: Praeger.

Miller, A. G. (1995). Constructions of the obedience experiments: A focus upon domains of relevance. *Journal of Social Issues*, 51(3), 33–53.

Miller, A. G., Collins, B. E., & Brief, D. E. (1995). Perspectives on obedience to authority: The legacy of the Milgram experiments. *Journal of Social Issues*, 51(3), 1–19.

Modigliani, A., & Rochat, F. (1995). The role of interaction sequences and the timing of resistance in shaping obedience and defiance to authority. *Journal of Social Issues*, 51(3), 107–123.

Riefenstahl, L. (1934). *Triumph of the Will* [Film]. (Available from International Historic Films, Chicago.)

Robinson, J. (1965). *And the crooked shall be made straight: The Eichmann trial, the Jewish catastrophe, and Hannah Arendt's narrative*. New York: Macmillan.

Rochat, F., & Modigliani, A. (1995). The ordinary quality of resistance: From Milgram's laboratory to the village of Le Chambon. *Journal of Social Issues, 51*(3), 195–210.

Shawn, K. (1989). *The end of innocence: Anne Frank and the Holocaust.* New York: Anti-Defamation League International Center for Holocaust Studies.

Skversky, M. (1998, Spring). Watching the program grow: Highlights from 1997–98. *Facing History and Ourselves News,* 5.

Staub, E. (1989). *The roots of evil: The origins of genocide and other group violence.* Cambridge, MA: Cambridge University Press.

Staub, E. (1993). The psychology of bystanders, perpetrators, and heroic helpers. *International Journal of Intercultural Relations, 17,* 315–341.

Waller, J. (1996). Perpetrators of the Holocaust: Divided and unitary self-conceptions of evildoing. *Holocaust and Genocide Studies, 10,* 11–33.

Wistrich, R. (1996). *Weekend in Munich: Art, propaganda and terror in the Third Reich.* London: Pavilion Books.

You can change the world: March of the Living Study Guide (1995, April). Miami, FL: Central Agency for Jewish Education.

Zillmer, E. A., Harrower, M., Ritzler, B. A., & Archer, R. P. (1995). *The quest for the Nazi personality: A psychological investigation of Nazi war criminals.* Hillsdale, NJ: Lawrence Erlbaum Associates.

9

A Science Museum Exhibit on Milgram's Obedience Research: History, Description, and Visitors' Reactions

Caryl Marsh
Museum Exhibitions Advisor

In 1992, to honor its 100th anniversary, the American Psychological Association (APA) launched a museum exhibition titled *Psychology: Understanding Ourselves, Understanding Each Other.* The exhibition opened at the Smithsonian Institution in Washington, D.C., where it attracted many enthusiastic visitors, as well as high praise from psychologists, the media, and the museum community.

The exhibition's goal was to introduce a broad, general science-museum audience to concepts, tools, methods, and results of 100 years of psychological research. APA staff devised and organized the exhibition in close collaboration with the Association of Science-Technology Centers and the Ontario Science Centre in Canada, with assistance from the Exploratorium in San Francisco and the Boston Children's Museum. Dozens of eminent U.S. and Canadian psychologists advised on content selection and development of exhibition components and reviewed all label copy.

An early version of the exhibition opened in 1991 at the Ontario Science Centre in Toronto, where it is on permanent display. APA's traveling version circulated to 14 science museums across the United States from 1992–1996. In 1997, APA's exhibition began a 5-year display at the Arizona Science Center in Phoenix. The exhibition has some 40 different three-dimensional participatory exhibits, including one that embodies the concepts of Milgram's obedience to authority experiment.

Psychologist advisors to the exhibition expressed strong positive as well as strong negative reactions to the inclusion of Milgram's research in the exhibition. Museum visitors expressed equally strong conflicting reactions to their experiences with the exhibit. Both sets of reactions seemed to replicate the controversial reactions to Milgram's original research. The following is an anecdotal account of these reactions during the development of the exhibition and since it has been on display.

REACTIONS DURING THE INITIAL DEVELOPMENT OF THE EXHIBIT COMPONENT

Four of us, experienced museum exhibit developers, visited the Archives of the History of American Psychology in Akron, Ohio, in the fall of 1986. We were searching for materials that we might transform into hands-on activities for the American Psychological Association's Centennial Exhibition. We brought different perspectives to the search. One of us was an anthropologist, director of traveling exhibitions for the Association of Science-Technology Centers. One, a biologist, was chief scientist at the Ontario Science Centre. The third was the Science Centre's head designer. I was the fourth. An exhibitions curator, as well as a social psychologist, I was the director of the exhibition for APA.

Entering the archives' main storage area, I noticed the Milgram apparatus. John Popplestone, the archives' director, had told me it was there. But I walked on to look at other things. Within minutes, Jerry Krause, the exhibit designer, was at my side, very excited. He asked, "Do you realize they have the original Milgram apparatus, the shock box?" I nodded and said that APA would probably never let us display it. Trained as a social psychologist, I was familiar with the Milgram research. I also knew that many psychologists were uncomfortable with it. Some even considered it an embarrassment. I explained that Milgram's research design, one that deceived the subject about the purpose of the experiment, was highly controversial. In fact, under current

APA guidelines and Federal regulations, it would now be very difficult, if not impossible, to get academic approval for Milgram's research design. Furthermore, Milgram's interpretation of his research results was also questioned.

Jerry persisted. He told me that most college students in Canada who had taken introductory psychology were familiar with the research. People would be fascinated to see Milgram's original apparatus. I simply nodded again. Jerry became more agitated. Although he never touched me, I felt as if he were shaking me by the shoulders. "Caryl Marsh," he said, "if you want this exhibition to amount to anything, you've got to take risks. It's got to have controversy!" I knew he was right. John Popplestone agreed and put the apparatus on the list of objects we would borrow for the exhibition.

Some days later, back in Washington, I was at dinner with several APA officials; one asked what objects from the Akron archives would be in the exhibition. I mentioned early intelligence tests, reaction-time experiments, psychophysics devices. "And," I added, "the Milgram apparatus." I might as well have dropped a bomb. The man asking the question, an enthusiastic supporter of the exhibition, exploded. He expressed all the strong feelings against the Milgram research I had anticipated. I listened quietly. Next day I telephoned the exhibition's overall content advisor, Shep White, at Harvard. He suggested I talk with Roger Brown. Brown's *Social Psychology: The Second Edition* (1986) opens with a chapter on social forces in obedience and rebellion. In it, he cited Milgram's obedience research as "the most famous series of experiments in social psychology" (p. 3).

When I met with Professor Brown and described the plans for the psychology exhibition, I asked what should be included from social psychology. He immediately replied that he thought Milgram's experiments were among the most important psychological research in the 20th century. I described to him the objections that had been raised. He agreed that we could refer all objectors to him. Social psychologists Philip Zimbardo and Elliot Aronson also strongly supported having Milgram's research in the exhibition.

The next major objections to the Milgram exhibit were raised in 1991, after the prototype exhibition had opened at the Ontario Science Centre in Toronto, Canada. This time the protests centered on the wording of the exhibit's labels. APA's Board of Scientific Affairs ruled that we must include in the exhibit alternative interpretations for the research. Three board members were asked to review all Milgram label copy and materials before final production of APA's traveling exhibition.

DESCRIPTION OF THE MILGRAM EXHIBIT

The transformation of psychology experiments into free-standing three-dimensional museum exhibition activities was a challenging task. Teams of Ontario Science Centre and APA staff, working with psychologist advisers, reviewed the research and tried out promising exhibit strategies with visitors at the Ontario Science Centre and other museums. The Milgram exhibit was the outcome of this kind of process. The germ of the idea for the exhibit came from an episode in the television program *Candid Camera*, which had appeared in the 1960s.

The core plan was to direct visitors down a path of black and white squares, instructing them to walk on the black squares only. At the end of the path would be the Milgram apparatus with an explanation of the original experiment. We assumed that visitors, having obeyed the directions to walk on the black squares, would grasp the concept of social influence.

The finished Milgram exhibit is an eye-catching, intriguing structure (Fig. 9.1). Viewed from a distance, one notices a sign well above eye level, in black block letters on a yellow background. The sign says: "ATTEN-TION!" Above it is another sign, in white letters on a blue background. The letters say: "Please walk on the black squares ONLY!" As people approach the signs, they see on the floor below them a path of alternating black and white squares extending into the distance. Bordering the path on the right and left sides is a light wood frame covered with canvas. The wood frame extends up to form a barrel-vaulted ceiling, more than 9 feet high, with a canvas cover. As people enter the path, they feel they are walking in a tentlike corridor. On the right and left are signs that repeat the message: "ATTENTION! Please walk on the black squares ONLY!" The path is 4 feet wide and 14 feet long (Fig. 9.2).

At the end of the path is the Milgram shock apparatus, carefully displayed in a plexiglas case (Fig. 9.3). Inside the case is a sign that reads, "This is the original apparatus used in the Milgram studies," and in smaller print, "Archives of the History of American Psychology. Akron."

The following are the explanatory labels below the display case in which the Milgram apparatus is shown:

Did you do as you were told?

On your way down the hallway did you obey the sign and walk on the black squares only? If you did, WHY? Perhaps, you walked on the black squares because of the authority of this museum—or perhaps you saw others doing it too.

Our society depends on us to comply with a huge array of requests, commands and rules every day.

We cross at marked crosswalks.

We line up behind the signs at bus stops, banks and movies.

But what triggers our obedience?

Social psychologists have identified two agents that command compliance.

AUTHORITY—we tend to obey authority figures more—possibly we believe they know best.

THE POWER OF THE SITUATION—circumstances often make it easier and simpler to obey than not to obey.

Would you hurt a stranger if someone in authority told you to?

Fig. 9.1 Exhibit at the Smithsonian Institution, viewed from a distance. Museum visitors lined up, waiting their turn to walk on the black-and-white squares path.
Note. Photograph by Hugh Talman. Used with permission of the American Psychological Association.

Fig. 9.2 Visitor walking on black squares only at the Smithsonian Institution exhibit.
Note. Photograph by Hugh Talman. Used with permission of the American Psychological Association.

Can you imagine the conditions under which you might?

Imagine that you have volunteered to take part in a memory experiment. You are told that as part of the experiment you will be required to give electrical shocks, ranging from mild to dangerously strong, to another person.

Would you do it?

How many people do you think would? Almost no one, right?

In experiments carried out by the American psychologist, Stanley Milgram, in the 1960's, it was discovered that almost 2 out of 3 subjects not only gave electrical shocks but went all the way to the strongest shock level.

Science and Deception: The Ethics of Milgram's Experiment

The manner in which the obedience experiments were performed has been strongly criticized, leading psychologists to examine more closely the ethics of deceiving participants and the obligation to inform subjects about the purpose of an experiment.

Stricter ethical standards have made it impossible for studies like those performed by Milgram to take place today.

Go to the rear of this exhibit to see an original film of this experiment and to learn more about compliance.

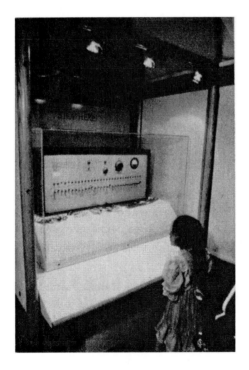

Fig. 9.3. Plexiglas case display of original Milgram apparatus at the Smithsonian Institution Exhibit. Apparatus courtesy of Archives of the History of American Psychology, Akron, Ohio.
Note. Photographs by Hugh Talman. Used with permission of the American Psychological Association.

At the rear of the exhibit on the back of the shock box display case is a panel with a small video screen and additional explanatory labels (see the following discussion). Facing the video panel is seating space for five or six visitors. Three buttons on the panel provide access to three different video sequences.

One video sequence is titled, "Why would an ordinary, law-abiding man give a lethal shock to an unseen stranger?" This is a 7-minute segment from Milgram's original black-and-white film of the obedience experiments. The second video is a 4-minute sequence with a brief introduction by Philip Zimbardo that describes early research on social influence. It includes actual footage from the original Lewin, Lippitt, and White studies of leadership styles comparing the effects of democratic, autocratic, and laissez-faire leaders on groups of 11-year-old boys and a scene from the classic Asch experiment on conformity. The third video is a 6-minute segment that shows Zimbardo's prison experiment with Zimbardo's explanatory comments (WGBH, 1989).

The text on the video panel, referred to previously, includes a detailed description of Milgram's original obedience experiments and their extensive replication, a facsimile of the newspaper advertisement used to recruit subjects, plus the following explanatory label that, in part, repeats the information below the Plexiglas case:

A Controversial Experiment

The manner in which the Milgram studies were conducted has been strongly criticized. Many objected to the use of deception in persuading the participants to comply. Others wondered whether the participants obeyed because they knew it was an experiment and were confident that no one was really being hurt.

The development of stricter ethical standards for the use of human subjects in psychological experiments has made it impossible for studies like those performed by Milgram to take place today.

Nevertheless Milgram's work was instrumental in focusing attention on how people respond to authority and the power of the situation.

The wording of this label was specified by APA's Board of Scientific Affairs. The somewhat secluded location of the video panel was the result of restrictions put on the use of the Milgram film by his widow, Alexandra Milgram. Mrs. Milgram thought that use of the film was unsuitable, possibly frightening, for young children. To obtain her permission to use the film, we had to agree to display it in a way that would prevent casual viewing by very young museum visitors. The secluded location achieved Mrs. Milgram's goal.

Unfortunately, we found that the location made the films less accessible to other visitors as well. The result was that many fewer visitors saw the film than walked the black-and-white squares path.

REACTIONS OF MUSEUM VISITORS
TO THE MILGRAM OBEDIENCE EXHIBIT

Sources of Information

To gain a better understanding of what visitors learn, museums in recent years have been studying their visitors. These studies have been both formal and informal, qualitative and quantitative. Because the psychology exhibition was the first major attempt to introduce the science of psychology to museum audiences, we, too, used several ways to gather information about visitors' reactions. We collected information about reactions to the entire exhibition, as well as to the individual components.

The exhibition itself has a place where visitors are invited to sit down and write their comments on 5-by-8-inch cards that read, "Tell us what you think about the Psychology Exhibition." Thousands of visitors have written their views. Additional information comes from hundreds of visitor interviews conducted by exhibition development staff at several different museums in which the exhibition was shown; from letters visitors sent after seeing the show; from reviews of the exhibition published in local newspapers and magazines as the exhibition circulated around the United States; from a formal entrance–exit study conducted by APA at three museums; and from observations by museum staff. There are also many photographs and a half-hour video that records typical visitor behavior in the exhibition (1992). Visitor reactions to the Milgram component of the psychology exhibition, reported in the next section, were culled from these varied sources.

Reactions

The Milgram exhibit was the one visitors most often spoke about in APA's exit study. Most visitors to the Milgram exhibit, 85 to 90%, did obey the instructions to walk on the black squares only. However, many fewer watched the films. Less than half the visitors continued past the display of the shock apparatus to the space where the films were displayed.

Overall, visitors, including psychologists, expressed the same range of verbal reactions to Milgram's research that is found in the literature (Blass, 1992; Miller, 1986). Comments about the research have ranged from high praise to profound condemnation. Similar views were voiced about our exhibit. The visitors and museum staff who perceived the exhibit as a deception were especially outspoken in Washington, D.C., and in San Francisco.

The following examples illustrate the range of reactions to Milgram's research and to our exhibit.

Visitors who accepted both the validity of the Milgram research and the validity of the exhibit format made the following comments:

- A woman in her 20s, at the Exploratorium in San Francisco said, "The exhibit at first seemed very innocent, walking on the black squares ... when I saw the apparatus ... I had heard of the experiment, I made the connection. Then, it seemed rather alarming." She said she watched the videotapes and at first thought: "I would never do that," and then, "I really asked myself, would I do that? I do tend to be obedient. It gave me a lot to think about." Her final comment: "Very valuable and interesting. Enables people to learn something about themselves, about their own behavior."

- A boy, aged 12, at the Boston Museum of Science; described the exhibit in detail and his careful exploration of it. He said he had read all the labels and watched all three of the video sequences. He told me: "The research was repeated in several different countries." And then, in a tone of amazement, he said: "Do you realize, two people out of three, over 60%, gave the strongest shock!" His tone suggested that he could not imagine anyone doing such a thing; yet he seemed to accept the research.

- One of the written "Tell Us What You Think" statements was by a father who described this interaction with his 5-year-old son:

  Brian said he would not obey a person who told him to hurt someone, but when his older brother was pestering us at one of the exhibits, I told him to punch him, and Brian hit him gently. I told him to really whack him, and Brian punched him right in the eye. Perhaps Milgram was right!
  [signed] Brian's Dad

Some visitors had no quarrel with Milgram's research but thought our exhibit was faulty.

- An exhibit designer at the Exploratorium said: "What people are really doing is entering into the activity as a kind of play with an expectation of a pleasant payoff. It seems unfair to make the connection between the walking on the black squares and the obedience of the Milgram experiment."
  "It [the exhibit] needs another activity, somehow bring people into the feeling of group pressure ... a little more about conformity."
- A social psychologist said: "It's not compelling. You need to make the task a little more difficult so that the obedience is more clear."
  I felt a little ripped off. Are you calling me obedient? I followed the rules (walked on the black squares) because in the museum I follow the rules and expect to get rewarded for doing so. In a way the task is too simple.

One visitor separated the black-and-white squares activity, which she liked and found useful, from the Milgram research which she rejected. In a long detailed letter following her visit, she wrote:

I am glad that the exhibition included "Please walk on the black squares only." My own immediate reaction was "*Why* should I?" I stood there for a minute or two calculating whether perhaps some white squares might be wired to ring a loud unpleasant bell—or perhaps give a mild tremor or shock. Then, I discarded those outcomes as unlikely given the milieu and intent of the exhibits to inform.

Finally because it was your show I decided to walk on the black squares only and not defy the instructions as I was tempted to do. And, importantly, I liked the fact that the sign said "Please————." So I learned, when I consider it all, how education and socialization is internalized if you:

a. Like the teacher
b. Ask for cooperation as a choice
c. Say "Please"

In the contrasting electric shock experiment, I find it difficult to accept the results ... Even though it expands our understanding of people's behavioral range, I dislike it intensely.

Fortunately, even in our crime infested-times many stories are published of self-sacrifice and heroism. Anecdotal rather than produced by an experimental lab, but reassuring that the world remains a battlefield of good and evil and we can pick our side and win.

Some visitors found the exhibit somewhat puzzling:

- A man in his 30s said he had "mixed reactions." He followed the instructions because of the authority of the museum, but wondered:

  Have I been made a fool? Is the museum trying to foster civil disobedience? Should I refuse to follow other instructions in the exhibition? It appears to be a demonstration that might encourage disorder. You want me to put things back into the Discovery Boxes [another exhibit].

  He said he thought "it was important to question what you're being told, but in the military, there is no time to question rules. I don't follow rules all the time." He said he had watched all three of the films "to learn more about psychology."

Some visitors engaged in the activity but did not understand the exhibit at all.

- A 10-year-old girl said she thought there would be an experiment at the end. Her friend thought that if one walked on the white squares buzzers would ring. "So we agreed to walk on the black squares. We looked at the display case but didn't really understand what it meant and how it related to walking on the black squares."

Some visitors who followed the instructions may have felt the irritation and impulse to disobey described by a Canadian newspaper reporter. In his published description of the exhibition, he wrote:

One of the more subtle exhibits involves a small enclosed passageway that leads to a glass case with a rather frightening electronic device inside. The floor is checkered in black and white tiles and we're instructed to walk on the black squares only.

Having carefully negotiated the route, avoiding white tiles at the risk of falling, one finally arrives at the machine. There, a little plaque informs us that we have once again proved just how obedient we are.

Very nice. Very sly. You glance around, checking to see if anyone noticed, then walk back, stepping heavily on white tiles.

Some psychologists thought the Milgram exhibit might contribute to giving psychology a bad name. It might reinforce the public's perception that "psychologists always lie." This observation was made ironically, but essentially stresses the point of view initially expressed by psychologists who opposed our including the Milgram research during the exhibition's initial development. One such psychologist also pointed out that essentially we, too, were deceiving the visitors by not giving them any reason to "walk on the black squares only."

Some visitors completely rejected both Milgram's research and the exhibit.

- An eminent MIT physicist commented, "I don't want anyone to tell me to walk somewhere. Basically, I do not believe the research. The field [psychology] is full of fraud. The task [walking on the black squares] doesn't seem relevant ... being asked to act without meaning."

- A woman in her 30s said:

  I don't want to know why or how people justify atrocious deeds like this. I did not want to participate by walking into the exhibit and help to perpetuate presentation of information like this. I feel this is an effort to manipulate me.

- A woman in her 40s said, "It's horrible. I think the research is horrible. The people have been tricked. I don't know why you would want to put something so horrible into the exhibition."

- Another woman in her 40s said, "It's the most immoral research I could imagine."

CONCLUDING THOUGHTS

The fact that the Milgram exhibit was the one most often mentioned by visitors exiting the psychology exhibition attests to the continuing relevance of the issues raised by Milgram's research. The exhibit's power to elicit compliance was even greater than we had anticipated. About 85 to 90% of the visitors walked only on the black squares as requested.

The strong objections raised by some psychologists to our including the Milgram material in APA's Exhibition was also expected. However, the similar objections expressed by some visitors and their extreme anger toward the museum for "tricking" them were a complete surprise. In fact, it was some time before I realized that indeed we had deceived them by not informing them *why* we asked them to walk only on the black squares.

The visitors' strong objections led me to ponder further the obedience/disobedience phenomenon. Rereading Milgram (1974), the following two statements caught my attention. In the preface to *Obedience to Authority* (1974), Milgram wrote:

> The dilemma inherent in obedience to authority is ancient, as old as the story of Abraham. What the present study does is to give the dilemma contemporary form by treating it as subject matter for experimental inquiry and with the aim of *understanding rather than judging it from a moral stand point.* (p.xi) [emphasis added]

But Milgram found the results of his studies disturbing. In the epilogue to *Obedience to Authority* he wrote:

> [The results] raise the possibility that human nature, or—more specifically—the kind of character produced in American democratic society, cannot be counted on to insulate its citizens from brutality and inhumane treatment at the direction of malevolent authority. A substantial proportion of people do what they are told to do, irrespective of the content of the act and without limitations of conscience, so long as they perceive that the command comes from a legitimate authority. (p. 189)

Milgram concluded, "This is a fatal flaw nature has designed into us, and which in the long run gives our species only a modest chance of survival" (p. 188).

The visitors' strong objections to our Milgram exhibit have led me to a different conclusion. I would hypothesize that obedience and disobedience are human capacities, ready to be modified by social forces. Most societies demand obedience. There are, indeed, some situations that require blind obedience. However, might it be more valuable for the society and for the individual to learn not only to obey but also when and how to question and disobey?

For example, a recent article in the *Washington Post* with the headline, "Retreat Before the Charge" (Warren, 1998), describes a human-rights camp that trains activists in the strategies of nonviolent protest. More than 100 young adult leaders of human rights and environmental groups from around the world engaged in a 6-day course of "direct action" workshops intended to inspire them to bolder, more confrontational strategies.

How might individuals who had experienced this training respond to an experiment based on Milgram's paradigm? Would they raise more questions? Refuse to participate?

To me, the importance of Milgram's research is that it demonstrates not only the power of the social situation to elicit obedience. It also shows the potential dangers of blind obedience. I believe we need to learn when and how to question and disobey, as well as when to obey.

ACKNOWLEDGMENT

I want to express my deep appreciation to Tom Blass for his patience and persistence in encouraging me to write this chapter.

REFERENCES

American Psychological Association (Producer). (1992). *Psychology: Understanding ourselves, understanding each other* [Videotape]. Washington, DC: American Psychological Association.

Blass, T. (1991). Understanding behavior in the Milgram obedience experiment: The role of personality, situations, and their interactions. *Journal of Personality and Social Psychology, 60,* 398–413.

Blass, T. (1992). The social psychology of Stanley Milgram. In M. P. Zanna (Ed.) *Advances in experimental social psychology,* (Vol. 25, pp. 277–329). San Diego, CA: Academic Press.

Brown, R. (1986). *Social psychology: The second edition.* New York: The Free Press.

Milgram, S. (1974). *Obedience to authority: An experimental view.* New York: Harper & Row.

Miller, A. G. (1986). *The obedience experiments: A case study of controversy in social science.* New York: Praeger.

Warren, R. (1998, June 20). Retreat before the charge. *The Washington Post,* p. C1.

WGBH (Boston) (Producer), & Zimbardo, Philip (Author/Narrator). In association with American Psychological Association, (1989). *The Power of the Situation* [videotape]. No. 19. *Discovering Psychology.* Santa Barbara, CA: Intellimation.

10

The Dynamics of Obeying
and Opposing Authority:
A Mathematical Model

François Rochat
The University of Michigan
Olivier Maggioni
Haute Ecole de Gestion, VD, Switzerland
Andre Modigliani
The University of Michigan

Obedience to authority is a ubiquitous phenomenon in our complex, hierarchically organized societies, but it is one that has been viewed with great ambivalence. Obedience has sometimes been praised for enabling people to organize and stand bravely together, doing their duty in the face of a common danger. One historical event that has become an epitome of both disciplined obedience and bravery against overwhelming odds occurred at Thermopylae Pass during the Persian–Greek wars fought in the Fifth century B.C. There, a small band of Spartan soldiers, under the command of their king, Leonidas, held off a far larger force of invading Persians by continuing to fight as commanded until the very last of them had been killed (Simonides, as cited in Bowra, 1961). But if obedience has at times been praised, it has at other times been denounced for contributing to the performance of callous, brutal, and cowardly acts. Some of the ambivalence associated with obedience is captured in Alfred, Lord Tennyson's famous poem, "The Charge of the

Light Brigade." Historically speaking, this ill-fated British charge against Russian troops during the Crimean War resulted from error and confusion in the issuing of commands; but although Tennyson acknowledges this in his poem, he still manages to make the disastrous charge seem heroic.

> Half a league, half a league,
> Half a league onward,
> All in the Valley of Death
> Rode the six hundred.
> "Forward the Light Brigade!
> Charge for the guns," he said.
> Into the Valley of Death
> Rode the six hundred.
>
> "Forward, the Light Brigade!"
> Was there a man dismayed?
> No, tho' the soldiers knew
> Someone had blundered:
> Theirs was not to make reply,
> Theirs was not to reason why,
> Theirs was but to do and die:
> Into the Valley of Death
> Rode the six hundred....

Although following orders may, depending on the circumstances, be either praiseworthy or blameworthy, Stanley Milgram was primarily interested in the darker side of obedience. In 1960, as an assistant professor of psychology at Yale University, he designed and began a series of social psychology experiments whose purpose was to lead to better understanding of obedience as it ordinarily develops in settings in which an authority figure is issuing direct orders to a subordinate. Milgram was particularly interested in situations in which the commands being given were manifestly harmful, the destructive effects being obvious to any subordinate. Indeed, in his experiments, participants were ordered by an experimenter to administer ever stronger electric shocks to a fellow participant, despite the latter's cries of pain and angry protests. Thus Milgram's research sought to study the behavior of subordinates in situations in which they were being required to follow the instructions of a legitimate authority no matter what the consequences might be, so long as the authority was formally in charge of the proceedings. These types of situations have a horrendous antecedent in the Holocaust, and Milgram was deeply concerned with what had happened to the Jews in Europe during the Nazi era of 1933 to 1945 (see Blass, 1992, 1993, 1998).

When Milgram began his experiments, he did not expect his participants to be so easily induced to give electric shocks to a man introduced to them as a fellow participant in the experiment, whom they believed was selected at random to be the "learner " in a so-called memory and learning project. But in fact, in his standard conditions, most participants did comply with the experimenter as he persistently prodded them to increase the level of the electric shocks. Milgram's experimental findings were not only very surprising but also very intriguing and quite rich. Yet they are not at all easy to understand.

Milgram's own explanation of his findings entailed arguing that obedient participants were somehow "captured" by a mental set that is associated with being an agent of authority—a set that he called the "agentic state"—which he believed led participants to feel no responsibility for the consequences of their actions (Milgram, 1974). This is not an entirely satisfying analysis, in part because it only adds a somewhat mystical quality to an explanation for obedience that had been offered by Herbert Simon well before Milgram conducted his experiments (Simon, 1945). Simon had maintained that all subordinates implicitly understand, from the very nature of their subservient roles, that they ought to hold aside their own personal preferences about their conduct and, instead, act in accordance with the desires (commands) of the authority. Because it is not their own preferences that guide their conduct but those of the authority, they are unlikely to feel responsible for the consequences of their actions. Here there is no special, "agentic" state of mind—merely a practical, common-sense understanding of what it means to be subject to an authority. Of course, Simon's framework does not help resolve the central question raised by Milgram's research: When and how will people come to defy the authority? That is, when and why will they cease to hold their own preferences in abeyance? Numerous attempts have been made to address these questions; perhaps the most thorough of these has been provided by Kelman and Hamilton (1989). In their book they examine carefully not only the social, legal, and psychological meanings of "legitimate" authority that can serve to create a presumption of obedience but also the interpersonal pressures and associated embarrassment that can create sufficient awkwardness to prevent participants from disobeying. (For reviews of the literature on the Milgram experiment, see Blass, 1991, 1992; Miller, 1986).

Most attempts to explain Milgram's findings have focused on the relative amount of obedience that he obtained in different experimental conditions. That is, the models that have been posited seek to identify parameters of the experimental situation whose values vary from one condition to another in a way that correlates with, and hence helps to explain, the differences in obedience across conditions. Our own attempts in this chapter will differ in three principal respects. First, we will be substantially less concerned with explaining differences in obedience across conditions (at least at this stage in our research) and much more interested in explaining differences in the timing and forcefulness of participants' opposition to the experimenter within the same experimental condition. Second, in explaining participants' opposition, we shall work with parameters whose values are not only expected to change over the course of an experimental session but are also assumed to change in response to one another. Hence, we are seeking to understand the dynamic relationship among variables that shape participants' behavior over time. Third, we shall attempt to express our understanding of participants' behavior in the form of a mathematical model. This model will allow us to generate simulated results that can then be compared to our observations of real participants.

We begin with a general discussion of the data that are available to us. Next we provide a description of an experimental condition on which we focus, followed by a description of our observations of participants' behavior in that condition. Once this has been accomplished, we take up the mathematical model.

Recently, efforts to better understand Milgram's results have been advanced by the fact that his original experimental data have now been made available to researchers through the archives of the Yale University Library. Milgram audiotaped almost all of his experimental sessions. Thus we have been able to listen to audiotapes of several of Milgram's experimental sessions and to analyze, minute-by-minute, the unfolding of participants' behavior as it developed over the course of an experimental session. This type of analysis has been a source of new findings (Modigliani & Rochat, 1995; Rochat & Modigliani, 1997) and has enabled us to better understand participants' behavior during the experiment as a social situation involving an interaction over time with the authority.

By examining only Milgram's published data, one can get a general sense for how participants responded differently to different experimental conditions. However, by listening to the audiotapes of actual sessions, one can obtain a much fuller and finer understanding of the experiment because one comes to appreciate that complying with the experimenter's orders, or refusing to do so, is an incremental process that develops in step-by-step fashion. An analysis of the outcome of this process without an analysis of the process itself tells us only part of the story of participants' obedience or resistance. In short, the audiotapes are of great interest because they give a sense of what was actually happening during the course of an experiment.

In the following pages we describe and analyze a typical experimental condition and its associated results. In his book, Milgram (1974) refers to this as the "Bridgeport condition." This experimental condition was conducted in Bridgeport, Connecticut, in the offices of the "Research Associates of Bridgeport," a fictitious group Milgram created in order to conduct his experiment outside of the academic setting of Yale University.

THE BRIDGEPORT CONDITION

Upon entering the offices of the Research Associates of Bridgeport, each of the participants ($n = 40$) was introduced to the "memory and learning project" by the experimenter. Two participants were present at each session. The other "participant" was actually an accomplice of the experimenter: a 47-year-old accountant of Irish-American descent who, according to Milgram, was seen by most observers as "mild-mannered and likeable" (Milgram, 1974, p. 16). The experimenter began the session by explaining to both participants that the purpose of the research was to better understand the effects of punishment on learning and that the experiment in which they were about to participate involved the administration of a test. One participant would be the "teacher," who would administer the test, and the other would be the "learner," who would attempt to master the test items as quickly as possible. Which participant played what role was ostensibly determined randomly by drawing slips of paper. Actually, however, the drawing was rigged so that the accomplice–participant always became the learner and the real participant always became the teacher. The experimenter then explained that each time the learner gave a wrong answer on the test, the teacher would be expected to punish him with an electric shock. In order to make this possible, the teacher was seated in front of a very large shock generator displaying 30 switches, each corresponding to a voltage level ranging from 15 to 450 volts; the learner was placed in an adjacent room and wired to leads ostensibly coming from the same shock generator. He was also strapped down in his chair so that he could not leave. (In reality, the learner was not wired to the shock generator, and he never received any shocks.) Next, the experimenter informed the teacher that each time the learner made an error on the test that was about to be administered, he (the teacher) should move up one switch on the shock generator, thus increasing the shock level by 15 volts.

As the administration of the test and the shocks got under way, the accomplice–learner began making a good many errors according to a prearranged plan. As a consequence, the teacher soon found himself delivering what he believed to be higher and higher intensity shocks, to which the learner reacted with grunts and then groans. After administering the 10th level (150 volts), he heard the learner cry out in pain and ask to be released from the experiment. However, the experimenter coolly insisted that the procedure continue. If the teacher did continue, then after delivering each higher shock, he heard the learner escalate his expressions of pain until they became agonized screams, and he heard the learner's pleas to be released grow increasingly desperate. Yet, if the teacher sought reassurances from the experimenter or otherwise sought to delay or halt the procedure, the experimenter simply prodded him to continue by saying, "Please go on," or "The experiment requires that you continue." If the teacher expressed concern about the victim's health or suffering, the experimenter further prodded him by saying, offhandedly, "No, although the shocks may be painful, they're not dangerous. Continue, please." Or he would say, "Whether the learner likes it or not, we must go on until he's learned all the items correctly. Go on, please." It was only after using four such prods in succession, with the participant refusing to resume his task each time, that the experimenter stopped making further requests and officially acknowledged that the participant had become fully defiant. If the participant did not refuse to continue, the procedure was halted after the delivery of 450 volts, and the participant was considered fully obedient. Whichever way the procedure ended, the experimenter then began a process of debriefing.

DESCRIPTION OF PARTICIPANTS' BEHAVIOR
OVER THE COURSE OF THE EXPERIMENT

Thirty-six experimental sessions in the Bridgeport Condition were taped, with four sessions not fully recorded; for these, we checked the written records of the shocks participants gave, as well as the written descriptions of their behavior. In studying the audiotapes of the condition, we examined participants' behavior from the time they entered the laboratory until the time they either completed their task or else refused to do so. We found that all verbal expressions that participants directed to the experimenter could rather easily be classified along a graduated scale that ranged from wholly cooperative to highly resistant. All such expressions were in fact coded into one of the following six categories, ordered from the most compliant to the most oppositional:[1]

> 1. *Acquiesces.* Participant verbally agrees with, accepts, or affirms a request from the experimenter or silently obeys/complies without comment. (For example: "All right. The next one's 'Slow—walk, truck, dance, music.' Answer, please.")
> 2. *Checks.* Participant seeks to review, clarify, verify, confirm, or amplify a relatively narrow aspect of the experimental task. (For example: "Do you want me to keep going?" "That's the end of the list; now what?" "Is that right what I read here? It says 'danger.'")
> 3. *Notifies.* Participant seeks to inform, point out, announce, forewarn, or, more generally, to introduce information that might arguably impede continuing with the procedure or might disqualify the participant from going on. (For example: "That man is yelling in there." "He wants to get out." "I don't hear nothing, anymore." "I think he should be checked in on." "Okay, but I refuse to take the responsibility.")
> 4. *Questions.* Participant expresses doubts or skepticism about the experimenter's statements or interrogates him by requesting additional information about the larger implications of the procedure or project. (For example: "Just how far do you intend to go with this thing?" "What if something's wrong with the man—he's had an attack or something?" "Can you look in on him to see if he's all right, please?")
> 5. *Objects.* Participant overtly dissents, argues, disagrees with the experimenter or invokes some personal impediment that he claims pre-

---

[1]All the following quotations are taken from Milgram's film and book (Milgram, 1965, 1974).

vents him from continuing. (For example: "Yeah, but there's too many items left here; I mean, Geez, what if he gets them wrong?" "It goes up higher and higher; I just don't like it, myself, to be honest with you." "Well, I'm sorry, I think when shocks continue like this, they are dangerous." "We came here out of our free will; if he doesn't want to continue, I don't want to go ahead.")

6. *Refuses.* Participant overtly declines to continue or directly rejects, rebuffs, dismisses the experimenter's requests or simply stops. (For example: "If he doesn't answer, I'm not going to go any further on this." "Well, I won't continue—not with the man screaming to get out." "Look, I'm not going to go any further until I know if that man is okay." "Well, whether I'm a weakling or what … I just won't do this, I'm sorry.")

Of course, few participants used this entire range of six categories, but all of them used at least the first two.

During the early part of the experimental session, before participants actually began their task of teaching and punishing, the audiotapes clearly convey the impression that almost all participants were generally in a cooperative mood, ready to carry out the procedures described to them during the opening minutes of the session. Once everything was ready for participants to begin their task, the experimenter repeated once again the task instructions. This gave participants a chance to ask questions or otherwise comment on the experimental procedure. No participant took this opportunity to question the procedure; all participants carried forward their cooperative inclinations and began to perform the task.

Participants' readiness to follow the experimenter's instructions did not last long, however. After administering just five shocks and reaching the 75-volt level, they were confronted with their fellow participant's first sign of pain, and 10% of them responded to this expression of discomfort by speaking to the experimenter (4 out of the 40 participants did so). The oppositional level of these initial remarks was not great, but they did amount at least to "checking." For these participants, then, this was the point when their initial, wholehearted readiness to assist the experimenter in his scientific work disappeared, for they were evidently beginning to experience some doubts about the well-being of their fellow participant. As the shock levels mounted and the complaints grew louder, all other participants eventually made similar apprehensive remarks revealing similar concerns. For instance, by

150 volts, 19 (47.5%) participants had at least checked with the experimenter about the experimental procedure. By 270 volts, all (100%) participants had at least checked with the experimenter about the experimental procedure. The second thoughts that participants now had about their task caused them to change their orientation and demeanor toward the experimenter. No longer did they simply acquiesce to the experimenter's instructions and carry out their task in a prompt, straightforward manner. Instead, they began to speak to him, to look for greater guidance and reassurance, even to progressively question him about the experimental procedure and, in some cases, eventually to object to his instructions, which ultimately led about half of the participants (21 out of the 40) to refuse to complete their task. In the course of their verbal exchanges with the experimenter, participants differed in how quickly they came to oppose the experimenter's requests in a relatively direct and firm manner—that is, by questioning, objecting to, or refusing his demands. Of the 40 participants, 12 (30%) took a firm oppositional stance quite early in the experimental session—at or before the 10th shock level (150 volts), at which the fellow participant first asked to be released. Another 14 (35%) opposed the experimenter in this fashion only after the 10th shock level but before or at the 22nd shock level (330 volts). The remaining 14 (35%) never reached this level of opposition at all.

Once participants had left the cooperation mode, many of them began to manifest their increasing reluctance behaviorally, as well as verbally, by hesitating and vacillating—alternately moving ahead with the procedure and then stopping, as if deliberating on whether or not to continue. All such interruptions and delays invariably led the experimenter to start prodding the stalled participants, sternly pressing them to resume their task. If they did continue, their fellow participant would cry out in pain and anger, demanding ever more desperately to be released from the experiment. The situation was made even worse by the fact that the experimenter never acknowledged the fellow participant's complaints and pleas but instead seemed utterly indifferent to his obvious suffering. Participants were thus caught between the learner's screams of pain and the experimenter's cold determination to go on with the experiment. Often participants seemed genuinely torn—simultaneously willing to continue with the task they were being told to carry out and not willing to inflict any further suffering on this man who had done nothing to deserve his fate. In short, and not surprisingly, exposure to such extreme conflict caused most participants to feel great ambivalence, confusion, uncertainty, and distress. This was unmistakably clear from their heavy breathing, stuttering, stammering, raised or cracking voices, grumbling, groaning, inappropriate laughter, expressions of frustration, and so forth.

One way participants sought to cope with their rising distress was by trying to ignore or rationalize the suffering of their fellow participant, but this was difficult because the shocks they had to inflict were becoming more and more painful, and his cries of pain ever more intense. After 330 volts the fellow participant actually stopped responding in any way, suggesting that he had either lost consciousness or was so severely injured that he could no longer make any sound. Another way for participants to at least shorten the acute distress of this period was to rush through the remaining switches on the shock generator, which a few did do, thereby completing the task quickly and fully complying with the experimenter. A fair number of participants dealt with the extreme stress by trying to convey their growing anguish to the experimenter, but the experimenter would coolly reply, "Well, whether the learner likes it or not, we must go on until he's learned all the word pairs correctly. Please go on." Sometimes participants' distress caused them to try resisting in a somewhat confused manner—for instance, one participant notified the experimenter that he would not go on with the procedure if it meant having to administer all the remaining shocks indicated on the shock generator. Yet, having made such a statement, he, as well as all other participants, still had no way out of the experiment other than by either completing the task or refusing to do it.

At bottom, it was precisely this dilemma that made the situation so distressing, for both of these courses of action required violating a personal code, either a moral commitment not to injure an innocent person or a promise to assist a scientist in carrying out his research project. In the end, then, all participants ended their torment in one of two ways: either they complied with the experimenter's wishes by going to the end of the experimental procedure, often in a resigned and mechanical fashion, or else they began to oppose the experimenter by firmly questioning and/or objecting to the procedure and then refusing to continue, irrespective of the amount of the pressure being exerted on them by the experimenter. Our observations indicate very clearly that the vacillation period was extremely demanding for most participants, which helps to explain why this period was followed by a more stable one consisting either of capitulation and compliance or of determined refusal and escape.

Did obedient and defiant participants differ in their behavior prior to reaching the final period of either capitulation or refusal? It will be recalled that, before the final period, participants differed considerably in how early in the procedure they had first firmly opposed the experimenter's demands—that is, first begun questioning, objecting to, or refusing his requests. Some participants had begun using these verbal categories by the time the shock level reached 150 volts, some only after this point, and some never used these categories at all. Of the 21 participants who ended up defiant, 12 (57.1%) opposed the experimenter in a firm manner before or at the 150-volt level. Of the 19 participants who ended up obedient, none (0%) opposed the experimenter firmly this early in the session. Looking at these findings the other way around, of the 12 participants who firmly opposed the experimenter early in the session, all of them (100%) ended up defiant. Of the 14 who firmly opposed him later, 9 (64.3%) ended up defiant. Finally, of the 14 participants who never opposed him firmly, none (0%) ended up defiant. Thus it appears that the timing of a participant's first firm opposition is important in shaping final outcomes. Firm, early opposition seems to be a sufficient condition for successful defiance, and, not surprisingly, total lack of such firm opposition is a sufficient condition for ending up obedient. There may, of course, have been other important differences among participants, but we were unable to detect them on the basis of the audiorecordings that we were using.

To summarize our observations of the 40 participants from the Bridgeport condition: All the participants started out in a helpful, cooperative mode; gradually this condition gave way to an increasingly turbulent period that was marked by hesitation, vacillation, and very high levels of stress; finally, they reached a more stable mode in which they resolved the ambivalence and tension by either acceding to or defying the experimenter's desires. This general profile does not, however, capture every participant's experience equally well. One third of them responded fairly early to the rising tension and turbulence of the vacillation period and managed to escape the situation relatively quickly by opposing the experimenter hastily and firmly. The rest were not as fortunate in that they were unable to translate their ambivalence and distress into an effective way of opposing the experimenter. An additional fifth did manage to mount an effective opposition later in the vacillation period, but the rest were doomed to traverse the whole of this acutely distressing interval. All of these finally emerged from the experiment obedient.

Although all participants' behaviors evolved over the course of the experiment—that is, unfolded over time—they did not do so in the same way nor in any systematic or predictable fashion. As we listened to the audiotapes, we found that even when participants were in the midst of their task, it did not seem possible to anticipate their upcoming courses of action. It was particularly difficult to do so once they had entered the period of turbulence. Of course, after the fact, when we can view the entirety of each participant's data, it becomes possible to know all the available paths through the situation and even to identify the turning points of many of them. Each participant travelled through time along a unique path of verbal behaviors that could be graphed and compared to other paths of other participants, thereby providing an overall picture of all the observed paths. This overall picture, in turn, allows for numerous variations (which might arise, for example, in future replications) and still holds true as a general description of participants' possible histories over the course of the experiment. Such a realization suggests an attempt to model participants' behavior over the course of the experiment. Before turning to such a task, we present an overall picture of participants' paths in the experiment (Fig. 10.1).

A MATHEMATICAL MODEL
OF PARTICIPANTS' BEHAVIOR

We begin with a few remarks about the nature of our methods and about the form of the model presented below.

Our method is typically hypothetico-deductive (i.e., once the choice of the hypothesis is made, the consequences of this hypothesis are drawn according to mathematical reasoning). Drawing in part on impressions formed while listening to Milgram's audiorecordings, we developed a mathematical model and set its parameters and then used this model to generate results that can be compared with Milgram's data—that is, with our earlier description of participants' behavior. Such a comparison permits us to evaluate the assumptions that underlie the model. If these assumptions seem indeed to be justified, then they and the other concepts we used to build the model should prove useful in deepening our understanding of Milgram's experimental findings.

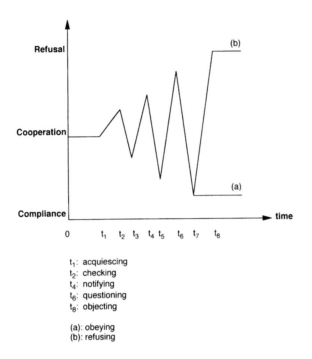

t₁: acquiescing
t₂: checking
t₄: notifying
t₆: questioning
t₈: objecting

(a): obeying
(b): refusing

Fig. 10.1.   Participants' sequence of behavior over the course of the experiment.

Because we are interested in the unfolding of participants' behavior over the course of an experimental session, time and changes over time must be taken into account. In order to do so, we develop a mathematical model that is associated with a set of theories about "dynamical systems." Such theories have a long history, dating back to Newton and Laplace in the 18th century. Researchers have continued to develop them by extending their areas of application from engineering to biology and from economics to the social sciences. Over the last 20 years, developments based on this set of theories have included catastrophe theory (Thom, 1972), chaos theory (Ruelle, 1989; Smale, 1980), and the theory of monotone systems (Hirsch, 1988).

The theory of dynamical systems provides the tools for studying how systems evolve over time. The main feature of mathematical systems is that they are defined by their state. The totality of all possible states of a system is called "state space" or "phase space." This space is described by the values of all the variables within it. For instance, in classical mechanics the variables might be the position and speed of a particle; in quantum mechanics, the particle's wave function; in ecology the size of two interacting populations; or in economics, the levels of supply and demand; and so forth. Thus the state of the system at a moment in time can be described by a point in state space. This point provides a geometrical representation of the state in the sense that it simultaneously shows, or denotes, the particular values of all the variables of the system.

As to the concept of change over time, if a specific state of the system is represented by a single point, then its evolution over time is represented by a path in state space—a path that describes the changing values of all variables over time. A dynamical system always has a law of evolution that explicitly or implicitly defines this path, that specifies how one moves from a given state to subsequent states. This law is deterministic, for it tells us that we can know the exact state of the system for any moment in time, providing only that we know its "initial condition"—its exact state when the evolution began. (A good introduction to this topic can be found in Hirsch, 1984).

HYPOTHESES AND MODEL

Our first task in building a model is to choose between two descriptions of time, namely a continuous one or a discrete one. After trying both, we chose the continuous description so that our model could be based on ordinary differential equations. Such equations are rarely used in the social sciences, but their advantage is in allowing for a qualitative discussion of the solutions of the model through the use of intuitively straightforward graphs. (It should be noted that when we tried using a discrete description of time, we obtained the same results).

Hypotheses About the State Space of Our System

The aim of our model is to account for participants' sequences of behavior in response both to the experimenter's orders and prods and to the fellow participant's expressions of protest and suffering. Hence our first variable is the participants' overt verbal behavior, which we call their (oppositional verbal) response, to be designated by r. There are a finite number of possible verbal responses for participants, and these responses are ordered in degrees. By choosing the continuous conception of time, we will be describing participants' verbal responses using the set of real numbers that lie between 0 and 1, which means that $r \in [0; 1]$, where 0 corresponds to following the experimenter's instructions faithfully and 1 corresponds to completely refusing to do so. (See Appendix D: Glossary of Symbols).

We need a second variable to account for participants' internal level of resistance, because we know that the oppositional level of their overt responses will not always match their inner state. Hence, our second variable is not directly observable, but we intend it to represent participants' psychological resistance to the experimenter's authority—a counterreaction to the experimenter's authoritative commands that is somewhat analogous to Brehm's concept of reactance (Brehm, 1966). We designate this second variable by s and, once again, assign it values that lie between 0 and 1—that is, $s \in [0; 1]$, where 0 corresponds to no resistance at all and 1 to a very high level of resistance.

We need to include two other variables, at least, to take into account the nature of the experimental situation in which participants find themselves. Our third variable is the level of pressure the experimenter is placing on participants, to be designated by p. When participants are carrying out the task, the experimenter remains quiet; however, whenever they hesitate to continue or stop altogether, then the experimenter presses them to go on. Finally, our fourth variable is the level of tension that participants are subjected to by a combination of the experimenter's increasingly insistent prodding and the knowledge that they are inflicting ever more severe pain on their fellow participant. This variable will be designated by Te.

The latter two variables, p (pressure) and Te (tension), are not independent, for their change over time is determined by other variables already in the system. Whenever a participant is complying with the experimenter's instructions, r will be close to 0 (= doing the task) and p will be low (= little or no prodding from the experimenter). But whenever a participant is refusing to follow the experimenter's instructions, r will be close to 1 (= opposing doing the task) and p will be high (= firmly prodded by the experimenter). In other words, when participants are rejecting the experimenter's instructions, the experimenter will put pressure on them to continue with the procedure; but when participants are following the experimenter's instructions, he will remain silent. This allows us to assume that p (pressure) equals r, that is, the pressure the experimenter puts on the participant equates with the level of opposition of the participant's response. This is translated into mathematical terms by the equation $p(t) = r(t)$, where t designates positive time $t \in \mathbf{R}_+$.

As an experimental session unfolds over time, participants either move ahead with their task, which causes their fellow participant to protest ever more forcefully, or else they oppose carrying out the task, which causes the experimenter to prod them with increasing firmness. Either way, tension (Te) will necessarily increase. This permits us to assume that Te is simply an increasing function of time—that it is not determined by any other parameter—because tension increases as either voltage or opposition increases over time. Thus if we consider that the experiment begins at time $t = 0$, the state space of the system is described by the variables $(r, s, t) \in [0; 1]^2 \times \mathbf{R}_+$.

Hypotheses About the Law of Evolution

It should be noted that some of our hypotheses are purely technical, and for this reason they are discussed in appendix A (Hfg0; Hf1; Hf3), whereas others are social psychological in nature and will be presented and discussed here.

We present our model in the form of differential equations where the dot designates the first derivative of the variables with respect to time, and f and g are the time-variation of the variables r and s:

$$\begin{cases} \dot{r} = g(p, s) \\ \dot{s} = f(r, s, Te) \end{cases} \tag{0}$$

This leads to the following hypothesis:

Hypothesis H0.   As described by the equations themselves, we are assuming that the variation over time in the opposition of participants' responses depends both on the amount of pressure (p) being put on them by the experimenter and on the participants' level of internal resistance (s). We are also assuming that variation over time in participants' internal resistance depends both on the level of their oppositional response and on the amount of tension developing when they so respond. In effect, then, we are assuming that the amount of tension exerted on participants directly influences their level of internal resistance and indirectly influences their verbal responses through its effects on their internal resistance.

In view of what we said earlier about the factors that determine the amount of pressure (p) and the amount of tension (Te), system (0) may be rewritten as system (1) in the following manner:

$$\begin{cases} \dot{r} = g(r, s) \\ \dot{s} = f(r, s, t) \end{cases} \qquad (1)$$

In actuality, it is not possible to associate specific functions with either f or g, for we simply do not know what these functions are. However, we can state certain hypotheses about the forms of these functions based primarily on insights gleaned from listening to Milgram's audiotapes but based also on our earlier observations about the experimental data, which led to Fig. 10.1. Indeed, listening to and analyzing Milgram's audiorecordings enabled us to recognize some of the notable features of participants' behavior as it evolved over the course of the experiment and, hence, to acquire some understanding of how participants' overt behavior changes as a function of their overt and covert levels of resistance and of the time elapsed since the start of the experimental session.

Hypothesis Hf2. There is a threshold R^*, such that if $s < R^*$, f decreases as t increases; this threshold is also such that if $s > R^*$, then f increases when t increases. Recall that f represents the variation (over time) of the resistance (s), which means that when the variation (f) is positive, the resistance (s) increases, whereas when the variation (f) is negative, the resistance (s) decreases. In other words, whenever a participant's internal resistance is below the threshold R^*, the function f will decrease as the experiment progresses, but whenever a participant's resistance is above this threshold, the function f will increase as the experiment continues to unfold. This hypothesis makes use of the assumption that, as the experiment unfolds, the tension participants experience always increases. In effect, because participants' tension increases monotonically with time, the threshold R^* can be seen as a boundary level for internal resistance, such that if a participant's internal resistance rises above this boundary or threshold, then his resistance will be further augmented as the level of tension increases; whereas if the participant's internal resistance remains below this threshold, then his resistance will be further attenuated as the level of tension increases. Put differently, the level of tension to which a participant is subjected will cause his internal resistance to either increase or decrease, depending on whether the level of his resistance is above or below the threshold. This is an interesting proposition that is rather clearly suggested by Milgram's data. It states that the tension participants experience will influence their internal resistance in opposite ways depending on whether the level of their internal resistance is relatively high or relatively low. (For a similar conclusion about the dynamics of human behavior, see Lewin (1958).

Hypothesis Hf3.   (The technical part of this hypothesis is discussed in appendix A). We imagine a curve whose equation $f = 0$ connects the points $(0; 0)$ and $(1; R^*)$. This curve is the graph of an increasing function, which means there is always a boundary path corresponding to $f = 0$.

The hypotheses about the function f presented here are illustrated in Fig. 10.2.

We now consider hypotheses about the function g.

Hypothesis Hg1.   Assume that if $s = 0$, then $g < 0$, and assume also that at the origin $(0; 0)$, $g(0; 0) = 0$. This will mean that if a participant has no internal resistance, his verbal responses will become less and less oppositional—that is, they will tend toward complete compliance.

Hypothesis Hg2.   There is a second threshold R^{**} such that:

1. If $r > 0$ and $s < R^{**}$ then $g < 0$.
2. If $r = 0$ and $s \leq R^{**}$ then $g = 0$.
3. If $1 > r \geq 0$ and $s > R^{**}$ then $g > 0$.
4. If $r = 1$ and $s \geq R^{**}$ then $g = 0$.

This means that beyond a certain threshold of internal resistance, the oppositional level of verbal responses will increase over time (along the gradation of verbal behavior described earlier), whereas below this threshold the oppositional level of verbal responses will decrease over time. In other words, when a participant's internal resistance exceeds the threshold, the opposition of his verbal responses will tend to increase toward defiance as the experiment proceeds; but when a participant's internal resistance is less than the threshold, his verbal responses will tend to decrease toward compliance as the experiment proceeds. These hypotheses about the function g are illustrated in Fig. 10.3.

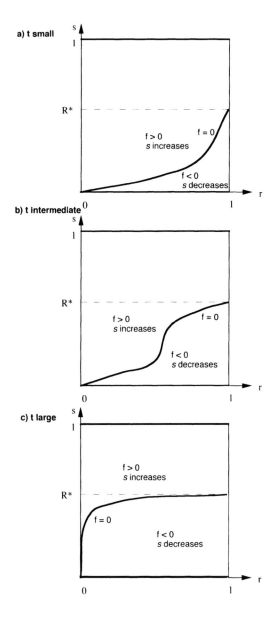

Fig. 10.2.   The square represents the state space, that is, each value of the variables response (r) and resistance (s) corresponds to a point whose coordinates are (r; s). R^* designates a threshold, which is a parameter of the model. The curve linking the points (0; 0) and (1; R^*) divides the square into two parts. In the part under the curve, the resistance (s) is decreasing, and in the part above the curve, the resistance (s) is increasing. This is also shown by the sign of the function f because this function represents the time derivative of the resistance (s).

The three figures (a), (b), and (c) show the change in the curve due to an increase of the tension (Te).

179

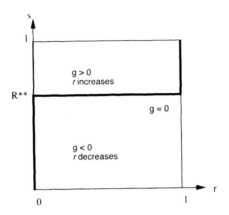

Fig. 10.3. As in Fig. 10.2, the horizontal segment whose height is R^{**} (R^{**} designates the second threshold, which is another parameter of the model) cuts the square into two parts. In the part above the threshold, the response (r) is increasing, whereas in the part under the threshold, the response (r) is decreasing. The function g represents the time derivative of the response (r); this function is not directly influenced by the increase in tension, and this is why the figure does not change over time.

Analysis of the Solutions of System (1)

We present the general idea of our analysis, and further development can be found in appendices B and C. As already noted, the state space is given by the square $[0; 1]^2$ over which system (1) defines a time-dependent vector field.[2] All paths taken together give what is called the phase portrait. The vector field changes over time. This change is related to the increasing tension participants experience as the experimental procedure unfolds—an increase due to the increase in both the voltage of the shocks being administered and the fellow participant's expressions of pain, as well as to the experimenter's determination to complete the experiment. Using the state space defined by the square $[0; 1]^2$, we can discuss how the solutions of system (1) be-

---

[2]The system (1) is a system of two differential equations. Such a system can be seen as a vector field. Indeed, for each point (r, s) of the square $[0; 1]^2$ we can calculate the components of its associated vector $\begin{pmatrix} g(r, s) \\ f(r, s, t) \end{pmatrix}$. Because the second component of the vector field, f(r, s, t), depends on time (variable t), this vector field evolves over time, and therefore is called a time-dependent vector field.

have by superimposing Fig. 10.2 and 10.3, and considering both earlier and later times.

Let us begin by illustrating the behavior of the solutions of system (1) and then proceed to examine the nature of this behavior and to discuss its implications for authority settings. We begin by considering the phase portrait when tension is fixed at a low level, which corresponds to early in time. Next, we consider the phase portrait when tension is fixed at a high level, which corresponds to late in time. Finally, we compare both of these phase portraits and draw conclusions about the behavior of the solutions when tension is increasing, which corresponds to a movement in time from earlier to later.

We consider the points **A** and **B** as two possible initial conditions representing two hypothetical participants. Fig. 10.4 shows the two points located in the state space. We represent the evolution over time of each of these points as a path starting at point **A** or at point **B**, with each step on the paths corresponding to the state of the systems at a given moment in time. It is as if the original points had begun to move (over time). This is illustrated in Fig. 10.5.

The actual form of these phase portraits depends on the values of the two thresholds (R^* and R^{**}) relative to one another. Thus we will con-

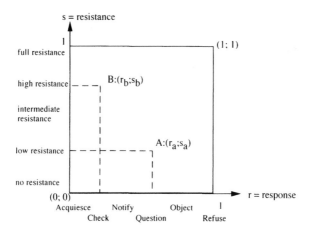

Fig. 10.4.   **A** and **B** are two points inside the square; this square represents the state space. The coordinates of **A** and **B** correspond to the specific values of the response (r) and the resistance (s). Point **A** corresponds to oppositional verbal response r_a = "questioning" and to internal resistance s_a = low. Point **B** corresponds to oppositional response r_b = "checking" and to resistance s_b = high.

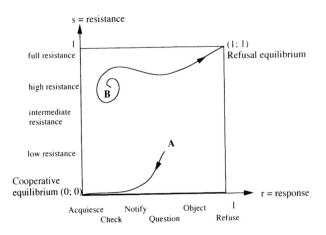

Fig. 10.5.   Here we can see that the solution that starts at point **A** leads to a decrease in both variables (r and s) and quickly converges toward the equilibrium of cooperation (0; 0). This means that participant A completes his task and ends up fully obedient. The other solution, which starts at point **B**, shows more oscillation. This participant begins by "checking" with the experimenter, then he "notifies" him, then moves back and forth between "acquiescing" and "checking," then becomes increasingly firm by notifying, questioning, objecting, and finally reaching the equilibrium of refusal (1; 1).

sider two cases $R^* > R^{**}$ and $R^* < R^{**}$. Because the case $R^* = R^{**}$ is rare, we will not consider it.

Case 1 : $R^{**} > R^*$.   When time (t) is early or intermediate, so that tension (Te) is at lower levels, the phase portrait is illustrated in Fig. 10.6.

For this case, we have two equilibrium points:[3] First there is the origin (0; 0), which corresponds to full cooperation, and second there is the vertex (1; 1), which corresponds to complete refusal. The hatched area represents the attraction domain[4] of the origin, which means that every path that starts and remains in this domain will eventually be drawn to the equilibrium point of cooperation (e.g., path **B**). All other

---

[3]If there exist particular values of the variables r and s—designated by r_0, s_0—such that $g(r_0, s_0) = 0$ and $f(r_0, s_0, t) = 0$ (for all t), then the point (r_0, s_0) is called an equilibrium (or equilibrium point). This is to say that when the initial condition of a solution of the system is (r_0, s_0), the time derivatives of the two variables are equal to zero, and thus the vector field vanishes at this point. Therefore, such a solution will stay forever at this point.

[4]In our model, all solutions tend toward an equilibrium point. For each equilibrium point there is an attraction domain that corresponds to the set of all initial conditions converging toward this point.

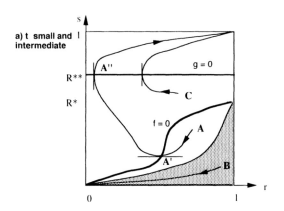

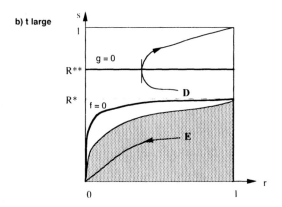

Fig. 10.6. The curves with an arrow represent the paths of the system whose initial conditions are given by the points **A, B, C, D, E**. All points starting in the hatched zone have a
path tending toward the equilibrium of cooperation (0; 0), which means that the hatched
zone is a domain of attraction. Part (a) shows the dynamics we would observe if tension
(Te) were fixed at a low or intermediate level. Part (b) shows the dynamics we would observe if tension (Te) were fixed at a high level. Comparing (a) and (b) reveals an increase
in the attraction domain.

183

paths will eventually be drawn to the equilibrium point of refusal $(1; 1)$. For example, in the solution starting at point **A**, the two variables, oppositional verbal response (r) and internal resistance (s), both begin by decreasing. When the path crosses the isocline[5] $f = 0$ at **A′** (where the tangent to the curve is horizontal), the derivative of the variable s changes sign, which means that s stops decreasing and begins increasing. From there to point **A″** internal resistance (s) continues to increase to ever higher levels, whereas verbal response (r) continues to decline in its opposition. When the path crosses the isocline $g = 0$ at point **A″** (where $s_r = R^{**}$ and where the tangent to the curve is vertical), the verbal response (r) stops declining and begins to increase to ever higher levels of opposition. Finally, the path drifts toward the equilibrium point of complete refusal.

As to point **B**, both variables decrease steadily, so that the path tends quickly toward the equilibrium of cooperation. As to point **C**, the path is similar to that of point **A**, except that internal resistance (s) increases steadily (see Fig. 10.6(a)).

When time (t) is later, so that tension has increased to high levels, the hatched area has increased as well, though it cannot go beyond the threshold R^*, as illustrated in Fig. 10.6(b). In this figure, the behavior of solutions **D** and **E** are similar to the ones for **C** and **A** in Fig. 10.6(a). However, the attraction domain almost fills the entire rectangle defined by 0 and R^*, causing the path of solution **E** to end in complete cooperation, unlike the path of solution **A**.

Thus far, we have considered the case in which tension is at low levels and the case in which tension is at high levels. Next we need to examine what happens when tension changes from being low to becoming high—that is, as time passes from early to late. This amounts to connecting the solutions found in the low-tension case (early in time) to those found in the high-tension case (later in time), thereby describing the behavior of the solutions of our model for all situations in which $R^{**} > R^*$.

All paths that start in the attraction domain of cooperation (such as point **B** in Fig. 10.6(a)) will be drawn toward the equilibrium point of cooperation. Conversely, all paths that start outside the rectangle defined by 0 and R^* (such as point **A** in Fig. 10.6(a)) will be drawn toward

---

[5]In most cases the equation $g(r, s) = 0$ (or $\dot{r} = 0$) defines a curve, called an isocline. At the point where a path (a solution) crosses this isocline its tangent is vertical. The equation $f(r, s, t) = 0$ (or $\dot{s} = 0$) defines another isocline. At the point where a path (a solution) crosses this isocline, its tangent is horizontal. The intersection of the two isoclines defines the equilibrium points.

the equilibrium point of refusal. However, any solution path that starts outside the attraction domain and with an internal resistance (s) that is below R* (as point A in Fig. 10.6(a)), embodies two distinct possibilities: Either the path quickly leaves the rectangle defined by 0 and R* and, hence, tends toward the equilibrium point of refusal, or else the attraction domain, which is constantly increasing over time, engulfs the path and captures it, creating a solution that tends toward the equilibrium point of cooperation.

Case 2. R** < R*.   In this case we have a new equilibrium point—to be designated by ε—at the intersection of the isoclines f = 0 and g = 0. Unlike the equilibria of cooperation and refusal, this equilibrium is an unstable one. It influences the transient behavior of solutions that are tending toward the equilibria (0; 0) and (1; 1). For small values of *t* (= low tension), the phase portrait is illustrated in Fig. 10.7.

Early in time all these solutions show large oscillations, especially the ones that start in the neighborhood of the unstable equilibrium ε. For instance, in Fig. 10.7, the solution starting at point A tends toward an equilibrium of refusal, but only after some oscillation. Path B oscillates as well, but it tends toward an equilibrium of cooperation. Early in time it is difficult to tell which equilibrium point a solution will ultimately be drawn to, because the attraction domain of cooperation

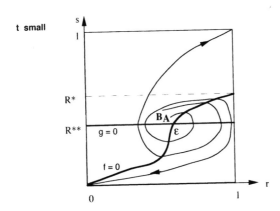

Fig. 10.7.   In the case in which the thresholds are such that R** < R*, the curves f = 0 and g = 0 have a new intersection point ε. This point is an unstable equilibrium point of the system. It can also be seen that the solutions of the system show large oscillations.

might be "rolled up" around the unstable equilibrium point ε, as shown in Fig. 10.8.

When the cases of low and high tension are examined together in order to assess what happens when tension increases, the result is identical to the case just discussed (as can be seen by adding Fig. 10.9 to Fig.

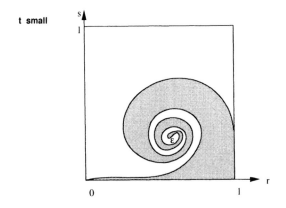

Fig. 10.8.   This figure shows what happens when the attraction domain of the equilibrium of cooperation (0; 0) wraps around the unstable equilibrium point ε. In such a case, initial conditions close to the unstable point of equilibrium ε will show large oscillations, making it practically impossible to determine a priori if they are tending toward the equilibrium of cooperation (0; 0) or toward the equilibrium of refusal (1; 1).

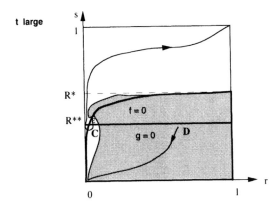

Fig. 10.9.   Despite the existence of an unstable equilibrium and oscillating solutions, when the tension (Te) increases, the attraction domain of the equilibrium of cooperation (0; 0) tends to fill the rectangle defined by 0 and R*.

10.7). The only notable difference is that early in time all paths or solutions are much more prone to oscillate—whether they ultimately tend toward an equilibrium of cooperation or refusal. In this case, then, early in the experiment hypothetical participants would show wide and repeated swings, both in the strength of their internal resistance and in the oppositional level of their verbal responses.

Conclusions

1. In the two cases considered above ($R^* > R^{**}$ and $R^* < R^{**}$), all solutions tend toward one or the other of two equilibria—that is, either an equilibrium of cooperation or an equilibrium of refusal. In both cases increases in tension cause an enlargement of the attraction domain of the equilibrium of cooperation, which eventually fills in the rectangle $[0; 1] \times [0; R^*]$. If a solution is to converge toward the equilibrium of refusal, the path must leave this area (the hatched area) quickly. In other words, those participants who end up disobedient tend to accomplish this by breaking off early in the experiment. This is a proposition that has been largely supported by analyses of Milgram's experimental data (Modigliani & Rochat, 1995).

Furthermore, case 2, $R^* < R^{**}$, shows that in this instance the solutions are subject to great oscillation. This pattern accurately captures the verbal behavior of certain real-life participants who check with and notify the experimenter, question the wisdom of the procedure, and object to the intensity of the shocks being given. Yet, between these acts of resistance, they resume the task and eventually complete the experiment. The last participant shown in Milgram's film, *Obedience*, is an excellent example (Milgram, 1965).

2. The correspondence found between the behavior of the solutions of our model and the behavior of actual participants lends support to our choice of variables—verbal response (r), resistance (s), pressure (p), and tension (Te)—as well as to our choice of two thresholds, R^* and R^{**}. The model should be applicable to all participants in any condition, provided only that the parameters are chosen appropriately (i.e., R^* and R^{**}, functions f and g, and initial conditions).

3. Further extending this approach, we could develop our hypotheses about functions f and g sufficiently to state the model on a software program that is capable of simulating participants' behavior over the course of the experiment. Thus we could move from a qualitative approach to a quantitative one. We could also attempt to specify some of the parameters of our model on the basis of experimental data.

OVERALL CONCLUSION

Studying Milgram's audio-recorded experimental sessions has given us the opportunity to improve our understanding of what happened to his participants over the course of their experimental sessions. This understanding is based partly on our listening to participants' verbal behavior during the experiment and partly on assumptions we have made about the underlying causes of this behavior—assumptions that we built into a mathematical model of the evolving experimental situation. We hoped that this model might offer a good general description of important features of participants' behavior and that it could help us identify the properties of participants and of their evolving situation that shaped their behavior.

We hypothesized, for example, that participants' changing (but invisible) level of internal resistance might play an important role in driving them toward an outcome of obedience or defiance. We further suggested that there might be important thresholds for internal resistance that, once crossed, tended to accelerate participants' movement toward one or another of these outcomes. Because levels of internal resistance are themselves a complex function of other variables that are also evolving (e.g., participants' level of verbal opposition, amount of pressure from the other actors, rising levels of tension), the task of understanding exactly how and why internal resistance might (or might not) come to exceed these thresholds is a complex one. All we can say at present is that we are able to generate patterns of simulated activity that are, in certain respects, strikingly similar to the behavior of experimental participants, and that we are able to do so by making reasonable assumptions about initial conditions, about the values of certain thresholds, and about the general forms of two functions relating our variables to one another. To take three examples of simulated findings that are similar to reality: first, virtually all participants who do not verbally oppose the experimenter's orders prior to the late portions of the experimental session end up obedient; second, most participants who end up disobedient do so by verbally opposing the experimenter quite early in the session; third, those who begin to verbally oppose the experimenter only later but do not manage to break off are prone to continue vacillating between cooperation and opposition throughout the session, ending up obedient about as often as disobedient. We hope to gain further insight into the psychological and social psychological meaning of the parameters we have chosen by studying whether they continue to generate results that mirror real participants' behavior when we modify their values in an effort to capture the diverse features of Milgram's other, and quite different, experimental conditions.

REFERENCES

Blass, T. (1991). Understanding behavior in the Milgram obedience experiment: The role of personality, situations, and their interactions. *Journal of Personality and Social Psychology, 60,* 398–413.

Blass, T. (1992). The social psychology of Stanley Milgram. In M. P. Zanna (Ed.), *Advances in experimental social psychology,* (Vol. 25, pp. 227–329). San Diego, CA: Academic Press.

Blass, T. (1993). Psychological perspectives on the perpetrators of the Holocaust: The role of situational pressures, personal dispositions, and their interactions. *Holocaust and Genocide Studies, 7,* 30–50.

Blass, T. (1998). The roots of Milgram's obedience experiments and their relevance to the Holocaust. *Analyse & Kritik, 20,* 46–53.

Bowra, C. M. (1961). *Greek lyric poetry from Alcman to Simonides.* Oxford, England: Clarendon Press.

Brehm, J. W. (1966). *A theory of psychological reactance.* New York: Academic Press.

Hartman, P. (1982). *Ordinary differential equations.* Boston: Birkhäuser.

Hirsch, M. W. (1984). The dynamical systems approach to differential equations. *Bulletin of the American Mathematical Society, 11*(1), 1–64.

Hirsch, M. W. (1988). Stability and convergence in strongly monotone dynamical systems. *Journal für reine angewandte Mathematik, 383,* 1–53.

Kelman, H. C., & Hamilton, V. L. (1989). *Crimes of obedience: Toward a social psychology of authority and responsibility.* New Haven, CT: Yale University Press.

Lewin, K. (1958). Group decision and social change. In T. M. Newcomb & E. L. Hartley (Eds.), *Readings in social psychology* (pp. 197–211). New York: Henry Holt.

Milgram, S. (1965). *Obedience.* [Film]. (Available from New York University Film Library).

Milgram, S. (1974). *Obedience to authority: An experimental view.* New York: Harper & Row.

Miller, A. G. (1986). *The obedience experiments: A case study of controversy in social science.* New York: Praeger.

Modigliani, A., & Rochat, F. (1995). The role of interaction sequences and the timing of resistance in shaping obedience and defiance to authority. *Journal of Social Issues, 51*(3), 107–123.

Rochat, F., & Modigliani, A. (1997). Authority: Obedience, defiance, and identification in experimental and historical contexts. In M. Gold (Ed.), *A new outline of social psychology* (pp. 235–246). Washington, DC: American Psychological Association.

Ruelle, D. (1989). *Elements of differential dynamics and bifurcation theory.* Boston: Academic Press.

Simon, H. A. (1945). *Administrative behavior.* New York: The Free Press.

Smale, S. (1980). *The mathematics of time.* New York: Springer-Verlag.

Thom, R. (1972). *Structural stability and morphogenesis.* Reading, MA: Benjamin.

Yoshizawa, T. (1966). *Stability theory by Lyapunov's second method.* Tokyo: Mathematical Society of Japan.

Yoshizawa, T. (1975). *Stability theory and the existence of periodic solutions and almost periodic solutions.* New York: Springer-Verlag.

APPENDIX A: ABOUT THE HYPOTHESES

We present the complementary hypotheses omitted in the text because of their technical features.

Hypothesis Hfg0:

The functions f and g are assumed to be continuously differentiable. In fact, being locally lipschitzian is a sufficient condition; see Hartman (1982).

Hypothesis Hf1:

If $s = 0$ or $s = 1$, then $f = 0$, which means that $f(r, 0, t) = f(r, 1, t) = 0$ for all r and t. This hypothesis means that, because participants' resistance cannot be a negative number nor any number greater than one, roughly speaking, "no resistance" corresponds to the minimum of $s(t)$ and 1 to "maximum resistance."

Hypothesis Hf3:

Except the cases $s = 0$ and $s = 1$, the equation $f(r, s, t_o) = 0$, for all t_o fixed, defines a curve connecting the points $(0, 0)$ and $(1, R^*)$. Furthermore, this curve is the graph of an increasing function. This hypothesis is mainly technical, but it can be seen as a complement to the hypotheses Hf2 and Hfg0.

APPENDIX B: THE EQUILIBRIA OF THE SYSTEM (1)

The equilibria are given by the intersection of the isoclines $f = 0$ and $g = 0$ (Fig. 10.2 and 10.3). In the case in which $R^{**} > R^*$, the only equilibria are the equilibrium of cooperation $(0, 0)$ and the equilibrium of refusal $(1, 1)$. In the case in which $R^{**} < R^*$, the isoclines have another point of intersection ε: (z, R^{**}), where z is such that, for this number, the increasing function, mentioned at Hf3, takes the value R^{**}. This point is an equilibrium only if we consider the tension Te fixed (see appendix C). As time increases, ε converges to the point $(0, R^{**})$, which can be seen as an asymptotic unstable equilibrium.

It should be noted that in this case, the point $(1, R^*)$ belongs to the intersection of the isoclines $f = 0$ and $g = 0$. This point is another equilibrium that corresponds to a participant's refusal associated with his intermediate resistance corresponding to the threshold R^*. This equilibrium is highly unstable and has no influence on the dynamics of the solutions. For this reason we did not consider it in the main text.

APPENDIX C: THE ANALYSIS OF THE BEHAVIOR OF THE SOLUTIONS

In this appendix we present a few remarks providing some details and some references that should prove helpful in understanding our statements about the behavior of the solutions of the system (1).

Existence and Unicity of the Solutions

With hypothesis Hfg0, our supposition was that the functions f and g were continuously differentiable. This condition assures us of the existence and unicity of the solutions, according to the classical mathematical theorems of ordinary differential equations (Hartman, 1982).

Completeness

Because the domain $[0; 1]^2$ is compact, the aforementioned classical theorems assure us that the solutions are semicomplete, that is, defined for all positive times.

The Analysis of the Phase Portraits at a Fixed Time

Because the function f depends on time, one might expect it to be incorrect to do an analysis of the phase portraits at a fixed time. Yet, providing that the nonautonomous system converges toward an autonomous system, which would correspond in our case to the maximum of the tension, it can be done. This condition can be translated into mathematical language, as Yoshizawa did some years ago (Yoshizawa, 1966, 1975).

APPENDIX D: GLOSSARY OF SYMBOLS

Numbers and Sets

R	the set of real numbers.
R_+	the set of positive real numbers (0 included).
$\in$	belongs to.
$[0; 1]$	the set of real numbers that are greater than or equal to zero and smaller than or equal to 1. Such sets are called intervals.

$[0; 1]^2$ is the set of all pairs of numbers (x, y), where x and $y \in$ $[0; 1]$. Geometrically speaking, $[0; 1]^2$ is represented by a square, as shown in Fig. 10.4.

Variables and Parameters

r the variable "response," which is a number belonging to the interval $[0; 1]$.

s the variable "resistance," which is a number belonging to the interval $[0; 1]$.

R^*, R^{**} respectively, the value of the first and the second threshold of resistance.

$\dot{r}, \dot{s}$ the dot on the variable is the first derivative of a variable with respect to time.

Hypotheses

H0   hypothesis #0 about the model

Hfg0   hypothesis #0 about the functions f and g

Hf1   hypothesis #1 about the function f

Hg2   hypothesis #2 about the function g

11

Reflections on the Stanford Prison Experiment: Genesis, Transformations, Consequences

Philip G. Zimbardo
Stanford University
Christina Maslach
University of California, Berkeley
Craig Haney
University of California, Santa Cruz

PROLOGUE
Philip G. Zimbardo

In a sense, this chapter does not fit well in the frame of this book on Milgram's paradigmatic research on obedience to authority. It is less about extreme forms of interpersonal compliance to the demands of unjust authority than it is about emerging conformity pressures in "total situations" in which the processes of deindividuation and dehumanization are institutionalized. However, in another sense, it is the natural complementary bookend to chapters tied to Milgram's obedience paradigm, which between them hold up the lessons of the power of social situations to overwhelm individual dispositions and even to degrade the quality of human nature.

Whereas a central contribution of Milgram's paradigm was to quantify aggression and thus the extent of obedience using a simple but impressive technology, the value of the Stanford Prison Experiment (SPE) resides in demonstrating the evil that good people can be readily induced into doing to other good people within the context of socially approved roles, rules, and norms, a legitimizing ideology, and institutional support that transcends individual agency. In addition, although the obedient participants in Milgram's many replications typically experienced distress for their "shocking" behavior, their participation lasted for only about one half hour, after which they learned that no one was really harmed. By contrast, participants in the SPE endured 6 days and nights of intense, often hostile, interactions that escalated daily in the level of interpersonal aggression of guards against prisoners. Take, as but one example of the confrontations that occurred repeatedly during the prison study, this statement found in a guard's diary: "During the inspection ... the prisoner ... grabbed my throat, and although I was really scared, I lashed out with my stick and hit him in the chin."

The authority that created the prison setting was typically not in sight of the participants, but rather I, in the role of prison superintendent, became an agency or remote agent overseeing the daily and nightly confrontations between these opposing forces. It became my job to hold in check the growing violence and arbitrary displays of power of the guards rather than to be the Milgramesque authority who, in becoming transformed from just to unjust as the learner's "suffering" intensified, demanded ever more extreme reactions from the participants. Indeed, it was just the opposite.

This chapter is the product of a 1996 APA symposium held in Toronto, Canada, honoring the 25th anniversary of the SPE. Editor Tom Blass thought that its basic themes could somehow mesh with the other contributions honoring and extending the classic work of Stanley Milgram. That symposium began with my overview of the genesis of the study, outlining some of the processes involved and the lessons learned from it. I highlighted the drama of the study with slides and archival footage, now contained in a video titled *Quiet Rage: The Stanford Prison Experiment* (Zimbardo, 1989). Christina Maslach presented the perspective of an "outsider" who witnessed the unimaginable transformations of character of the participants—and of herself—and heroically challenged the authority to end the study. Craig Haney, who had assisted in all phases of the study, along with William Curtis Banks, described how current conditions in real prisons could benefit from application of the lessons of the SPE. We follow that same sequential flow here, giving very personal accounts of our experiences in this loosely connected, tripartite structure.

But before doing so, I want to exercise the prerogative of seniority to interject some reflections on my personal association with Star ley Milgram that links us intimately beyond the facts of our most salient research. So allow me to share a few remembrances of the "good old days" before we turn to our analysis of the Stanford Prison Experiment.

Stanley and I were high school classmates at James Monroe High School in the Bronx, he being considered the smartest kid and I voted the most popular. We sometimes talked about the reasons for seemingly strange or irrational behavior by teachers, peers, or people in the real world that violated our expectations. Not coming from well-to-do homes, we gravitated toward situational explanations and away from dispositional ones to make sense of such anomalies. The rich and powerful want to take personal credit for their success and to blame the faults of the poor on their defects. But we knew better; it was usually the situation that mattered, by our account.

After graduation in 1950, we went to separate colleges and graduate schools but were reunited briefly a decade later at Yale University. Stanley had started as a new assistant professor in 1960, whereas I left Yale to start my career at New York University. I returned the next year to teach part time in the School of Education and met with him on several occasions. Stanley began his landmark obedience studies in 1961, and, when I asked about his research, Stanley chose not to share his ideas or emerging data with me (or anyone else, I gather). He said that he preferred to wait until his work was published, and then he would be pleased to discuss it. But I still regret this lost opportunity to share ideas at their most exciting stage of emergence.

We exchanged correspondence in 1965; I congratulated Stanley on winning the American Association for the Advancement of Science (AAAS) prize, and he responded with the hope of increasing our contact in the future. He called me a while later to say he was using my book *The Cognitive Control of Motivation* (Zimbardo, 1969) as a text in his methodology course because it represented the most rigorous and interesting studies testing predictions from dissonance theory. Obviously flattered, I worked at renewing our relationship, planning a jointly authored social psychology textbook along with Bob Abelson (that unfortunately never materialized), calling him more often, and meeting him at conventions. Several interesting conversations deserve mention here. I realized one day while teaching about the Milgram paradigm that we all focus on the obedient participants and ignore the heroic ones who resisted the situational pressures to obey the authority. I wondered what they did after they refused to continue shocking the "learner." Did they get out of their assigned seat and run to aid the victim in apparent distress or insist that the experimenter do so? When I posed this question to Stanley, he searched his memory and answered, "Not one, not ever!" That means that he really demonstrated a more fundamental level of obedience that was total—100% of the participants followed the programmed dictates from elementary school authority to stay in your seat until granted permission to leave. We both discussed but did not act on the need for psychologists to study the dissidents, the rebels, the whistle-blowing heroes. Demonstrating the power of the situation to make good people do evil deeds somehow held more appeal to us than the more difficult reverse process of showing how ordinary people could be induced to do heroic deeds within a Milgram-like paradigm.

At APA in 1971, I modified my planned invited address to include graphic procedural slides and some hot new data I had just obtained from a study that had ended only weeks before, the Stanford Prison Experiment. Stanley was in the audience and was excited, in our conversation afterwards, about the conceptual similarity of our research and really delighted that I would soon be diffusing some of the critical heat off him regarding the ethics of such "dark side of human nature" research.

One of my greatest surprises from Stanley came at the height of his career when he confided in me that he felt his research was underappreciated and not sufficiently respected by his social psychology colleagues. I was at first stunned because his obedience studies are the most cited in every introductory and social psychology text I know. But perhaps what he meant was that, unlike Leon Festinger, his work did not generate countless dissertations nor instigate more than a few dozen studies claiming to prove or disprove his theory (see Blass, 1992). And in that sense, Stanley was right. He was the master at demonstrating phenomena in captivating scenarios. His research revealed vital aspects of human nature and social processes, and his readers, his film observers, were, in a sense, the control condition. It was their accounts of what ought to have happened, how they would have behaved, that served as the base rate against which Stanley's results could be evaluated. Stanley Milgram, for all his genius, was not a theoretician who inspired many others to support or challenge his derivations. He was a keen observer of human nature, a brilliant empiricist, who could translate abstract conceptions and socially intriguing questions into elegant experimentally valid plots for his actors to play out and improvise—which leads to my final link in the connection between Stanley and me.

Only after Stanley died did I become aware of our mutual admiration for Allen Funt, creator of *Candid Camera*. I consider Funt to be one of the most creative, intuitive social psychologists on the planet. For 50 years he has been contriving experimental scenarios in which ordinary people face a challenge to their usual perceptions or functioning. He manipulates situations to reveal truths about compliance, conformity, the power of signs and symbols, and various forms of mindless obedience. I persuaded Funt to allow me to work with him in preparing sets of his videos for distribution to teachers of introductory psychology and others for social psychology. In preparing a viewer/instructor's manual to accompany the videos and laser disks (Zimbardo & Funt, 1992), I came across an article (Milgram & Sabini, 1979) that Stanley had written earlier with John Sabini about the vital lessons of *Candid Camera* for psychologists and his respect for its creator (see Zimbardo & Funt, 1992).

I end this prologue with one final surprise. When interviewing Funt for an invited article in *Psychology Today* (Zimbardo, 1985)—as part of my long-term persuasive effort to get him to share those videos with academicians—I was intrigued by Funt's assertion that he had absolutely no formal psychological background or training that might have provided a scaffold for his *Candid Camera* paradigms. Just as my probing was reaching a dead end in trying to discover some relevant historical contributions, Funt recalled having worked his senior year at Cornell University as a research assistant for some German professor in the School of Home Economics. His job was to observe, from behind a one-way mirror, different feeding patterns of mothers and nurses as they fed food to their babies or to foundlings. The year was 1934. Funt strained his memory further on questioning and remembered that the professor was "a Kurt, something or other." It was indeed Kurt Lewin, the seminal figure in experimental social psychology, intellectual grandfather to Stanley Milgram, Allen Funt, me, and a whole generation of social psychologists. I think that Stanley would have enjoyed hearing that story.

THE SPE: WHAT IT WAS, WHERE IT CAME FROM, AND WHAT CAME OUT OF IT
Philip G. Zimbardo

The serenity of a summer Sunday morning in Palo Alto, California, was suddenly shattered by the sirens of a police squad car sweeping through town in a surprise mass arrest of college students for a variety of felony code violations. They were handcuffed, searched, warned of their legal rights, and then taken to police headquarters for a formal booking procedure. Let's return to that scene on August 14, 1971, to recall what those arrests were all about.

Synopsis of the Research

The police had agreed to cooperate with our research team in order to increase the "mundane realism" of having one's freedom suddenly taken away by the police rather than surrendering it voluntarily as a research participant who had volunteered for an experiment. The city police chief was in a cooperative and conciliatory mood after tensions had run high on Stanford's campus following violent confrontations between his police and student anti-Vietnam War protesters. I capitalized on these positive emotions to help defuse these tensions between police and college students and thereby to solicit the invaluable assistance of police officers in dramatizing our study from the outset.

These college students had answered an ad in the local newspaper inviting volunteers for a study of prison life that would run up to 2 weeks for the pay of $15 a day. They were students from all over the United States, most of whom had just completed summer school courses at Stanford or the University of California, Berkeley. Seventy of those who had called our office were invited to take a battery of psychological tests (the California Personality Inventory) and engage in interviews conducted by Craig Haney and Curtis Banks, who were graduate students at that time. We were assisted by David Jaffe, an undergraduate who played the role of prison warden. I played the role of prison superintendent, in addition to being the principal investigator, which would later prove to be a serious error in judgment.

Two dozen of those judged most normal, average, and healthy on all dimensions we assessed were selected to be the participants in our experiment. They were randomly assigned to the two treatments of mock prisoner and mock guard. Thus there were no systematic differences between them initially nor systematic preferences for role assignments. Virtually all had indicated a preference for being a prisoner because they could not imagine going to college and ending up as a prison guard. On the other hand, they could imagine being imprisoned for a driving violation or some act of civil disobedience and thus felt they might learn something of value from this experience should that ever happen.

The guards helped us to complete the final stages in the construction of the mock prison in the basement of the Stanford University psychology department. The setting was a barren hallway, without windows or natural light. Office doors were fitted with iron bars, and closets were converted to dark, solitary confinement areas. The "yard" was the 30-foot-long hallway in front of the three prison cells—converted from small staff offices. Three offices were set up in an adjacent hallway for the staff: one for the guards to change into and out of their uniforms, one for the warden, and the third for the superintendent. Provision was made for space in the hallway to accommodate visitors on visitors' nights. There was only a single door for access and exit, the other end of the corridor having been closed off by a wall we erected. A small opening in that wall was provided for a video camera and for inconspicuous observation. The cells were bugged with microphones so that prisoner conversations could be secretly monitored.

The guards were invited also to select their own military-style uniforms at a local army surplus store and met as a group for a general orientation and to formulate rules for proper prisoner behavior on the Saturday before the next day's arrests. We wanted the guards to feel as if it were "their prison" and that soon they would be hosting a group of prisoner-guests.

The would-be prisoners were told to wait at home or at the address they provided us, and we would contact them on Sunday. After the surprise arrest by the police, they were brought to our simulated prison environment, where they underwent a degradation ceremony as part of the initiation into their new role. This is standard operating procedure in many prisons and military institutions, according to our prison consultant, a recently paroled ex-convict, Carlo Prescott. Nine prisoners filled three cells, and three guards staffed each of the 8-hour shifts, supplemented by backups on standby call. Additional participants were also on standby as replacements if need be, one of whom was called on midweek to take the place of a released prisoner. The prisoners wore uniforms that consisted of smocks with numbers sewn on front and back, ankle chains, nylon stocking caps (to simulate the uniform appearance from having one's hair cut off), and rubber thongs on their feet, but no underwear. Among the coercive rules formulated by the guards were those requiring the prisoners to refer to themselves and each other only by their prison number and to the guards as "Mr. Correctional Officer."

Much of the daily chronology of behavioral actions was videotaped for later analysis, along with a variety of other observations, interviews, tests, diaries, daily reports, and follow-up surveys that together constituted the empirical data of the study. Of course, we were studying both guard and prisoner behavior, so neither group was given any instructions on how to behave. The guards were merely told to maintain law and order, to use their billy clubs as only symbolic weapons and not actual ones, and to realize that if the prisoners escaped the study would be terminated.

It is important to realize that both groups had completed informed-consent forms indicating that some of their basic civil rights would have to be violated if they were selected for the prisoner role and that only minimally adequate diet and health care would be provided. The university Human Subjects Review Board approved of the study with only minor limitations that we followed, such as alerting Student Health Services of our research and also providing fire extinguishers because there was minimal access to this space. Ironically, the guards later used these extinguishers as weapons to subdue the prisoners with their forceful blasts.

It took a full day for most of the guards to adapt to their new, unfamiliar roles as dominating, powerful, and coercive. Initial encounters were marked by awkwardness between both groups of participants. However, the situation was radically changed on the second day, when several prisoners led all the others in a rebellion against the coercive rules and restraints of the situation. They tried to individuate themselves, ripped off their sewn-on prisoner numbers, locked themselves into their cells, and taunted the guards. I told the guards that they had to handle this surprising turn of events on their own. They called in all the standby guards, and the night shift stayed overtime. Together, they crushed the prisoner rebellion and developed a greater sense of guard camaraderie, along with a personal dislike of some of the prisoners who had insulted them to their face. The prisoners were punished in a variety of ways. They were stripped naked, put in solitary confinement for hours on end, deprived of meals and blankets or pillows, and forced to do push-ups, jumping jacks, and meaningless activities. The guards also generated a psychological tactic of dividing and conquering their enemy by creating a "privilege cell" in which the least rebellious prisoners were put to enjoy the privilege of a good meal or a bed to sleep on. This tactic did have the immediate effect of creating suspicion and distrust among the prisoners.

We observed and documented on videotape that the guards steadily increased their coercive and aggressive tactics, humiliation, and dehumanization of the prisoners day by day. The staff had to remind the guards frequently to refrain from such abuses. However, the guards' hostile treatment of the prisoners, together with arbitrary and capricious displays of their dominating power and authority, soon began to have adverse effects on the prisoners. Within 36 hours after being arrested, the first prisoner had to be released because of extreme stress reactions of crying, screaming, cursing, and irrational actions that seemed to be pathological. The guards were most sadistic in waking prisoners from their sleep several times a night for "counts," supposedly designed for prisoners to learn their identification numbers but actually to use the occasion to taunt them, punish them, and play games with them, or rather on them. Deprivation of sleep, particularly REM sleep, also gradually took a toll on the prisoners. Interestingly, the worst abuses by the guards came on the late-night shift, when they thought the staff was asleep and they were not being monitored.

That first prisoner to be released, Prisoner 8612, had been one of the ringleaders of the earlier rebellion, and he jolted his fellow prisoners by announcing that they would not be allowed to quit the experiment even if they requested it. The shock waves from this false assertion reverberated through all of the prisoners and converted the simulated experiment into "a real prison run by psychologists instead of run by the state," according to one of the prisoners. After that, some prisoners decided to become "good prisoners," obeying every rule and following all prison procedures faithfully in zombie-like fashion. Powerful conformity pressures eliminated individual differences among the prisoners. But another generalized reaction was to imitate the behavior of Prisoner 8612 and passively escape by acting "crazy" and forcing the staff to release them prematurely. On each of the next three days a prisoner took that path out of the SPE. A fifth prisoner was released after he broke out in a full body rash following the rejection of his appeal for parole by our mock parole board. The parole board heard prisoner requests for early parole and refutations by the guards. The board consisted of secretaries, graduate students, and others, headed by our prison consultant, who was familiar with such hearings because his own parole requests had been turned down at least 16 times.

Although most of the time during the day and night the only interactions that took place were between prisoners and guards, it should be noted that probably as many as 100 other people came down to our basement prison to play some role in this drama. On Visitors' Night, about two dozen parents and friends came to see their prisoners. A former prison chaplain visited, interviewed all but one of the inmates, and reported that their reactions were very much like those of first-time offenders he had observed in real prisons. Our two parole boards consisted of another 10 outsiders. Perhaps as many as 20 psychology graduate students and faculty looked in from the observation window or at the video monitor during the experiment or played more direct roles inadvertently. Others helped with interviews and various chores during the study. Finally, a public defender came to interview the remaining inmates on the last day. He came at the request of the mother of one of the prisoners, who had been informed by the Catholic priest (who had visited our prison earlier) that her son wanted legal counsel to help him get out of the detention facility in which he was being held. He too likened their mental and behavioral state to those of real prisoners and jailed citizens awaiting trial.

We had to call off the experiment and close down our prison after only 6 days of what might have been a 2-week long study of the psychological dynamics of prison life. We had to do so because too many normal young men were behaving pathologically as powerless prisoners or as sadistic, all-powerful guards. Recall that we had spent much time and effort in a selection process that chose only the most normal, healthy, well-adjusted college students as our sample of research participants. At the beginning of the study there were no differences between those assigned randomly to guard and prisoner roles. In less than a week, there were no similarities among them; they had become totally different creatures. Guard behavior varied from being fully sadistic to occasionally acting so to being a tough guard who "went by the book" and, for a few, to being "good guards" by default. That is, they did not degrade or harass the prisoners, and even did small favors for them from time to time, but never, not once, did any of the so-called good guards ever contest an order by a sadistic guard, intervene to stop or prevent despicable behavior by another guard, or come to work late or leave early. In a real sense, it was the good guards who most kept the prisoners in line because the prisoners wanted their approval and feared things would get worse if those good guards quit or ever took a dislike to them.

Building on this brief synopsis of an intensely profound and complex experience, I next want to outline why this study was conducted as it was and what we learned from it. Before doing so, I should preview the next section of this chapter by noting that the immediate impetus for terminating the study came from an unexpected source, a young woman, recently graduated with a PhD from our department, who had agreed to assist us with some interviews on Friday. She came in from the cold and saw the raw, full-blown madness of this place that we all had gradually accommodated to day by day. She got emotionally upset, angry, and confused. But in the end, she challenged us to examine the madness she observed—that we had created. If we allowed it to continue further, she reminded us of our ethical responsibility for the consequences and well-being of the young men entrusted to our care as research participants.

Genesis of the Experiment: Why Did We Do This Study?

There were three reasons for conducting this study, two conceptual and one pedagogical. I had been conducting research for some years earlier on deindividuation, vandalism, and dehumanization that illustrated the ease with which ordinary people could be led to engage in antisocial acts by putting them into situations in which they felt anonymous or in which they could perceive others in ways that made them less than human, as enemies or objects. This research is summarized in Zimbardo (1970). I wondered, along with my research associates, Craig Haney and Curt Banks, what would happen if we aggregated all of these processes, making some participants feel deindividuated and others dehumanized within an anonymous environment, that constituted a "total environment" (see Lifton, 1969) in a controlled experimental setting. That was the primary reason for conducting this study.

A related second conceptual reason was to generate another test of the power of social situations over individual dispositions without relying on the kind of face-to-face imposition of authority surveillance that was central in Stanley Milgram's obedience studies (see Milgram, 1992). In many real-life situations, people are seduced to behave in evil ways without the coercive control of an authority figure demanding their compliance or obedience. In the SPE, we focused on the power of roles, rules, symbols, group identity, and situational validation of ordinarily ego-alien behaviors and behavioral styles. We were influenced here by earlier reports of "brainwashing" and "milieu control" coming out of accounts of the Korean War and Chinese Communist indoctrination methods (Schein, 1956).

Pedagogically, the study had its roots in a social psychology course I had taught the previous spring, after the student strikes against the university as part of anti-Vietnam War activities. I invited students to reverse roles and instruct me on 10 topics that interested me but that I had not had the time to investigate. They were primarily topics and issues that were at the interface of sociology and psychology or of institutions and individuals, such as the effects of being put into an old-age home, media distortion of information, and the psychology of imprisonment. The group of students, headed by David Jaffe, who chose the prison topic conducted a mock prison experiential learning session over a weekend just before they were to make their class presentation. The dramatically powerful impact this brief experience had on many of them surprised me and forced us to consider whether such a situation could really generate so much distress and role identification or whether the students who chose to study prisons, among the many other options available to the class, were in some way more "pathological" than the rest of the ordinary students. The only way to resolve that ambiguity was to conduct a controlled experiment that eliminated self-selection factors, and so we did.

Ten Lessons Learned From the SPE

1. Some situations can exert powerful influences over individuals, causing them to behave in ways they would not, could not, predict in advance (see Ross & Nisbett, 1991). In trying to understand the causes of complex, puzzling behavior, it is best to start with a situational analysis and yield to the dispositional only when the situational fails to do a satisfactory causal job.

2. Situational power is most salient in novel settings in which the participants cannot call on previous guidelines for their new behavior and have no historical references to rely on and in which their habitual ways of behaving and coping are not reinforced. Under such circumstances, personality variables have little predictive utility because they depend on estimations of future actions based on characteristic past reactions in certain situations—but rarely in the kind of situation currently being encountered. Personality tests simply do not assess such behaviors but rely on asking about typical reactions to known situations—namely, a historical account of the self.

3. Situational power involves ambiguity of role boundaries, authoritative or institutionalized permission to behave in prescribed ways or to disinhibit traditionally disapproved ways of responding. It requires situational validation of playing new roles, following new rules, and taking actions that ordinarily would be constrained by laws, norms, morals, and ethics. Such validation usually comes cloaked in the mantle of ideology; value systems considered to be sacred and based on apparently good, virtuous, valued moral imperatives (for social psychologists, ideology equals their experimental "cover story").

4. Role playing—even when acknowledged to be artificial, temporary, and situationally bound—can still come to exert a profoundly realistic impact on the actors. Private attitudes, values, and beliefs are likely to be modified to bring them in line with the role enactment, as shown by many experiments in dissonance theory (Festinger, 1957; see Zimbardo & Leippe, 1991). This dissonance effect becomes greater as the justification for such role enactment decreases—for example, when it is carried out for less money, under less threat, or with only minimally sufficient justification or adequate rationale provided. That is one of the motivational mechanisms for the changes we observed in our guards. They had to work long, hard shifts for a small wage of less than $2 an hour and were given minimal direction on how to play the role of guard, but they had to sustain the role consistently over days whenever they were in uniform, on the yard, or in the presence of others, whether prisoners, parents, or other visitors. Such dissonance forces are likely to have been major causes for the internalization of the public role behaviors into private supporting cognitive and affective response styles. We also have to add that the group pressures from other guards had a significant impact on being a "team player," on conforming to or at least not challenging what seemed to be the emergent norm of dehumanizing the prisoners in various ways. Finally, let us

take into account that the initial script for guard or prisoner role playing came from the participants' own experiences with power and powerlessness, of seeing parental interactions, of dealing with authority, and of seeing movies and reading accounts of prison life. As in Milgram's research, we did not have to teach the actors how to play their roles. Society had done that for us. We had only to record the extent of their improvisation within these roles—as our data.

5. Good people can be induced, seduced, initiated into behaving in evil (irrational, stupid, self-destructive, antisocial) ways by immersion in "total situations" that can transform human nature in ways that challenge our sense of the stability and consistency of individual personality, character, and morality (Lifton, 1969). It is a lesson seen in the Nazi concentration camp guards; among destructive cults, such as Jim Jones' Peoples Temple or more recently the Japanese Aum cult; and in the atrocities committed in Bosnia, Kosovo, Rwanda, and Burundi, among others. Thus any deed that any human being has ever done, however horrible, is possible for any of us to do—under the right or wrong situational pressures. That knowledge does not excuse evil; rather, it democratizes it, shares its blame among ordinary participants, rather than demonizes it. Recently, a program at the U.S. Air Force Academy (code-named SERE) that was designed to train cadets for survival and escape from enemy capture had to be terminated early because it got out of control. As part of a "sexual exploitation scenario," women cadets were beaten repeatedly, degraded, humiliated, put in solitary confinement, deprived of sleep, and made to wear hoods over their heads—all much like the SPE. But in addition, the women cadets in this course were subjected to simulated rapes by interrogators that were realistic enough to cause posttraumatic stress disorder. These "rapes" were videotaped and also watched by other cadets, none of whom ever intervened. The grandfather of one abused female cadet, himself a World War II hero, said, "I can't believe that all these men, these elite boys, could stand around and watch a young woman get degraded and not one had enough guts to stop it" (Palmer, 1995, p. 24). After watching our "good guards" be similarly immobilized when witnessing SPE abuses, I can now understand how that could happen.

6. Human nature can be transformed within certain powerful social settings in ways as dramatic as the chemical transformation in the captivating fable of Dr. Jekyll and Mr. Hyde. I think it is that *transformation of character* that accounts for the enduring interest in this experiment for more than a quarter of a century. A recent analysis of the SPE by an

Australian psychologist (Carr, 1995) reports that undergraduate students in that country who learn about the study are left surprised, disturbed, and mystified by it. He notes:

> Judging by the reactions of our own students, it has even more impact than either Asch's "line-length" study (Asch, 1951) or Milgram's (1963) obedience study. What seems to strike home is that Zimbardo's situation impacted much more deeply on his subjects, reportedly corrupting their own innermost beliefs and feelings—and all this without involving the direct pressure to change which runs through the classic conformity and obedience studies. (Carr, 1995, p. 31)

7. Despite the artificiality of controlled experimental research such as the SPE or any of Milgram's many variations on the obedience paradigm, when such research is conducted in a way that captures essential features of "mundane realism," the results do have considerable generalizability power. In recent years, it has become customary to deride such research as limited by context-specific considerations, as not really credible to the research participants, or as not tapping the vital dimensions of the naturalistic equivalent. If this were so, there would be no reason to ever go through the enormous efforts involved in doing such research well. We believe that much of that criticism is misguided and comes from colleagues who don't know how to do such research or how to make it work or who misunderstand the value of a psychologically *functional* equivalent of a real-world process or phenomenon. Several previous chapters in this volume document eloquently the generalizability of Milgram's experiments.

I would like to call attention to two parallels to the SPE: one recent, the other from an earlier era. On July 22, 1995, news headlines chronicled, "Guards abused inmates in immigration center" (Dunn, 1995, p. A6). The article, reprinted in the *San Francisco Chronicle* from the *New York Times*, reported on an investigation of a New Jersey detention center holding immigrants awaiting deportation. It outlined "a culture of abuse that had quickly developed at the detention center," in which "underpaid and poorly trained guards had beaten detainees, singling out the midnight shift as particularly abusive." Investigators found that "guards routinely participated in acts meant to degrade and harass, such as locking detainees in isolation and repeatedly waking them in the middle of the night." This was all possible in part because "the detention center had become a closed and private world." Such an account mirrors exactly what transpired in the SPE: The worst abuses were by guards on our midnight shift, who thought they were not being monitored by the research team; they degraded, harassed, and woke the prisoners repeatedly every night, and at times hit them and locked them in isolation—and they were also underpaid and poorly trained to be guards.

Historian Christopher Browning (1992) provides a chilling account of a little-known series of mass murders during the Holocaust. A group of older reserve policemen from Hamburg, Germany, was sent to Poland to round up and execute all the Jews living in rural areas because it was too costly and inconvenient to ship them to the concentration camps for extermination. In his book, appropriately titled *Ordinary Men*, Browning documents how these men were induced to commit the atrocities of shooting Jewish men, women, and children, doing the killing up close and personal, without the technology of the gas chambers to distance the crimes against humanity. The author goes on to note, "Zimbardo's spectrum of guard behavior bears an uncanny resemblance to the groupings that emerged within Reserve Police Battalion 101" (p. 168). He shows how some became sadistically "cruel and tough," enjoying the killings, whereas others were "tough, but fair" in "playing the rules," and a minority qualified as "good guards" who refused to kill and did small favors for the Jews.

So we side with Kurt Lewin, who argued decades ago for the science of experimental social psychology. Lewin asserted that it is possible to take conceptually and practically significant issues from the real world into the experimental laboratory, where it is possible to establish certain causal relationships in a way not possible in field studies and then to use that information to understand or make changes in the real world (Lewin, 1951; Lewin, Lippitt, & White, 1939). In fact, in his presidential speech to the American Psychological Association, psycholinguist George Miller (1969) startled his audience by advocating a radical idea for that time, that we should "give psychology away to the public." The exemplars he later used, in a *Psychology Today* (1980) interview, as being ideal for public consumption of psychological research were the Stanford Prison Experiment and Milgram's obedience studies.

From another perspective, the SPE does not tell us anything new about prisons that sociologists and narratives of prisoners have not already revealed about the evils of prison life. What is different is that by virtue of the experimental protocol, we put selected good people, randomly assigned to be either guard or prisoner, and observed the ways in which they were changed for the worse by their daily experiences in the evil place.

8. Selection procedures for special tasks, such as being prison guards—especially those that are relatively new to the applicants—might benefit from engaging the participants in simulated role playing rather than, or in addition to, screening on the basis of personality testing. As far as I know, current training for the very difficult job of prison guard, or correctional officer, involves minimal training in the psychological dimensions of this position.

9. It is necessary for psychological researchers who are concerned about the utility of their findings and the practical application of their methods or conclusions to go beyond the role constraints of academic researcher to become advocates for social change. We must acknowledge the value-laden nature of some kinds of research that force investigators out of their stance of objective neutrality into the realm of activism as partisans for spreading the word of their research to the public and to those who might be able to implement its recommendations through policy actions. Craig Haney and I have tried to do so collectively and individually in many ways with our writings, public testimonies, and development of special media to communicate to a wider audience than the academic readers of psychology journals.

For starters, we published the SPE first to U.S. audiences in articles in the *New York Times Magazine* (Zimbardo, Haney, Banks, & Jaffe, 1973) and in *Society* (Zimbardo, 1972), as well as to international audiences (Haney, Banks, & Zimbardo, 1973; Zimbardo & Haney, 1978); we extended the implications to education in a *Psychology Today* magazine piece (Haney & Zimbardo, 1975) and in an educational journal (Haney & Zimbardo, 1973); and we related psychology to legal change (Haney, 1993b). I have also specified how the SPE gives rise to considering new role requirements for social advocacy by psychologists (Zimbardo, 1975). Most recently, we have just published an article in *American Psychologist* on how the lessons learned from the SPE could improve the ill health of America's out-of-control correctional system (Haney & Zimbardo, 1998). Appearances on national television and radio shows, such as *The Phil Donahue Show* and *That's Incredible*, in which I discussed the SPE, have also extended the audience for this research. In each case, some of the participants from our prison study were involved. We have carried the message to college and high school students and also to civic groups through colloquia and distribution of a dramatic slide–tape show (Zimbardo & White, 1972; available on the INTERNET, http://www.ZIMBARDO.COM/ PRISONEXP) and the provocative video *Quiet Rage* (1992), as well as in the PBS video series *Discovering Psychology* (1989; Program #19, "The Power of the Situation"). Finally, I have given invited testimony relating the SPE to various prison conditions before Congressional Subcommittees on the Judiciary (The Power and Pathology, 1970; The Detention and Jailing, 1973).

10. Prisons are places that demean humanity, destroy the nobility of human nature, and bring out the worst in social relations among people. They are as bad for the guards as the prisoners in terms of their destructive impact on self-esteem, sense of justice, and human compassion. They are designed to isolate people from all others and even from the self. Nothing is worse for the health of an individual or a society than to have millions of people who are without social support, social worth, or social connections to their kin. Prisons are failed social-political experiments that continue to be places of evil and even to multiply, like the bad deeds of the sorcerer's apprentice, because the public is indifferent to what takes place in secret there and because politicians use them and fill them up as much as they can to demonstrate only that they are "tougher on crime" than their political opponents. At present, such misguided thinking has led to the "three strikes" laws in California and a few other states. Meant to curtail violent crime, the statute was so broadly written as to include drug offenses as "serious felonies," thus filling prisons with a disproportionate number of nonviolent, young minority drug offenders—for a minimum of 25 years to a maximum life term. The cost to taxpayers figures to be about one million dollars per inmate for 25 years of warehousing and medical care and to be even greater for older inmates (see Zimbardo, 1994). The costs of extensive prison construction and of hiring many guards to oversee the many prisoners starting to fill these new prisons is already diminishing the limited state and county funds available for health, education, and welfare. A "mean-spirited" value system pervades many correctional operations, reducing programs for job training, rehabilitation, and physical exercise, and even limiting any individuality in appearance. Projections are dire at best for the future of corrections in the United States.

I was able to terminate my failed prison experiment, but every citizen is paying for, and will continue to pay an enormous price in taxes for, the failed experiments taking place in every state of this union—the failed U.S. prison system. This system has failed by any criteria: of recidivism, of prison violence, of illegal activities practiced in prisons, of second offenders often committing more serious second-time-around crimes than initially, of low morale of corrections staff, and of deadly prison riots. Among the most outrageous examples of the evil that prison settings can generate come from the recent reports of guards "staging fights among inmates and then shooting the combatants," 50 of whom have been shot and 7 killed in the past 8 years (Holding, 1996). Federal investigators have been checking out such reports (*Los Angeles Times*, 1998). Obviously, sometimes it is the guards we must be protected from, as we saw in the SPE.

Ethics of the SPE

Was the SPE study unethical? No and Yes. No, because it followed the guidelines of the Human Subjects Research Review Board that reviewed it and approved it (see Zimbardo, 1973). There was no deception; all participants were told in advance that, if they became prisoners, many of their usual rights would be suspended and they would have only minimally adequate diet and health care during the study. Their rights should have been protected by any of the many citizens who came to that mock prison, saw the deteriorated condition of those young men, and yet did nothing to intervene—among them, their own parents and friends on visiting nights, a Catholic priest, a public defender, many professional psychologists, graduate students, secretaries, and staff of the psychology department, all of whom watched live action videos of part of the study unfold or took part in parole board hearings or spoke to participants and looked at them directly. We might also add another no, because we ended the study earlier than planned, ended it against the wishes of the guards, who felt they finally had the situation under their control and there would be no more disturbance or challenge by the prisoners.

Yes, it was unethical because people suffered and others were allowed to inflict pain and humiliation on their fellows over an extended period of time. This was not the distress of Milgram's participants imagining the pain their shocks were having on the remote victim–learner. This was the pain of seeing and hearing the suffering you as a guard were causing in peers, who, like you, had done nothing to deserve such punishment and abuse. And yes, we did not end the study soon enough. We should have terminated it as soon as the first prisoner suffered a severe stress disorder on Day 2. One reason we did not was because of the conflicts created by my dual roles as principal investigator, thus guardian of the research ethics of the experiment, and as prison superintendent, thus eager to maintain the integrity of my prison.

Positive Consequences

1. The study has become a model of the "power of the situation" in textbooks and in the public mind. Along with Milgram's obedience studies, the SPE has challenged people's views that behavior is primarily under the influence of dispositional factors, which is the view promoted by much of psychology, psychiatry, religion, and law.

2. The study's results, as presented in my testimony before a Congressional Judiciary Committee, influenced federal lawmakers to change a law so that juveniles jailed in pretrial detention (as was the case in our study) would not be housed with adult prisoners because of the anticipated violence against them, according to Congressman Birch Bayh.

3. The study has been presented to a great many civic, judicial, military, and law enforcement groups to enlighten them and arouse their concern about prison life and has influenced guard training in some instances (see Newton & Zimbardo, 1975; Pogash, 1976). Its role-playing procedures have been used to demonstrate to mental health staff how their mental patients perceive and respond to situational features of the ward and staff insensitivity toward them (see Orlando, 1973). Its results have been generally replicated in another culture, New South Wales, Australia (Lovibond, Mithiran, & Adams, 1979).

4. Ideas from the SPE have been the source of three research programs that I have carried out in the past 20 or more years, most notably on the psychology of shyness and ways of treating it—first in the unique Shyness Clinic that I started at Stanford and now in the local community—to liberate shy people from their self-imposed silent prisons (see Zimbardo, 1977, 1986; Zimbardo, Pilkonis, & Norwood, 1975). The second long-standing research program influenced by my personal experiences in the SPE is the study of time perspective, how people come to develop temporal frames to partition their experiences but then come to be controlled by their overuse of past, present, or future time frames (see Gonzalez & Zimbardo, 1985; Zimbardo & Boyd, in press). Temporal distortion was a fact of life in the SPE, with 80% of the conversations (monitored secretly) among mock prisoners focused around the immediate present and little about the past or future. Also apparent in the SPE was the fact that many healthy, normal young men began behaving pathologically in a short time period. Thus I began to

study the social and cognitive bases of "madness" in normal, healthy people in controlled laboratory experiments (see Zimbardo, Andersen, & Kabat, 1981; Zimbardo, LaBerge, & Butler, 1993). We have found that pathological symptoms may develop in up to one third of normal participants in the process of trying to make sense of their unexplained sources of arousal (Zimbardo, 1999).

5. At the personal level, there are several positive effects of the SPE that are a source of pride for me.

Carlo Prescott, our prison consultant, has been a good citizen and out of prison for the past 27 years after having served 17 previous years and being released just months before his involvement in the SPE. Because of his role in the SPE, Carlo got a job, had his own radio program for some years, taught college courses on imprisonment, lectured in the community, and gained new status and enhanced self-esteem. We have maintained a close, supportive relationship over all the intervening years.

Doug Korpi, Prisoner 8612, a ringleader of the prisoner rebellion, was the first prisoner to suffer an extreme emotional stress reaction that forced us to release him after only 36 hours. Doug was so disturbed by his loss of control in this situation that he went on to get a PhD in clinical psychology, in part to learn how to gain greater control over his emotions and behavior. He did his dissertation on shame (of the prisoner status) and guilt (of the guard status), completed his internship at San Quentin Prison, and has been a forensic psychologist in the San Francisco and California corrections system. It is his moving testimony that gave us the title for the video *Quiet Rage*, when he talked to us about the sadistic impulse in guards that must be guarded against because it is always there in such situations of differential power, ready to slip out, to explode, as a kind of "quiet rage." Here is a case of the obvious initially negative effect of the power of the SPE being transformed into a positive and enduring consequence for the individual and society.

Craig Haney went on to graduate from Stanford with a law degree, as well as a PhD from the psychology department. He is now on the faculty of University of California, Santa Cruz, teaching courses in psychology and law, as well as in the psychology of institutions. Craig is one of the nation's leading consultants on prison conditions and one of only a handful of psychological experts working with attorneys who still represent prisoner class-action suits in the United States. Craig outlines his views on the relationship between lessons of the SPE and corrections in the final section of this chapter.

Christina Maslach, now a psychology professor at University of California Berkeley, who contributed the next section of this chapter, utilized her experience in the SPE to become the pioneering researcher on "job burnout," the loss of human caring among health care professionals. Her work helps to identify those at risk for burnout, and she also adopts a situationist perspective in recommending how to change institutions that promote burnout as opposed to the traditional therapeutic focus on changing "defective workers." She has also studied the flip side of deindividuation processes, focusing instead on the positive aspects of individuation; that is, the things that make people feel uniquely special.

Finally, I end with the ultimate tribute to the crossover impact of the SPE into popular culture. "Stanford Prison Experiment" is also the name of a rock band from Los Angeles whose very loud music represents "a fusion of punk and noise," according to their leader, who learned about the SPE as a student at UCLA. Having heard their music and "hung out" with the quartet at a recent concert at San Francisco's famous Fillmore auditorium, I can attest to their high energy and tympanic destructive tendencies.

It is reasonable to conclude that there is something about this little experiment that has enduring value not only among social psychologists but also among the general public. I now believe that special something is the dramatic transformation of human nature, not by Jekyll–Hyde chemicals but rather by the power of the situation. Thus I end the first part of this trilogy being pleased that my colleagues and I have been able "to give psychology a way into the public consciousness" in an informative, interesting, and entertaining format that enables all of us to understand something so basic, although disturbing, about our conception of human nature. I think that Stanley Milgram would be pleased that our well-worn, circuitous paths have crossed again in this tribute to him.

AN OUTSIDER'S VIEW OF THE UNDERSIDE OF THE STANFORD PRISON EXPERIMENT
Christina Maslach

My Role in the Stanford Prison Experiment

In August of 1971, I had just completed my doctorate at Stanford University, where I was the office mate of Craig Haney, and was preparing to start my new job as an assistant professor of psychology at the University of California, Berkeley. Relevant background also should include mention that I had recently gotten involved romantically with Phil Zimbardo, and we were even considering the possibility of marriage. Although I had heard from Phil and other colleagues about the plans for their prison simulation study, I had not participated in either the preparatory work or the initial days of the actual simulation. Ordinarily I would have been more interested and maybe become involved in some way, but I was in the process of moving, and my focus was on preparing for my first teaching job. However, I agreed when Phil asked me, as a favor, to help conduct some interviews with the study participants. The interviews were to be done on Friday, nearly a week after the start of the study, to assess some of the subjective impact of participation on the guards, as well as the prisoners. I came down to Palo Alto on Thursday night to visit the "prison" and get some sense of what was going on.

When I went downstairs to the basement location of the prison, I viewed the yard from the observation point at the end of the hall (where the video camera was set up). Not much was happening at that point, and there was not much to see. I then went to the other end of the hall, where the guards entered the yard; there was a room outside the yard entrance, which the guards used to rest and relax when not on duty or to change into or out of their uniforms at the start or end of their shifts. I talked to one of the guards there who was waiting to begin his shift. He was very pleasant, polite and friendly, surely a person anyone would consider a really nice guy.

Later on, one of the research staff mentioned to me that I should take a look at the yard again, because the new late-night guard shift had come on, and this was the notorious "John Wayne" shift. John Wayne was the nickname for the guard who was the meanest and toughest of them all; his reputation had preceded him in various accounts I had heard. Of course, I was eager to see who he was and what he was doing that attracted so much attention. When I looked through the observation point, I was absolutely stunned to see that their John Wayne was the "really nice guy" with whom I had chatted earlier. Only now he was transformed into someone else. He not only moved differently, but he talked differently—with a Southern accent. (I discovered later that he was modeling his role on a prison movie character.) He was yelling and cursing at the prisoners as he made them go through "the count," going out of his way to be rude and belligerent. It was an amazing transformation from the person I had just spoken to—a transformation that had taken place in minutes just by stepping over the line from the outside world into that prison yard. With his military-style uniform, billy club in hand, and dark, silver-reflecting sunglasses to hide his eyes (adopted by Phil from the movie *Cool Hand Luke*), this guy was an all-business, no-nonsense, really mean prison guard.

At around 11 p.m., the prisoners were being taken to the toilet prior to going to bed. The toilet was outside the confines of the prison yard, and this had posed a problem for the researchers, who wanted the prisoners to be "in prison" 24 hours a day (just as in a real prison). They did not want the prisoners to see people and places in the outside world, which would have broken the total environment they were trying to create. So the routine for the bathroom runs was to put paper bags over the prisoners' heads so they couldn't see anything, chain them together in a line, and lead them down the hall into, around, and out of a boiler room and then to the bathroom and back. It also gave the prisoners an illusion of a great distance between the yard and the toilet, which was in fact only in a hallway around the corner.

When the bathroom run took place that Thursday evening, Phil excitedly told me to look up from some report I had been reading: "Quick, quick—look at what's happening now!" I looked at the line of hooded, shuffling, chained prisoners, with guards shouting orders at them—and then quickly averted my gaze. I was overwhelmed by a chilling, sickening feeling. "Do you see that? Come on, look—it's amazing stuff!" I couldn't bear to look again, so I snapped back with, "I already saw it!" That led to a bit of a tirade by Phil (and other staff there) about what was the matter with me. Here was fascinating human behavior unfolding, and I, a psychologist, couldn't even look at it? They couldn't believe my reaction, which they may have taken to be a lack of interest. Their comments and teasing made me feel weak and stupid—the out-of-place woman in this male world—in addition to already feeling sick to my stomach by the sight of these sad boys so totally dehumanized.

A short while later, after we had left the prison setting, Phil asked me what I thought about the entire study. I'm sure he expected some sort of great intellectual discussion about the research and the events we had just witnessed. Instead, what he got was an incredibly emotional outburst from me (I am usually a rather contained person). I was angry and frightened and in tears. I said something like, "What you are doing to those boys is a terrible thing!" What followed was a heated argument between us. That was especially scary for me, because Phil seemed to be so different from the man I thought I knew, someone who loves students and cares for them in ways that were already legendary at the university. He was not the same man that I had come to love, someone who is gentle and sensitive to the needs of others and surely to mine. We had never had an argument before of this intensity. Instead of being close and in tune with each other, we seemed to be on opposite sides of some great chasm. Somehow the transformation in Phil (and in me as well) and the threat to our relationship was unexpected and shocking. I don't remember how long the fight went on, but I felt it was too long and too traumatic.

What I do know is that eventually Phil acknowledged what I was saying, apologized for his treatment of me, and realized what had been gradually happening to him and everyone else in the study: that they had all internalized a set of destructive prison values that distanced them from their own humanitarian values. And at that point, he owned up to his responsibility as creator of this prison and made the decision to call the experiment to a halt. By then it was well past midnight, so he decided to end it the next morning, after contacting all the previously released prisoners, and calling in all the guard shifts for a full round of debriefings of guards, prisoners, and then everyone together. A great weight was lifted from him, from me, and from our personal relationship (which celebrated its 25th wedding anniversary on August 10, 1997).

Lessons To Be Learned: Dissent, Disobedience, and Challenging the System

So what is the important story to emerge from my role as "the Terminator" of the Stanford Prison Experiment? I think there are several themes I would like to highlight.

First, however, let me say what the story is not. Contrary to the standard (and trite) American myth, the Stanford Prison Experiment is not a story about the lone individual who defies the majority. Rather, it is a story about the majority—about how everyone who had some contact with the prison study (participants, researchers, observers, consultants, family, and friends) got so completely sucked into it. The power of the situation to overwhelm personality and the best of intentions is the key story line here.

So why was my reaction so different? The answer, I think, lies in two facts: I was a late entrant into the situation, and I was an "outsider." Unlike everyone else, I had not been a consenting participant in the study when it began and had not experienced its powerful defining events. Unlike everyone else, I had no socially defined role within that prison context. Unlike everyone else, I was not there every day, being carried along as the situation changed and escalated bit by bit. Thus the situation I entered at the end of the week was not truly the "same" as it was for everyone else—I lacked their prior consensual history, place, and perspective. For them, the situation was construed as being still within the range of normalcy; for me, it was not—it was a madhouse.

My overall reaction—that the situation was crazy and harmful—was similar to that of Prisoner 416, who was also a late entrant (he joined the study on Wednesday as a replacement for another prisoner, 8612, who had been released early). He, too, found the situation to be a madhouse. He said later: "It was a prison to me. I don't regard it as an experiment or simulation. It was a prison run by psychologists instead of run by the state." Prisoner 416 chose to resist the powerful pressures he was facing from guards and inmates by going on a hunger strike, refusing to eat his food in protest. He believed that his rebellion might serve as a catalyst for renewed prisoner solidarity and opposition against the guards or that, if it was not, he would get physically ill and would have to be released. He was wrong; even after only 4 days it was too late to stir the other prisoners out of their zombie-like conformity to the rules. So instead of becoming the defiant hero who mobilized collective resistance to the brutality of the guards and the sadism of the John Waynes there, he was just a lonely troublemaker, despised by prisoners and tormented by the guards for not eating his awful food. In any case, Prisoner 416 soon became an "insider" in the situation because he tried to work within a set of definitions of that situation, establishing a uniquely defined role as rebel and disobedient prisoner, whereas I was an outsider without a clear role on that momentous night.

Would I have been so vocally opposed were I one of the research team? Would I have been able to stand up to the authority that Phil represented if I were still a graduate student dependent on his good will for a recommendation and not feeling the independence of my new position as a professor? Would I have cared enough to challenge him and his research enterprise had I not had a prior personal relationship that enabled me to see how much he had been adversely transformed by his own role in this drama? I just don't know. I would hope that I would have still acted out of the same ethical principles, but in retrospect, I can't be certain.

My reactions are interesting to consider in light of Milgram's obedience research. I have always been struck by the difference between dissent and disobedience in those studies; although many participants dissented, saying that they didn't want to give electric shocks to the learner, some even crying at the prospect of what they thought they were doing to that poor victim, only a minority of the participants actually disobeyed and stopped pressing the shock keys (in the baseline conditions). Verbal statements did not translate often into behavioral acts. In the SPE, there was a great deal of dissent of many different kinds, as prisoners and guards argued about what was happening within the prison. But disobedience was rare. It first emerged in the prisoner rebellion, but that was quickly crushed by the guards, not to resurface until Prisoner 416's solitary hunger strike. In the case of Prisoner 416, disobedience meant refusing to go along with the rules of the situation. But that disobedience did not ultimately change the situation—indeed, it backfired, making the prison setting even more toxic. The guards pitted the other prisoners against Prisoner 416, forcing them to choose between keeping their warm blankets and pillows while Prisoner 416 remained all night in the "solitary confinement" of a dark, small closet or giving up their bedding in return for the release of Prisoner 416 from solitary. It is sad to report that the majority of prisoners—his buddies—opted to leave him in solitary confinement.

As an outsider, I did not have the option of specific social rules that I could disobey, so my dissent took a different form—of challenging the situation itself. This challenge has been seen by some as a heroic action, but at the time it did not feel especially heroic. To the contrary, it was a very scary and lonely experience being the deviant, doubting my judgment of both situations and people, and maybe even my worth as a research social psychologist. I had to consider also in the back of my mind what I might do if Phil continued with the SPE despite my determined challenge to him. Would I have gone to the higher authorities, the department chair, dean, or Human Subjects Committee, to blow the whistle on it? I can't say for sure, and I am glad it never came to that. But in retrospect, that action would have been essential in translating my values into meaningful action. When one complains about some injustice and the complaint only results in cosmetic modifications while the situation flows on unchanged, then that dissent and disobedience are not worth much. What did it matter to the classic original Milgram study that one third of the participants disobeyed and refused to go all the way? Suppose it was not an experiment; suppose Milgram's "cover story" were true, that researchers were studying the role of punishment in learning and memory and would be testing about one thousand participants in a host of experiments to answer their practical questions about the educational value of judiciously administered punishment. If you disobeyed, refused to continue, got paid, and left silently, your heroic action would not prevent the next 999 participants from experiencing the same distress. It would be an isolated event without social impact unless it included going to the next step of challenging the entire structure and assumptions of the research. Disobedience by the individual must get translated into systemic disobedience that forces change in the situation or agency itself and not just in some operating conditions. It is too easy for evil situations to co-opt the intentions of good dissidents or even heroic rebels by giving them medals for their deeds and a gift certificate for keeping their opinions to themselves.

For me, the important legacy of the prison experiment is what I learned from my personal experience and how that helped to shape my own subsequent professional contributions to psychology. What I learned about most directly was the psychology of dehumanization—how basically good people can come to perceive and treat others in such bad ways; how easy it is for people to treat others who rely on their help or good will as less than human, as animals, inferior, unworthy of respect or equality. That experience in the SPE led me to do the pioneering research on burnout—the psychological hazards of emotionally demanding human service work that can lead initially dedicated and caring individuals to dehumanize and mistreat the very people they are supposed to serve. My research has tried to elucidate the causes and consequences of burnout in a variety of occupational settings; it has also tried to apply these findings to practical solutions (e.g., Maslach, 1976, 1982; Maslach, Jackson, & Leiter, 1996; Maslach & Leiter, 1997; Schaufeli, Maslach, & Marek, 1993). I also encourage analysis and change of the situational determinants of burnout rather than focusing on individual personalities of the human caregivers. So my own story in the Stanford Prison Experiment is not simply whatever role I played in ending the study earlier than planned but my role in beginning a new research program that was inspired by my personal experience with that unique study.

THE SPE AND THE ANALYSIS OF INSTITUTIONS
Craig Haney

The SPE, Milgram, and the Spirit of the Times

For me, the Stanford Prison Experiment was a formative, career-altering experience. I had just finished my second year as a psychology graduate student at Stanford when Phil Zimbardo, Curtis Banks, and I began to plan this research. My interests in applying social psychology to questions of crime and punishment had just begun to crystallize, with Phil Zimbardo's blessing and support. But the study also represented the intersection of several preexisting interests and experiences. Like many undergraduates, I'm sure, I was drawn to social psychology in part because of the dramatic lessons that Stanley Milgram's (1963; 1965) research taught us about human nature and his brilliance in adapting the methods of psychological research to demonstrate enduring truths about the power of the social world to shape and transform us.

In fact, I was in the audience at the University of Pennsylvania when Milgram debated the formidable Martin Orne (Orne, 1973) about the role of "demand characteristics" in the Milgram studies. Even then it seemed apparent to me that in most of the real-world social contexts in which analogues to the Milgram paradigm might be found—primarily in institutional settings—the demand characteristics, although different in nature, would be at least as powerful as those that attached to the laboratory. Indeed, as a college senior I had taken a graduate anthropology seminar with Erving Goffman and was much influenced by his perspective on "asylums," the social psychological characteristics of total institutional environments, and the tremendous power of socially defined roles to shape not only attitudes and behavior but also individual identities (Goffman, 1961). I had come to Stanford because Phil Zimbardo's (1970) extraordinary paper on deindividuation had excited me about the possibility of doing social psychological research that combined the rigor of Milgram's obedience paradigm and the richness of Goffman's ethnography.

I was at Stanford for 2 years before we conducted the SPE. During that time I took several classes with Walter Mischel and was fascinated by what were then still revolutionary ideas—that personality variables often explained only a small portion of the variance in social behavior and that more careful attention to often ignored dimensions of situations might provide much greater insight into the nature of social interactions (Mischel, 1968). And I had the good fortune of working with David Rosenhan on his extremely clever demonstration of the ways in which the prevailing assumptions, procedures, and atmosphere in both private and state mental hospitals so profoundly shaped and influenced the perceptions of the staff that they not only could not discern sanity from madness but also often processed the normal behavior of pseudopatients as further signs of their psychopathology (Rosenhan, 1973).

These were exciting times in which to be a graduate student. The paradigms in psychology were changing, and a new emphasis on structures, contexts, and situations was emerging. Stanley Milgram's research both grew out of and contributed enormously to this changing zeitgeist. Although his specific focus was obedience to authority, implicit in Milgram's research was a general recognition of the power of real-world social contexts to dramatically alter human behavior. His demonstration of the lengths to which participants would go to obey "authorized" commands provided an empirical backdrop against which others studied less extreme but more prevalent situations and circumstances. And his use of normal individuals to explore the boundaries between normal and abnormal behavior indirectly reinforced the notion that extreme situations and not deviant personalities or aberrant dispositions were often at the root of collective evil, social pathology, and societal dysfunction.

Mischel's broad and systematic analysis of the limits of personality assessment built on and amplified this portion of Milgram's message about the relative power of situations over dispositions. Zimbardo had earlier examined different sets of dehumanizing and deindividuating social conditions that radically transformed individual dispositions by producing aggressive behavior from within its normal, societally regulated constraints. Goffman and Rosenhan, each in different ways, explored the intersection of social roles, procedures, perceptions, and identities in similar real-world settings in which the authorization derived not from an individual authority figure but from the structure of an institutional setting and the social psychological context it created. In the SPE, Zimbardo, Banks, and I extended a number of these notions to the institution of the prison—in many ways our society's concrete and steel embodiment of the dispositional hypothesis itself. But we were all indebted to Milgram for the way in which his demonstrations dramatically reframed the issues that we subsequently studied. Whether or not any of us drew consciously and directly from the Milgram paradigm in formulating our own research agendas, his work was an especially salient part of the prevailing intellectual atmosphere in which our ideas were generated.

Viewed with the benefit of hindsight, I suppose, this kind of intellectual history makes my involvement in the SPE seem natural, logical, and almost inevitable—all the more because Phil Zimbardo and I shared a deep belief that social psychology could and should be used to improve the human condition. I was Phil's teaching assistant in a course offered in the spring quarter before we conducted the SPE. In the spirit of those times the course had been titled Social Psychology in Action, and we were surrounded with activist students who worked with us on devising ways to make the discipline of social psychology more germane to the important issues of the day. During one of these classes—in which students regularly took a significant role in helping to set the classroom agenda—he and I were both moved by the eloquence and insight of an ex-convict, Carlo Prescott, whom one of the students knew and recommended that we invite to speak to the class. I think we realized simultaneously that the institution of prison represented a crucible in which many of the psychological forces we were both interested in studying combined and interacted (although I am sure that neither one of us anticipated the many ways in which this single project we were about to launch would have such a significant impact on our subsequent professional lives). In the ensuing weeks, as the plan for the prison study began to take shape, we relied heavily on the expertise of our ex-convict consultant to educate us about the realities of prison life.

This academic activism and desire to connect to the real world were part of the spirit of the times, and Milgram had something to do with them as well. His were some of the first—and certainly the most dramatic—social psychological studies conducted in the early 1960s to highlight the potential application of this discipline to pressing social problems. Although he was not generally known as a social-political activist, Milgram's work inspired generations of activist social scientists who applied theory and data to questions of social policy and the pursuit of social change. It is impossible to calculate the number of students who were inspired by the sheer dramatic force of these studies to pursue careers exploring unexamined dimensions of human nature, but I count myself among them. His work pushed against the limits of not only the ethical bounds of experimental research but also the political limits of incisive social psychological commentary. Phil has noted that Milgram believed the SPE took some of the critical heat off his research, and I'm certain that it did. But it is also true that his work provided a preexisting context for ours, helping to expand our sense of what it was possible to accomplish in an experimental setting and even to embolden us in the critical uses to which we were willing and able to put our laboratory-based empirical knowledge.

The SPE and the Power of Institutions

When Phil Zimbardo, Curt Banks, and I began to discuss some way of both assessing the effects of prison environments and demonstrating their powerful, transforming effects, I was strongly committed to the idea that we should select normal healthy participants and randomly assign them to their prison roles. But, frankly, we were all somewhat skeptical about how effectively we could create the equivalent of a functional prison environment that would have the capacity to sustain itself over a 2-week period. I wondered whether the roles we had created would hold together (we had provided some but not many institutional supports for them) and whether the guards and prisoners would take their tasks seriously or, to make things easier on themselves, capitalize on what could have been perceived as a gamelike atmosphere (we had decided that we would not intervene in a heavy-handed way to direct events in one direction and not another). And all of us shared concerns over whether significant, measurable changes in attitudes and behavior would occur over the relatively short period of time the study was designed to last.

We really had only Stanley Milgram's research to draw on directly as a still relatively recent and not yet widely replicated example of the power of a laboratory situation to bend identities and transform behavior. However, as Phil has already noted, the two paradigms were very different in several critical ways. Milgram, after all, had focused on obedience, measuring the effects of an ever-present authority. In fact, when the authority figure was not present, Milgram had showed that the force of his instructions dissipated rather rapidly (Milgram, 1974). Our study was designed to see whether placing participants in a more conventionally designed, and in some ways familiar, role would give the situation a lastingness that it did not appear to have in Milgram's research. Also, of course, there was no real script for our participants to follow—they literally made it up as they went along (as do real guards and prisoners, who must generate behavior in conformity to what they perceive to be the demands of the prison situation).

Although I did not realize it at the time, I could not have wished for a better social laboratory in which to observe the extraordinary power of institutions and the relative malleability of personality in the face of such situational influence. I was the person primarily responsible for interviewing the volunteers from which we selected our participants. Banks and I reviewed the personality profiles and interview notes that had been collected on them, selected our "abnormally normal" group of participants, and then randomly assigned them to their prison roles. Like everyone else close to the study, I too became immersed in its logic and was transformed by its power. But my close contact with the subjects beforehand also gave me perhaps the best vantage point from which to observe the dramatic transformations that were occurring in them over an unbelievably short period of time. Not long after I finished my work on the SPE I began to study actual prisons and eventually focused also on the social histories that helped to shape the lives of the people who were confined inside them. But I never lost sight of the perspective on institutions that I gleaned from observing and evaluating the results of 6 short days inside our simulated prison.

In this regard, I want to share a few personal anecdotes from the SPE that illustrate both the subtle power of the situation that we had created and the remarkable tenacity of the culturally shared belief in personality as the causal locus of behavior (especially behavior that is unexpected or extreme). The role we had constructed for Banks and me—"psychological counselors" at the prison—was designed to keep us in close proximity to the inner workings of the prison so that we could collect data and make as many observations as possible as events unfolded. The job of counselors gave us an excuse to interact periodically with the prisoners (whom we could not see when they were in their cells). From time to time during the study we brought them out of their cells for interviews and also to fill out various questionnaires that we had decided beforehand would be needed to document the subtle changes that we thought might take place in them over the course of the study.

Almost immediately after the experiment began I sensed that major changes were taking place in the participants' perceptions of and relationship to me. The prisoners—all of whom I had interviewed before the study began and with whom I felt some bond or connection—now looked at me with skepticism and distrust, refusing any real openness or genuine communication. In their eyes, although my function at the prison was ostensibly to inquire after their well-being and monitor their psychological health, I was no longer the person with whom they had earlier easily and comfortably interacted. I was one of "them"—a member of the prison administration whose interests now diverged significantly from theirs and whose expressions of honest concern were of no real import given my unwillingness and inability to measurably improve their lot by changing prison conditions (something that, for obvious reasons, I could not do).

In a different way, one that was less noticeable at first but that became more profound over time, the guards, too, withdrew. Just as with the prisoners, I also had interviewed all of them before the experiment began and felt I had gotten to know them as individuals, albeit only briefly. Perhaps because of this, I really felt no hostility toward them as the study proceeded and their behavior became increasingly extreme and abusive. But it was obvious to me that because I insisted on talking privately with the prisoners—ostensibly "counseling" them—and occasionally instructed the guards to refrain from their especially harsh and gratuitous mistreatment, they now saw me as something of a traitor. Thus, describing an interaction with me, one of the guards wrote in his diary: "The psychologist rebukes me for handcuffing and blindfolding a prisoner before leaving the (counseling) office, and I resentfully reply that it is both necessary (for) security and my business anyway." Indeed, he had told me off. In a bizarre turn of events, I was put in my place for failing to uphold the emerging norms of a simulated environment I had helped to create by someone whom I had randomly assigned to his role.

As the prison atmosphere evolved and became thick and real, I sensed the growing hostility and distrust on all sides. On one of the nights that it was my turn to sleep overnight at the prison, I had a terribly realistic dream in which I was suddenly imprisoned by guards in an actual prison that Zimbardo, Banks, and I supposedly had created. Some of the prisoners in our study, the ones who in retrospect had impressed me as most in distress, were now decked out in elaborately militaristic guard uniforms. They were my most angry and abusive captors, and I had the unmistakable sense that there was to be no escape or release from this awful place. I awoke drenched in sweat and shaken from the experience. The dream required no psychoanalytic acumen to interpret and should have given me some pause about what we were doing. But it didn't. I pressed on without reflection. After all, we had a prison to run and too many day-to-day crises and decisions to allow myself the luxury of pondering the ultimate wisdom of this noble endeavor that had already started to go wrong.

In the ensuing years, much of my time has been spent studying real prisons and engaging in constitutional litigation over conditions of confinement. Because the psychological well-being of the prisoners is largely at issue in these cases and I am pressed to formulate strategies for making institutional environments more humane, I have often thought back on my brief but intense experience in the SPE and the dynamic it revealed. The speed with which the psychological counselor's role in our simulated prison became impossibly ambivalent and irresolvably contradictory gave me some insight into the untenable position that "helpers" face when placed within settings devoted to oppressive control.

Indeed, psychologists often are consigned to a kind of interpersonal "no-man's land" inside real prisons. The ambiguity of their role is a curse rather than a blessing, because they must exist in environments in which the institutional definition of who you are is all that others have to rely on in gauging their interactions with you. When it is not clear who you are—because the role you occupy does not allow for clarity of purpose—the only rational stance for guards and prisoners alike is to be wary of you. Because psychologists increasingly lack power in prisons in which punishment, not rehabilitation, has become the raison d'être of corrections, they become more marginalized and irrelevant. This, I think, is one of the real costs of the shift to punishment models of imprisonment over the last several decades—the way in which the rehabilitative purpose of imprisonment that empowered psychologists to act as a restraining edge against the worst abuses of imprisonment exists no more. That buffering presence has been stripped away, leaving only the good intentions of the staff and the occasional intervention of the courts to tame the raw force of the institutional imperatives created inside our current prisons.

The second anecdote speaks to the unexpected depth and tenacity of the concept of psychological individualism—precisely what the SPE was designed to challenge. Less than 2 days into the study, on another of the nights that I had overnight duty at the prison, I returned from a late dinner to find that one of the prisoners, Prisoner 8612, had suffered an "emotional breakdown" and was demanding to be released. Caught completely by surprise—only 36 hours had passed in our planned 2-week simulation—I talked at length with the young man, took him to a quiet room outside the basement corridor that served as our prison "yard," and gave him an opportunity to relax and perhaps regain his composure. He told me that he could not stand the constant hassling of the guards following his role as one of the ringleaders of the Day 2 prisoner rebellion. As I learned later, when he had told that to Zimbardo and Prescott earlier during dinner time, Prescott ridiculed him as a soft white boy who would not last a day in San Quentin. Zimbardo offered him a Faustian deal: He would arrange for the guards not to bother Prisoner 8612 at all in return for the prisoner's providing him with a "little information" about prisoner activities from time to time, adding that he need not decide now but could think it over and give his decision later. Instead of rejecting that offer to become a "snitch," he began considering it, thinking he could become a "double agent." But he was now really confused; and when he left the superintendent's office, Prisoner 8612 announced to his fellow inmates, lined up for a count, that they could not get out, that the staff would not release them. He then went into his cell, lay down on his cot, and became increasingly agitated.

After allowing Prisoner 8612 to rest for a while, I returned, hoping that he would reconsider. But he was adamant and upset even more than before. By now it was the middle of the night, and I knew I could not easily contact Zimbardo, my mentor and "boss." It was clear that the decision over what to do with this unstable prisoner was going to be mine alone. Although in retrospect it seems an easy call, at the time it was a daunting one. I was a 2nd-year graduate student, we had invested a great deal of time, effort, and money into this project, and I knew that the early release of a participant would compromise the experimental design we had carefully drawn up and implemented. As experimenters, none of us had predicted an event like this, and, of course, we had devised no contingency plan to cover it. On the other hand, it was obvious that this young man was more disturbed by his brief experience in the Stanford Prison than any of us had expected any of the participants to be even by the end of the 2 weeks. So I decided to release him.

When Zimbardo and Banks came to the prison the next morning, I had a lot of explaining to do. Understandably, because neither one of them had actually seen how upset the prisoner had become—shouting, crying, emotionally enraged, thinking irrationally—they were skeptical

of my decision to let him go. I could tell they doubted my judgment. After a fair amount of discussion I was relieved that they finally agreed
that I really had made the appropriate choice. But then a different task
faced us: how to account for this extreme and, from our point of view,
entirely premature and unexpected emotional reaction. We quickly
seized on an explanation that felt as natural as it was reassuring—he
must have broken down because he was weak or had some kind of de-
fect in his personality that accounted for his oversensitivity and overre-
action to the simulated prison conditions! In fact, we worried that
there had been a flaw in our screening process that had allowed a "dam-
aged" person somehow to slip through undetected. It was only later that
we appreciated this obvious irony, that we had "dispositionally explained" the first truly unexpected and extraordinary demonstration of
situational power in our study by resorting to precisely the kind of
thinking we had designed the study to challenge and critique.

I don't think this ironic, self-contradictory behavior can be dismissed
simply by attributing it to our naiveté. In a culture steeped in the assumptions of psychological individualism, few of us are immune to its pull.
Dispositional thinking and the fundamental attribution error to which it
leads loom large even for those of us strongly committed to alternative
ways of viewing the social world. We are not only socialized and schooled
in its logic but find comfort in what it lulls us into thinking about ourselves and our relationship to the various social problems that we observe
in the world around us. Christina Maslach's poignant commentary on
what she experienced in her brief contact with the SPE underscores how
much we—the experimenters—were motivated to avoid looking directly at the consequences of the environment that we had created.

Attributing prisoner breakdowns to defective dispositions and regarding the cruelty of the guards as some fascinating social psychological dynamic that required study rather than intervention allowed us to
ignore the painful, obvious truth. Like the experimenters in the SPE,
many people find solace in the fundamental attribution error and the
way it reassures us that we are not responsible for the harsh social or institutional conditions to which others succumb. If we can attribute de-
viance, failure, and breakdowns to the individual flaws of others, then
we are absolved. In subsequent writing about psychology and law, I
have often tried to critically address the extraordinary hold that psychological individualism continues to have over legal thinking (e.g.,
Haney, 1982, 1983) and the law's resistance to contextualizing (espe-

cially) criminal behavior (e.g., Haney, 1995; 1996). However, this personal lesson taken directly from the pages of the SPE has humbled me about the difficulty of the task.

Institutional Change in the Years Since Milgram and the SPE

As I noted earlier, in the years that have passed since the SPE was conducted I have spent a large part of my professional life studying actual prisons, touring and inspecting penal systems across the country, as well as in different parts of the world, conducting in-depth interviews with hundreds of prisoners and correctional staff members, and becoming involved in litigation that challenged the cruel and unusual nature of conditions of confinement in a number of penal institutions. I have no doubt that much of my basic orientation to these issues was influenced in large part by the early lessons I had learned both from Stanley Milgram's obedience paradigm and, certainly, from the SPE's demonstration of the power of institutional environments.

The history of this kind of litigation carries some final lessons, I think, for the meaning and significance of both the Milgram experiments and the SPE and their potential role in producing social and institutional change. Given the significant head start we had on these issues in the late 1960s and early 1970s, when the paradigm changes I talked about earlier were in full swing, we should have made great progress by now—not only in understanding but in actually limiting the potential for institutional excess and abuse that had been highlighted both in Milgram's research and the SPE. Of course, we have not. The prison system in the United States continues in an unprecedented and worsening "crisis" that threatens to become permanent (e.g., Haney, 1997a; Haney & Zimbardo, 1998). Many penal institutions are plagued by unheard-of levels of overcrowding and the abandonment of rehabilitative programs and goals. Court cases continue to uncover shocking levels of brutality and mistreatment of prisoners, as Milgramesque scenarios are played out in SPE-like settings across the country.

In addition, there has been a destructive politicization of the process by which we inflict legal punishment, one in which politicians shamelessly compete for the title of "toughest on crime," with no concern for the social and economic costs of frequently ineffective and irrelevant law-and-order programs. Indeed, incarceration levels have soared for the last 2 decades, whereas crime rates have remained largely stable or actually decreased in most places and the amount of recidivism actually increased in many. Factor in the extraordinary disproportions in the rates of imprisonment of our minority citizens—what might be called the racialization of prison pain—and the renewed use of long-term, solitary-like confinement and punitive isolation in a new penal form known as the "supermax" prison that keeps prisoners in a potentially damaging, asocial, behavioral "deep freeze" for years on end (e.g., Haney & Lynch, 1997), and you begin to fathom the dimensions of this crisis.

Many of us involved in the systematic study of prison conditions also have assisted in the effort to bring unconstitutional penal institutions under legal scrutiny in the United States. Along with the constitutional and civil-rights attorneys who pursue these issues, we have established a very mixed and, I think, instructive record in this regard. Most such efforts have been extremely successful in the initial stage of documenting unconstitutional conditions and obtaining preliminary court-ordered relief, especially with trial court judges who could be brought close to the realities of the prison environments in question and whom we could persuade to see and feel at least some of the impact of the conditions of confinement whose effects on prisoners were at issue. For me, among other things, this has included: participating in a trial in which the totality of conditions in a maximum security prison in Washington State were found unconstitutional (*Hoptowit v. Ray*, 1982); a successful constitutional challenge to conditions inside the "lockup" or disciplinary segregation units in several California prisons, including Folsom, San Quentin, and Soledad (e.g., *Toussaint v. McCarthy*, 1984); an examination of the deficiencies in mental health and medical services provided to prisoners in the entire California prison system that resulted in a substantial federal court-ordered overhaul and improvements (*Coleman v. Wilson*, 1995); and, most recently, an evaluation of the harmful effects of isolated confinement inside a futuristic, so-called supermax prison, Pelican Bay, where, in addition to unremitting monotony and the deprivation of all forms of normal social contact, prisoners were exposed to mistreatment and brutality at the hands of the correctional staff (Haney, 1993a; *Madrid v. Gomez*, 1995).

Yet these initial successes are often followed by a series of legal and practical setbacks that blunt the significance of the litigation in effecting meaningful institutional change. In the legal arena itself it is generally the case that the higher the level to which these cases are taken on appeal, the less sympathetic a hearing prisoner-petitioners receive from the court. Although there may be some historical and ideological idio-syncrasies that help to account for this pattern, I think a social psycho-logical dynamic may be at work as well. Like at least some of Milgram's participants, only judges who most directly face the consequences of the (correctional) authorization they are asked to provide may be able to place the most effective and meaningful limits on what is acceptable. Elsewhere I have argued that our law sometimes demonstrates a per-verse genius for distancing decision makers from the morally ambigu-ous effects of their decisions; for example, that it employs an elaborate panoply of procedural mechanisms to morally disengage executioners, as well as capital jurors, from the harsh reality of the tasks they are asked to perform in death penalty cases (Haney, 1997b). In prisoners' rights cases, appellate judges in far-off venues who know little of the re-alities of prison life and have only the cold written record of a hearing to review may find it difficult to fully grasp the psychological conse-quences of the treatment in question. The common placement of penal institutions in remote locales where few people can observe what goes on inside the prison walls only compounds the problem because it helps to neutralize public sentiment on these issues.

The practical setbacks derive primarily from the inability of at least some courts to effectively manage the process of implementing institu-tional change. Here, too, I think there may be a social psychological dy-namic at work (cf. Haney & Pettigrew, 1986). The law is still dominated by a largely dispositional view of human behavior that also pervades its vision of legally mandated institutional change. The implementation of court orders in prison litigation often takes the form of little more than a series of judicial directives, followed by some process of official moni-toring to make sure that those directives are followed. Yet many of the lessons of both the Milgram paradigm and the SPE are ignored here. That is, we know that the social and institutional context that gives rise to unconstitutional conditions and mistreatment in an actual prison must be radically transformed if the behavior of those who have created and maintained this environment is to be altered.

Although in one sense both Milgram and the SPE demonstrated the extraordinary power of authority and the potency of socially defined roles and both offered the possibility that such power and potency could be harnessed to accomplish good as well as evil, both studies also under-scored the importance of specific situational conditions to control and change behavior. Good people and even good intentions are not enough.

This is especially true in a complex institutional context in which there are likely to be contending views and preferences about who is actually in charge (i.e., the court or the preexisting power structure). Indeed, Milgram (1974) showed very effectively that ambivalent or contradictory authority figures lost their power to effectively compel compliance. My earlier anecdote about the ambiguity of the helping role in an oppressive place of confinement is consistent with this perspective. Thus legally mandated institutional change, in prisons and elsewhere, would do well to mind the social psychological lessons of Milgram and the SPE: Behavior changes when critical dimensions in the powerful situations that support it are changed as well.

CONCLUSION

In the years since the SPE and the Milgram studies were completed, continuing intellectual and academic progress has been made in documenting the situational origins of behavioral influence and control. Outside of the academy, however, there was an ensuing ideological backlash that undid much of the progress toward developing both popular understanding and political recognition of the importance of social context, structure, and situation. For much of this period, social maladies were typically attributed to individual-level pathology and short-comings. Indeed, in some quarters, crime, poverty, mental illness, and racial differences in achievement, general well-being, and economic attainment were not only dispositionalized and essentialized but also biologized and geneticized.

Against this despairing and victim-blaming perspective, the lessons of the Milgram studies and the SPE have withstood the test of time. As my colleagues in the SPE and I have acknowledged, these events left an indelible impression on each of us. I believe that the rest of my professional life has been influenced by the clarity of the observations that we made in the SPE, and its basic lessons have guided much of the research I have done and no doubt influenced the questions on which I have worked. Like Stanley Milgram before us, my colleagues Zimbardo, Banks, Maslach, and I have seen a controlled and absolutely unambiguous demonstration that few people ever do—the way in which good, normal people can be turned into something else—rapidly, measurably, profoundly. Indeed, Zimbardo, Banks, and I took something else with us from this experience—the sometimes painful-to-watch chronicle of how this could happen to ourselves. Like most hard lessons, I suppose, the value of this one can only be gauged by the uses to which it is put. And there is still much constructive work to be done.

REFERENCES

Blass, T. (1992). The social psychology of Stanley Milgram. In M. P. Zanna (Ed.), *Advances in experimental social psychology*, (Vol. 25, pp. 277–329). San Diego, CA: Academic Press.

Browning, C. R. (1992). *Ordinary men: Reserve Police Battalion 101 and the final solution in Poland*. New York: HarperCollins.

Carr, S. (1995). Demystifying the Stanford Prison Study. *British Psychological Society, Social Psychology Section, Newsletter No. 33*, 31–34.

Coleman v. Wilson, 912 F. Supp. 1282 (1995).

Dunn, A. (1995, July 22). Guards abused inmates in immigration center. *San Francisco Chronicle*, p. A6.

Festinger, L. (1957). *A theory of cognitive dissonance*. Stanford, CA: Stanford University Press.

Goffman, E. (1961). *Asylums: Essays on the social situation of mental patients and other inmates*. Garden City, NY: Anchor Books.

Gonzalez, A., & Zimbardo, P. G. (1985, March). Time in perspective: The time sense we learn early affects how we do our jobs and enjoy our pleasures. *Psychology Today*, pp. 21–26.

Haney, C. (1982). Psychological theory and criminal justice policy: Law and psychology in the Formative Era. *Law and Human Behavior, 6*, 191–235.

Haney, C. (1983). The good, the bad, and the lawful: An essay on psychological injustice. In W. Laufer & J. Day (Eds.), *Personality theory, moral development, and criminal behavior* (pp. 107–117). Lexington, MA: Lexington Books.

Haney, C. (1993a). Psychology and legal change: The impact of a decade. *Law and Human Behavior, 17*, 371–398.

Haney, C. (1993b). Infamous punishment: The psychological effects of isolation. *National Prison Project Journal, 8*, 3–21.

Haney, C. (1995). The social context of capital murder: Social histories and the logic of capital mitigation. *Santa Clara Law Review, 35*, 547–609.

Haney, C. (1996). Psychological secrecy and the death penalty: Observations on "the mere extinguishment of life." *Studies in Law, Politics, and Society, 16*, 3–68.

Haney, C. (1997a). Psychology and the limits to prison pain: Confronting the coming crisis in Eighth Amendment law. *Psychology, Law, and Public Policy, 3*, 499–588.

Haney, C. (1997b). Violence and the capital jury: Mechanisms of moral disengagement and the impulse to condemn to death. *Stanford Law Review, 49*, 1447–1486.

Haney, C., Banks, W. C., & Zimbardo, P. G. (1973). Interpersonal dynamics in a simulated prison. *International Journal of Criminology and Penology, 1*, 69–97.

Haney, C., & Lynch, M. (1997). Regulating prisons of the future: The psychological consequences of supermax and solitary confinement. *New York University Review of Law and Social Change, 23*, 477–570.

Haney, C., & Pettigrew, T. (1986). Civil rights and institutional law: The role of social psychology in judicial implementation. *Journal of Community Psychology, 14*, 267–277.

Haney, C., & Zimbardo, P. G. (1973). Social roles, role-playing, and education. *Behavioral and Social Science Teacher, 1*, 24–45.

Haney, C., & Zimbardo, P. G. (1975, June). Stimulus/Response: The blackboard penitentiary: It's tough to tell a high school from a prison. *Psychology Today*, pp. 26, 29–30, 106.

Haney, C., & Zimbardo, P. G. (1998). The past and future of U.S. prison policy: Twenty-five years after the Stanford Prison Experiment. *American Psychologist, 53*, 709–727.

Holding, R. (1996, November 8). State sends investigators to Corcoran. *San Francisco Chronicle*, pp. A1, A19.

Hoptowit v. Ray, 682 F.2d 1237 (1982).

Los Angeles Times. (1998, March 19). FBI probes slayings at state prisons: Civil rights inquiry at Pelican Bay, Susanville.

Lewin, K. (1951). *Field theory in social science.* New York: Harper.

Lewin, K., Lippitt, R., & White, R. K. (1939). Patterns of aggressive behavior in experimentally created "social climates." *Journal of Social Psychology, 10,* 271–299.

Lifton, R. J. (1969). *Thought reform and the psychology of totalism.* New York: Norton.

Lovibond, S. H., Mithiran, X., & Adams, W. G. (1979). The effects of three experimental prison environments on the behavior of non-convict volunteer subjects. *Australian Psychologist, 14,* 273–287.

Madrid v. Gomez, 889 F. Supp. 1146 (1995).

Maslach, C. (1976, September). Burned-out. *Human Behavior*, pp. 16–22.

Maslach, C. (1982). *Burnout: The cost of caring.* Englewood Cliffs, NJ: Prentice-Hall.

Maslach, C., Jackson, S. E., & Leiter, M. P. (1996). *The Maslach Burnout Inventory* (3rd ed.). Palo Alto, CA: Consulting Psychologists Press.

Maslach, C., & Leiter, M. P. (1997). *The truth about burnout.* San Francisco, CA: Jossey-Bass.

Milgram, S. (1963). Behavioral study of obedience. *Journal of Abnormal and Social Psychology, 67,* 371–378.

Milgram, S. (1965). Some conditions of obedience and disobedience to authority. *Human Relations, 18,* 57–76.

Milgram, S. (1974). *Obedience to authority: An experimental view.* New York: Harper & Row.

Milgram, S. (1992). *The individual in a social world: Essays and experiments* (2nd ed.). New York: McGraw-Hill.

Milgram, S., & Sabini, J. (1979). Candid Camera. *Society, 16,* 72–75.

Miller, G. A. (1969). Psychology as a means of promoting human welfare. *American Psychologist, 24,* 1063–1075.

Miller, G. A. (1980, January). Giving psychology away in the 80s (An interview with E. Hall). *Psychology Today*, pp. 38ff.

Mischel, W. (1968). *Personality and assessment.* New York: Wiley.

Newton, J. W., & Zimbardo, P. G. (1975). *Corrections: Perspectives on research, policy and impact.* (ONR Technical Report No. Z-13). Summary of proceedings of the third annual conference on Corrections in the United States Military, Stanford, CA. June, 1974. Stanford University: Stanford, CA.

Orlando, N. J. (1973). The mock ward: A study in simulation. In O. Milton & R. G. Wahler (Eds.), *Behavior disorders: Perspectives and trends* (3rd ed., pp. 162–170). Philadelphia: Lippincott.

Orne, M. (1973). Communication by the total experimental situation: Why it is important, how it is evaluated, and its significance for the ecological validity of findings. In P. Pliner, L. Krames, & T. Alloway (Eds.), *Communication and affect: Language and thought* (pp. 157–191). New York: Academic Press.

Palmer, L. (1995, May 28). Her own private Tailhook. *New York Times Magazine,* 23–26.

Pogash, C. (1976, March 25). Life behind bars turns sour quickly for a few well-meaning Napa citizens. *San Francisco Chronicle*, pp. 10–11.

Rosenhan, D. (1973). On being sane in insane places. *Science, 170,* 250–258.

Ross, L., & Nisbett, R. (1991). *The person and the situation.* New York: McGraw-Hill.

Schaufeli, W. B., Maslach, C., & Marek, T. (Eds.). (1993). *Professional burnout: Recent developments in theory and research.* Washington, DC: Taylor & Francis.

Schein, E. H. (1956). The Chinese indoctrination program for prisoners of war: A study of attempted brainwashing. *Psychiatry, 19,* 149–172.

The detention and jailing of juveniles. Hearings before the Subcommittee to Investigate Juvenile Delinquency, of the U.S. Senate Committee on the Judiciary. (September, 1973) (pp. 141–161). (testimony of Philip Zimbardo). Washington, DC: U. S. Government Printing Office.

The power and pathology of imprisonment. Hearings before Subcommittee #3 of the Committee on the Judiciary, House of Representatives, 92nd Cong., 1st Sess. on Corrections, Part ll, Prisons, Prison Reform and Prisoner's Rights: California (1974) (testimony of Philip Zimbardo). *Congressional Record* (Serial No. 15, October 25). Washington, DC: U.S. Government Printing Office.

Toussaint v. McCarthy, 597 F. Supp. 1388 (1984).

Zimbardo, P. G. (1969). *The cognitive control of motivation.* Glenview, IL: Scott, Foresman.

Zimbardo, P. G. (1970). The human choice: Individuation, reason, and order versus deindividuation, impulse, and chaos. In W. J. Arnold & D. Levine, (Eds.), *1969 Nebraska Symposium on Motivation* Vol. 27, (pp. 237–307). Lincoln, NE: University of Nebraska Press.

Zimbardo, P. G. (1972). Pathology of imprisonment. *Society, 6,* 4, 6, 8.

Zimbardo, P. G. (1973). On the ethics of intervention in human psychological research: With special reference to the Stanford Prison Experiment. *Cognition, 2,* 243–256.

Zimbardo, P. G. (1975). On transforming experimental research into advocacy for social change. In M. Deutsch & H. Hornstein (Eds.), *Applying social psychology: Implications for research, practice, and training* (pp. 33–66). Hillsdale, NJ: Lawrence Erlbaum Associates.

Zimbardo, P. G. (1977). *Shyness: What it is, What to do about it.* Reading, MA: Addison-Wesley.

Zimbardo, P. G. (1985, June). Laugh where we must, be candid where we can. [A conversation with Allen Funt.] *Psychology Today,* pp. 42–47.

Zimbardo, P. G. (1986). The Stanford shyness project. In W. H. Jones, J. M. Cheek, & S. R. Briggs (Eds.), *Shyness: Perspectives on research and treatment* (pp. 17–25). New York: Plenum Press.

Zimbardo, P. G. (1989). *Discovering psychology: A PBS-TV introductory psychology course.* Washington, DC: Annenberg/CPB Project.

Zimbardo, P. G. (1989). *Quiet rage: The Stanford Prison Experiment video.* Stanford, CA: Stanford University.

Zimbardo, P. G. (1994). *Transforming California's prisons into expensive old age homes for felons: Enormous hidden costs and consequences for California's taxpayers.* San Francisco, CA: Center for Juvenile and Criminal Justice.

Zimbardo, P. G. (1999). Discontinuity theory: Cognitive and social searches for rationality and normality—may lead to madness. In M. Zanna (Ed.), *Advances in experimental social psychology* (Vol. 31, pp. 345–486). San Diego, CA: Academic Press.

Zimbardo, P. G., Andersen, S., & Kabat, L. G. (1981). Induced hearing deficit generates experimental paranoia. *Science, 212,* 1529–1531.

Zimbardo, P. G., & Boyd, J. N. (in press). Putting time in perspective: A new individual differences metric. *Journal of Personality and Social Psychology.*

Zimbardo, P. G., & Funt, A. (1992). *Candid camera classics in social psychology: Viewer's guide and instructor's manual.* New York: McGraw-Hill.

Zimbardo, P. G., & Haney, C. (1978). Prison behavior. In B. B. Wolman (Ed.), *International encyclopedia of psychiatry, psychology, and neurology* (Vol. 4, pp. 52–53). New York: Human Sciences Press.

Zimbardo, P. G., Haney, C., Banks, W. C., & Jaffe, D. (1973, April 8). The mind is a formidable jailer: A Pirandellian prison. *New York Times Magazine*, pp. 36ff.

Zimbardo, P. G., LaBerge, S., & Butler, L. (1993). Physiological consequences of unexplained arousal: A posthypnotic suggestion paradigm. *Journal of Abnormal Psychology, 102*, 466–473.

Zimbardo, P. G., & Leippe, M. R. (1991). *The psychology of attitude change and social influence.* New York: McGraw-Hill.

Zimbardo, P. G., Pilkonis, P. & Norwood, R. (1975, May). The silent prison of shyness. *Psychology Today*, pp. 69–70, 72.

Zimbardo, P. G., & White. G. (1972). *The Stanford Prison Experiment slide-tape show*, Stanford University.

Author Index

Adams, A. M., 64, *88*
Adams, W. G., 212, *235*
Adorno, T. W., 139, *141*
Allport, G., 129, *141*
Ancona, L., *54*, 59
Andersen, S., 213, *236*
Anderson, G. M., 36, *54*
Archer, R. P., 139, *143*
Arendt, H., 125, *141*
Aronson, E., 14, *21*
Arroyo, J. A., 64, *87*
Asch, S. E., 62, *87*, 207
Ashmore, R. D., 64, *88*
Assiter, A., 36, *54*
Aubert, R., 108, *110*

Baldwin, M. W., 72, *87*
Balmore, S., 134, *141*
Bandura, A., 134, 136, 137, *141*
Banks, W. C., 209, *234*, *237*
Bargh, J. A., 66, *87*, 89
Baumeister, R. F., 63, 87
Baumrind, D., 14, *21*
Bell, S. T., 64, *87*
Bellinger, D. N., 14, *21*
Bem, D. J., 64, *87*

Bem, S. L., 75, *87*
Bentler, P. M., 81, *87*
Berscheid, E., 64, 65, *88*
Bierbrauer, G. A., 46, *54*
Birnbach, R., 113, *123*
Blass, T., 9, 10, 11, *21*, *22*, 37, 41, 42,
    44, 51, *54*, *55*, 62, 69, 82, *87*,
    114, 121, *123*, 130, 137, 139,
    141, 154, *159*, 163, 164, *189*,
    196, *234*
Block, W., 36, *54*
Bock, D. C., 48, *55*, 59
Borofsky, G. L., 139, *141*
Bowra, C. M., 161, *189*
Boyd, J. N., 212, *236*
Brand, D. J., 139, *141*
Brannon, L. A., 10, *22*
Branscombe, N. R., 64, *87*
Brant, W. D., 52, *55*
Brehm, J. W., 175, *189*
Brief, D. E., 11, *22*, 44, *55*, 61, 62, 63,
    66, 67, 68, 71, 73, 78, 85, *88*,
    125, 134, *141*, *142*
Brock, T. C., 10, *22*
Brown, R., 147, *159*
Browne, M. N., 36, *55*
Browning, C., *55*, 131, *141*, 208, *234*
Bryant, A., 113, *123*
Butler, L., 213, *237*

Caballero, R. B., 49, *57*
Carr, S., 207, *234*
Cassel, C. K., 36, *55*
Chapman, G., 116, *123*
Collins, B. E., 11, *22*, 44, *55*, 61, 62, 63, 66, 67, 68, 71, 73, 78, 85, *88*, 125, 134, *141*, *142*
Corey, M., 47, 51, *57*, 59
Costanzo, E. M., 49, *55*
Crouch, M., 128, *141*

Dawidowicz, L., 126, 127, 128, 129, *142*
Deaux, K., 64, *88*
DeLeon, G., 29, *34*
Dertke, M. C., 39, *57*
Dion, K., 64, 65, *88*
Dlin, E., 134, *141*
Dobson, J., 36, *56*
Dunkel-Schetter, C., 71, *88*
Dunn, A., 207, *234*

Eagly, A. H., 50, *55*, 64, *88*
Edwards, D. M., 48, *55*, 58, 59
Evancic, C., 64, *88*
Evans, R. I., 40, *55*

Ferrell, O. C., 36, *55*
Festinger, L., 205, *234*
Fiske, S. T., 63, *88*
Fogelman, E., 108, *109*
Foley, L. A., 64, *88*
Ford, T. E., 64, *88*
Forsyth, D., 43, *55*
Foushee, H., 113, 117, *123*
Franks, P., 48, *55*, 58, 59
French, J. R. P., Jr., 41, *55*, 114, *123*
French, S., 36, *55*
Frenkel-Brunswik, E., 139, *141*
Friedgood, D., 48, *55*, 58, 59
Funt, A., 197, *236*

Gardiner, G., 36, *55*
Geen, R. G., *57*, 59
Geller, D. M., 14, *22*
Gergen, K. J., 51, 52, *55*
Giampetro-Meyer, A., 36, *55*
Gillen, B., 44, 45, *57*, 64, 65, *88*
Ginnett, R., 116, *123*
Goffman, E., 30, *34*, 221, *234*
Goldhagen, D., *55*, 87, *88*, 129, 131, *142*
Gomez, M. N. G., 49, *57*
Gonzalez, A., 212, *234*
Goodson, J. L., Jr., 64, *88*
Green, M. J., 36, *55*
Greenwood, J. D., 39, *55*
Guimond, S., 36, 44, 45, *56*

Haber, S., 15, *23*
Hackman, J., 120, *123*
Haesler, A., 92, 93, *109*
Hamilton, V. L., 27, *34*, 46, *56*, 163, *189*
Haney, C., 209, 229, 230, 231, 232, *234*, *235*, *237*
Harrower, M., 139, *143*
Hartman, P., *189*, 190
Hastorf, H. C., 63, 65, *88*
Hawkins, H. L., 39, *57*
Helm, C., 39, *56*
Helmreich, R., 113, 117, *123*, *124*
Herbert, T., 71, *88*
Higbee, K. L., 45, *56*
Hilberg, R., 136, *142*
Hirsch, M. W., 173, 174, *189*
Holding, R., 211, *235*
Holland, C. D., *56*, 59
Hollander, E. P., 21, *22*

Imbar, S., 134, *141*

Jackson, S. E., 220, *235*

Jaffe, D., 209, *237*
Janoff-Bulman, R., 72, *88*
Jones, E. E., 63, *88*

Kabat, L. G., 213, *236*
Kanki, B., 117, *124*
Kaplan, S. J., 73, 83, *89*
Karnik, K., 64, *88*
Katz, F. E., 36, *56*
Kaufmann, H., 45, *56*
Keller, S., 92, 94, 95, 96, 98, 99, 103, 106, *110*
Kelman, H. C., 27, *34*, 135, 136, 137, 140, *142*, 163, *189*
Kilham, W., 47, 49, 50, 51, *56*, 59
King, J., 64, *88*
Koh, H. H., 36, *56*
Kooman, A., 45, *56*
Krackow, A., 51, *55*
Kubasek, N. K., 36, *55*
Kuriloff, P. J., 64, *87*
Kuttner, P., 29, *34*
Kwak, K., 36, 44, 45, *56*

LaBerge, S., 213, *237*
LaFrance, M., 64, *88*
Langevin, P., 36, 45, *56*
Lanzmann, C., 136, *142*
Lasserre, A., 93, 94, *110*
Laurent, J., 36, *56*
Leary, M. R., 63, *88*
Leippe, M. R., 205, *237*
Leiter, M. P., 220, *235*
Lerner, M. J., 72, *88*
Levinger, G., 73, *89*
Levinson, D. J., 139, *141*
Levy, D. A., 61, 62, 63, 66, 67, 68, 73, 78, 85, *88*
Lewin, K., 178, *189*, 208, *235*
Lifton, R. J., 140, *142*, 203, 206, *235*
Lippitt, R., 208, *235*
Lipstadt, D., 126, *142*
Lobb, B., 116, *123*

Lobban, G., 48, *55*, 58, 59
Lobel, T. E., 64, *88*
Longo, L. C., 64, *88*
Longridge, T., 113, *123*
Lottes, I., 64, *87*
Lovibond, S. H., 212, *235*
Lozowick, Y., 131, *142*
Lucido, D. J., 15, *23*
Lutsky, N., 135, *142*
Lynch, K., 31, *34*
Lynch, M., 231, *234*

Mackay, H. C. G., 48, *55*, 58, 59
MacLellan, C., 36, *56*
Madon, S., 64, *88*
Makhijani, M. G., 64, *88*
Mann, L., 47, 49, 50, 51, *56*, 59
Mantell, D., *56*, 59, 115, *123*
Martin, J., 116, *123*
Maslach, C., 220, *235*
Maslow, A. H., 12, *22*
Masters, B., 36, *56*
Matthaus, J., 132, *142*
Maughan, M. R. C., 45, *56*
McGuire, W. J., 12, *22*
Mecham, M., 112, *123*
Meeus, W., 121, *123*
Merritt, A., 113, *123*
Milgram, A., 16, *22*
Milgram, J., 16, *22*
Milgram, S., 10, 11, 15, 16, 17, 18, 20, 22, 29, 30, 31, *34*, 35, 36, 37, 38, 39, 40, 41, 42, 43, 44, 45, 47, 48, 51, 53, *56*, *57*, 58, 59, 61, 69, *88*, 92, 104, 105, *110*, 114, 115, *123*, 125, 130, 132, 133, 134, 135, 136, 137, 139, 140, *142*, 158, *159*, 163, 165, 167, 187, *189*, 197, 204, 207, 221, 224, 233, *235*
Miller, A., 139, *142*
Miller, A. G., 11, *22*, 37, 44, 45, *57*, 63, 64, 65, *88*, 114, *124*, 125, 128, 139, *142*, 154, *159*, 164, *189*

Miller, F. D., 41, *57*
Miller, G. A., 208, *235*
Mills, J., 14, *21*
Miranda, F. S. B., 49, *57*
Mischel, W., 222, *235*
Mitchell, G., 36, *55*
Mithiran, X., 212, *235*
Mixon, D., 45, 46, *57*
Modigliani, A., 108, *110*, 137, 138, *142*,
    143, 164, 187, *189*
Morelli, M., 36, 39, 40, *56*, *57*
Morgen, K., 29, *34*
Murray, B., 16, *22*

Nail, P. R., 85, *88*
Newton, J. W., 212, *235*
Nisbett, R., 204, *236*
Norwood, R., 212, *237*

Olsen, N., 72, *89*
Orlando, N. J., 212, *235*
Orne, M., 221, *235*
Osgood, C. E., 62, 75, *89*

Paldiel, M., 108, *110*
Palmer, L., 206, *235*
Pareyson, R., *54*, 59
Patten, S. C., 40, *57*
Pearson, K. N., 44, *57*
Penner, L. A., 39, *57*
Perlman, D., 10, *22*
Pettigrew, T., 232, *234*
Pilkonis, P., 212, *237*
Plater, M. A., 64, *89*
Podd, M. H., *57*, 58, 59
Pogash, C., 212, *236*
Polefka, J., 63, 65, *88*
Powers, P. C., *57*, 59
Powers, W. T., 71, *89*

Raaijmakers, Q., 121, *123*
Radlove, S., 44, 45, *57*, 64, 65, *88*
Rands, M., 73, *89*
Raven, B., 41, 43, *55*, *57*, 114, *123*
Reis, H. T., 72, *89*
Riefenstahl, L., 133, *142*
Ring, K., 47, 51, *57*, 59
Ritzler, B. A., 139, *143*
Roberts, A. R., 28, 29, *34*
Robinson, J., 130, *142*
Rochat, F., 108, *110*, 137, 138, *142*,
    143, 164, 187, *189*
Rogers, R. W., *57*, 59
Rokhsar, J., 134, *141*
Rosenhan, D., *57*, 59, 222, *236*
Ross, L., 45, *57*, 68, *89*, 204, *236*
Rubin, J. Z., 41, 43, *57*
Ruelle, D., 173, *189*

Sabini, J., 17, 18, *22*, 197, *235*
Salvi, M., 108, *110*
Sanford, R. N., 139, *141*
Schein, E. H., 204, *236*
Schenker, C., 44, 45, *57*, 64, 65, *88*
Schlenker, B. R., 63, 64, *89*
Schmitt, B., 29, *34*
Schneider, D. J., 63, 65, *88*, *89*
Schneider, W., 66, *89*
Schurz, G., 49, 51, *57*
Schwartz, A., 29, *34*
Sedikides, C., 72, *89*
Shalala, S. R., *58*
Shanab, M. E., 47, 49, *58*
Shavit, T., 64, *88*
Shawn, K., 129, *143*
Shelton, G. A., 52, *58*
Sherif, M., 10, *22*
Shiffrin, R. M., 66, *89*
Siegler, M., 36, *55*
Silberklang, D., 134, *141*
Silver, M., 11, *23*
Simon, H. A., 163, *189*
Skversky, M., 127, *143*
Smale, S., 173, *189*
Smith, E. R., 64, *87*

Spector, B. J., 36, *58*
Spector, P., 39, *57*
Spillane, R., 116, *123*
Staub, E., 132, 136, 137, 138, 140, *143*
Stocking, C. B., 36, *55*
Stone, A., 39, *57*
Suci, G. J., 62, 75, *89*

Takooshian, H., 10, 11, 15, 20, *23*, 44,
    58
Tannenbaum, P. H., 62, 75, *89*
Tarnow, E., 114, *124*
Tavris, C., 15, 16, *23*
Taylor, S. E., 63, 66, *88*, *89*
Thom, R., 173, *189*
Thomas, R. E., 64, *89*
Tice, D. M., 64, *89*
Trudeau, J. V., 63, *89*

Voronov, A., 37, *58*

Waller, J., 140, *143*

Wallston, K., 47, 51, *57*, 59
Walster, E., 64, 65, *88*
Warren, N. C., 48, *55*
Warren, R., 158, *159*
Waters, J., 28, 29, *34*
Wegner, D. M., 66, *89*
Weigold, M. F., 63, *89*
Weiner, B., 69, *89*
White, G., 209, *237*
White, R. K., 208, *235*
Wiener, E., 117, *124*
Wish, M., 73, 83, *89*
Wistrich, R., 135, *143*

Yahya, K. A., 47, 49, *58*
Yaron, M., 134, *141*
Yoshizawa, T., *189*, 191

Zamorano, M. A. M., 49, *57*
Zillmer, E. A., 139, *143*
Zimbardo, P. G., 16, *23*, 115, *124*, 195,
    197, 203, 205, 209, 210, 211,
    212, 213, 221, 230, *234*, *235*,
    236, *237*

Subject Index

Agentic state theory, 69–71, 163
Airline cockpit study, *see* Obedience, excessive
Alumni, 11–12, 15, 24
American Psychological Association (APA), 145–146
American Psychological Foundation (APF), 10, 23–24, 44
    Distinguished Teaching in Psychology, 10, 23–24
Association of Holocaust Organizations, 126–127, 128
Attribution theory, 69–71
Audiotape analysis, *see* Bridgeport condition
Authority characterization, 37–44, 53
    experiment of, 41–44
    expert authority, 39–44
    legitimate authority, 38–44, 162–163
    social power, 41–42
Awards, 10, 23–24

Behavior, learner
    learner defined, 61
    learner identity, 71–72, 83
Behavior, teacher
    Bridgeport condition, 167–172

    acquiesces, 167, 168, 170–171
    audiotape analysis, 165–166, 168, 188
    checks, 167, 168–169
    distress, 169–172
    notifies, 167
    objects, 167–168, 169–170
    questions, 167, 169, 170
    refuses, 168, 169, 170–171
    summarization of, 171–172, 188–189
    time factor in, 171–172, 173–174
person-perception
    agentic state, 69–71
    and attribution theory, 69–71
    cognitive system structure, 63, 65–66, 85–86
    defiant disobedience, 68, 74, 79
    disobedience style, 67–68, 73–74, 79
    and experimenter identity, 71–72, 83
    and implicit personality theory, 64–67, 74–77, 85
    and learner identity, 71–72, 83
    meanings in, 63, 65–66
    obedience vs. disobedience, 66, 67–68, 77–79
    polite disobedience, 68, 74, 79

polite obedience, 73–74
and responsibility, 69–71, 79–82, 85
responsibility-clock procedure, 70–71
and social system analysis, 63, 71–73, 83–85
teacher defined, 61
and teacher identity, 62–63, 66–68, 77–79
Bridgeport condition
description of, 165–166
mathematical model of, 172–187
dynamical systems theory, 173–174
hypotheses for, 174–180, 188, 190, 191–192
hypothetico-deductive method, 172
systems solution analysis, 180–187, 190–191
and obedience studies
agentic state, 163
legitimate authority, 162–163
obedience ambivalence, 161–162
teacher behavior, 167–172
acquiesces, 167, 168, 170–171
audiotape analysis, 165–166, 168, 188
checks, 167, 168–169
distressed, 169–172
notifies, 167
objects, 167–168, 169–170
questions, 167, 169, 170
refuses, 168, 169, 170–171
summarization of, 171–172, 188–189
time factor in, 171–172, 173–174

Candid Camera, 197
Charlie's Coffeepot (Milgram), 29
City and the Self, 14, 23
City University of New York (CUNY), 3, 9, 10, 11, 19, 24, 25–26

Code of Federal Regulations (CFR), 112
Coercive power, 41
Communication, hesitant, 115, 116–117
Conformity and Independence, 23
Cultural research, 59t
airline captain authority, 113–114
gender differences, 48–49
Germany, 4, 35–36
United States, 4, 35–36

Defiant disobedience, 68, 74, 79
Disobedience styles, 67–68, 73–74, 79
defiant, 68, 74, 79
polite, 68, 74, 79
Distinguished Teaching in Psychology, 10, 23–24
Dynamical systems theory, 173–174

Eichmann in Jerusalem: A Report on the Banality of Evil (Arendt), 125
Enlightenment effects, 51–53
Ethics
obedience museum exhibit, 151–153
Stanford Prison Experiment (SPE), 203, 211–212
Euphemistic labels, 136
Experiment 5, 47
Experiment 8, 47
Experiment 11, 52
Expert authority, 39–44

Facing History and Ourselves, 127
Films, 10, 139
City and the Self, 14, 23
Conformity and Independence, 23
Human Aggression, 23
Invitation to Social Psychology, 23, 30

Nonverbal Communication, 23
Obedience, 14, 23, 37, 42–43
*Quiet Rage: The Stanford Prison
    Experiment*, 194, 209–210,
    213
Shoah, 136

Gender differences, 38, 47–50, 54
    studies on, 48–49
Germany, *see also* Grueninger, Paul;
        Holocaust education
    cross-cultural research, 4, 35–36
    culture of, 132
    Holocaust, 3–4
        and identity management, 86–87
        and impression management, 86
        as research influence, 3–4,
            125–126
Grueninger, Paul
    defiant disobedience of, 91–92, 95,
        96, 102, 104–105, 107–108
    Milgram paradigm comparison, 92,
        101–106
    and Nazi persecution, 91, 92–95
    refugee protection
        motivation for, 91–92, 94–95, 96,
            99–101, 108–109
        techniques of, 97–99, 109
        as rescuer, 95–97
        and Swiss refuge, 93–95, 96–97
        government attitude, 92, 93–95,
            97, 99, 109
        New Order, 97
        tradition of, 92–93, 96, 99, 100,
            106–107

Harvard University, 2, 6, 10, 11, 24
*Hitler's Willing Executioners: Ordinary
        Germans and the Holocaust*
        (Goldhagen), 131
Holocaust, *see also* Grueninger, Paul
    and identity management, 86–87

and impression management, 86
as research influence, 3–4, 125–126
Holocaust education
    approaches to, 126
    Holocaust/laboratory social forces
        disobedience, 137–138
        euphemistic labels, 136
        responsibility displacement, 137
        situation definition, 132–135
        task routinization, 135–136
    non-obedience theories, 130–132
        anti-Semitism, 131
        and German culture, 132
        victim proximity, 131–132
    obedience studies' absence
        college, 128, 130
        high school, 126–128, 129
        middle school, 126–128, 129
        and psychology emphasis,
            128–130
        and racism emphasis, 129
        reasons for, 128–130
        time factor, 129
    obedience studies' influence,
        125–126, 130, 138–141
    purpose of, 126
Human Aggression, 23
Hypothetico-deductive method, 172

Identity management, 61–62, *see also*
        Person-perception
    and Holocaust, 86–87
    identity defined, 62
Implicit personality theory, 64–67,
    74–77, 85
Impression management, 61–62, *see
        also* Person-perception
    and Holocaust, 86
    process of, 63–64
    social impression defined, 62, 63–64
Informational power, 41
Institutional study, *see* Stanford Prison
        Experiment (SPE)
Invitation to Social Psychology, 23, 30

James Monroe High School, 2
Jews, *see* Grueninger, Paul; Holocaust;
　　Holocaust education

Legitimate authority, 38–44, 162–163
Line-oriented flight training (LOFT),
　　120–121, 122
Lost child study, 15

Map study, 5, 31
Mathematical model, *see* Bridgeport
　　condition
Milgram, Stanley
　classroom work
　　awards, 10, 23–24
　　courses, 16–20, 24
　　experiential influence, 17–18, 19
　　films, 10, 14, 23
　　obedience activities, 18–21
　　peer-grading, 19–20
　　personal style, 12, 13–16, 24
　　as researcher, 12
　　research/teaching collaboration,
　　　16–17
　　as speaker, 12
　　student alumni, 11–12, 15, 24
　　as teacher, 3, 9–12, 24
　　as thinker, 12
　　as writer, 6–7, 12, 29
　as friend, 32–34
　as mentor, 28–32
　personal history
　　childhood, 1–2
　　cross-cultural research, 4
　　death, 3, 10
　　education, 1–2
　　family, 1, 3, 5–6
　　Holocaust interest, 3–4
　　inventions, 6
　　musical production, 6–7, 12
　　research influences, 3–7, 125–126
　　science interest, 5, 16

　　story writing, 6–7, 12, 29
　　teaching career, 3
　　travel, 4–5
　as research supervisor, 26–28
　Milgram paradigm comparison, *see
　　also* Holocaust education;
　　Person-perception
　and excessive obedience, 111,
　　　115–117, 122
　　closeness effect, 115
　　hesitant communication, 115,
　　　116–117
　　situation definition acceptance,
　　　115, 116, 117
　and Holocaust refugees, 92,
　　　101–106
　Stanford Prison Experiment (SPE),
　　　221–224, 230–234
Monaco, Jackie, 15
Museum exhibit study, *see* Obedience,
　　museum exhibit of
Musical production, 6–7, 12

National Transportation Safety Board
　　(NTSB), 111, 112–113,
　　117–121
Nonverbal Communication, 23

Obedience, 14, 23, 37, 42–43
Obedience, excessive
　captain authority sources, 111,
　　　112–114
　　Code of Federal Regulations
　　　(CFR), 112
　　corporate culture hierarchy, 113
　　cultural comparison, 113–114
　　and employee conformity, 114
　　flight hours, 112–113
　　flight rules, 113
　　military values, 113
　　organizational norms, 113
　　and social power, 114

union seniority, 112
case study, 117–120
Milgram paradigm comparison, 111,
    115–117, 122
    closeness effect, 115
    excessive obedience, 115
    hesitant communication, 115,
        116–117
    situation definition acceptance,
        115, 116, 117
obedience optimization, 111–112,
    121–122
    database for, 122
    role-playing, 121
plane crash rates, 111
    line-oriented flight training
        (LOFT), 120–121, 122
    monitoring/challenging errors,
        120–121
Obedience, museum exhibit of
collaboration for, 145
controversy regarding, 146–148,
    157–159
description of, 148–153
    and ethics, 151–153
goal of, 145
reactions to, 153–157
    disobedience, 156
    exhibit confusion, 156
    exhibit rejection, 155, 157, 158
    obedience, 153–154, 157
    and psychology reputation,
        156–157
    research rejection, 155–156, 157
    research validity, 154
    social situation influence,
        158–159
title of, 145
as visitor information resource, 153
Obedience optimization, 111–112,
    121–122
database for, 122
role-playing, 121
Obedience paradigm issues
authority characterization, 37–44,
    53

experiment of, 41–44
    expert authority, 39–44
    legitimate authority, 38–44
    social power, 41–42
gender differences, 38, 47–50, 54
    studies on, 48–49
interest in, 36–37
obedience rate changes, 38, 50–53,
    54
    enlightenment effects, 51–53
obedience rate prediction/outcome,
    38, 44–47, 53–54
overview, 37–38, 53–54
Obedience rate
changes in, 38, 50–53, 54
    enlightenment effects, 51–53
prediction/outcome dichotomy, 38,
    44–47, 53–54
*Obedience to Authority: An Experimen-
    tal View* (Milgram), 17, 29, 37,
    158
Obedience vs. disobedience, 66, 67–68,
    77–79
    defiant disobedience, 68, 74, 79
    disobedience style, 67–68, 73–74, 79
    polite disobedience, 68, 74, 79
    polite obedience, 73–74
Ordinary Men (Browning), 208

Person-perception
experimenter identity, 71–72, 83
identity management, 61–62
    and Holocaust, 86–87
    identity defined, 62
impression management, 61–62
    and Holocaust, 86
    process of, 63–64
    social impression defined, 62,
        63–64
learner behavior
    learner defined, 61
    and learner identity, 71–72, 83
meaning construction, 63–65
    symbolic meanings, 64

process of, 63–64
self-perception, 62, 87
systems theory perspective, 71–72
teacher behavior
   agentic state, 69–71
   and attribution theory, 69–71
   cognitive system structure, 63,
      65–66, 85–86
   defiant disobedience, 68, 74, 79
   disobedience style, 67–68, 73–74,
      79
   and experimenter identity, 71–72,
      83
   and implicit personality theory,
      64–67, 74–77, 85
   and learner identity, 71–72, 83
   meanings in, 63, 65–66
   obedience vs. disobedience, 66,
      67–68, 77–79
   polite disobedience, 68, 74, 79
   polite obedience, 73–74
   and responsibility, 69–71, 79–82,
      85
   responsibility-clock procedure,
      70–71
   and social system analysis, 63,
      71–73, 83–85
   teacher defined, 61
   and teacher identity, 62–63,
      66–68, 77–79
Polite disobedience, 68, 74, 79
Polite obedience, 73–74
Power
   coercive, 41
   expert, 39–44
   informational, 41
   legitimate, 38–44, 162–163
   referent, 41
   reward, 41
   social
      and authority, 41–42
      and excessive obedience, 114
      and Stanford Prison Experiment
         (SPE), 193–194, 203,
         204, 206, 212

Prison study, *see* Stanford Prison Experiment (SPE)
Proximity effect
   to experimenter, 115
   to victim, 131-132

Queens College, 2
*Quiet Rage: The Stanford Prison Ex-
   periment*, 194, 209–210, 213

Referent power, 41
Responsibility
   and agentic state theory, 69–71, 163
   and Holocaust, 137
      responsibility-clock procedure,
         137
   and person-perception, 69–71,
      79–82, 85
      responsibility-clock procedure,
         70–71
Responsibility-clock procedure, 70–71,
   137
Reward power, 41

Self-destructive obedience, *see* Obedience, excessive
Shoah, 136
Situation definition
   and excessive obedience, 115, 116,
      117
   and Holocaust, 132–135
Situation influence
   obedience museum exhibit, 158–159
Stanford Prison Experiment (SPE),
   193–194, 203, 204, 206, 212
Social change, institutional, 195,
   209–210, 212, 230–233
Social impression, 62, 63–64

Social power
   and authority, 41–42
   and excessive obedience, 114
   and Stanford Prison Experiment
      (SPE), 193–194, 203, 204,
      206, 212
Stanford Prison Experiment (SPE)
   ethics of, 203, 211–212
   and institutional analysis
   Milgram experiment influence,
      221–224
   prison change, 230–233
   prison power, 224–230
   institutional change from, 195
   lessons learned
      character transformation,
         206–207
      dissonance effect, 205–206
      generalizability, 207–208
      participant selection, 209
      personality variables, 205
      prison system failure, 210–211
      role validation, 205
      situational analysis, 204
      social change, 195, 209–210,
         212, 230–233
      total situation effect, 206, 212
   Milgram paradigm comparison,
      193–194
      legitimate authority, 194
      research influence, 221–224,
         230–234
      time factor, 194
   outsider perspective, 194–195,
      214–220
      and dissent, 218–220
      lessons learned, 217–220
      personal role, 214–217
   positive consequences
      cultural influence, 214
      personal, 213–214

   research influence, 212–213,
      233–234
   social change, 212, 230–233
   total situation model, 212
   purpose of, 203–204
   research synopsis, 198–203
      participant behavior, 200–203
      participant selection, 198–199
      prison setting, 199–200
   total situation effect, 193–194, 203,
      204, 206, 212
Story writing, 6–7, 12, 29
Subway study, 6, 17–18, 20
Switzerland, *see* Grueninger, Paul
Systems theory, 71–72

Task routinization, 135–136
Television, 10
Tenth Level, The, 44
Theater, 10
Therapeutic community (TC), 29
Time factor
   in Bridgeport condition, 171–172,
      173–174
   in obedience studies' absence, 129
   in Stanford Prison Experiment (SPE),
      194

United States, 4, 35–36
United States Holocaust Memorial
   Museum, 126–127, 128

ValuJet Airlines, 116

Yale University, 3, 4, 10, 11